The Virtuous and Violent Women of Seventeenth-Century Massachusetts

The Virtuous and Violent Women of Seventeenth-Century Massachusetts

EMILY C. K. ROMEO

UNIVERSITY OF MASSACHUSETTS PRESS
Amherst and Boston

Printed in the United States of America

ISBN 978-1-62534-513-4 (paper); 512-7 (hardcover)

Designed by Deste Roosa
Set in Adobe Caslon Pro
Printed and bound by Books International, Inc.

Cover design by adam b. bohannon
Cover art by Erica Guilane-Nachez / stock.adobe.com.

Library of Congress Cataloging-in-Publication Data

Names: Romeo, Emily C. K., author.
Title: The virtuous and violent women of seventeenth-century
Massachusetts
/ Emily C.K. Romeo.
Description: Amherst : University of Massachusetts Press, [2020] | Includes bibliographical references and index. |
Identifiers: LCCN 2020017791 | ISBN 9781625345127 (hardcover) | ISBN 9781625345134 (paperback) | ISBN 9781613767627 (ebook) | ISBN 9781613767634 (ebook)
Subjects: LCSH: Puritan women—Massachusetts—Social conditions—17th century. | Puritans—Massachusetts—History—17th century. | Puritans—Rhode Island—Providence—History—17th century. | Violence—Massachusetts—History—17th century. | Family violence—Law and legislation—Massachusetts—History—17th century. | Married women—Legal status, laws, etc.—Massachusetts—History—17th century. | Sex role—Religious aspects—Puritans.
Classification: LCC F67 .R66 2020 | DDC 305.409744/09032—dc23
LC record available at https://lccn.loc.gov/2020017791

British Library Cataloguing-in-Publication Data
A catalog record for this book is available from the British Library.

A portion of chapter 2 was first published in a previous form as "An Almost Inconceivable Foe: Anglo-American Women and Violence against Colonial Authority in Seventeenth-Century New England," in *Journal of Women's History* 31, no. 2 (Summer 2019), 80–100. Copyright © 2019 Journal of Women's History. Reprinted with permis-sion by Johns Hopkins University Press.

FOR TONY, JOEY, AND NIC

CONTENTS

PREFACE

This book explores acts of violence by Anglo-American women in colonial Massachusetts, from the everyday to the extraordinary, within the unique environment of Puritan New England. Examining women's violence reveals, in unique ways, the pervasiveness of violence throughout Puritan society. It also uncovers commonalities among women's violent actions. Behaviors that appear dramatically dissimilar on the surface—over-correcting children, fighting neighbors and tax collectors, attacking Indians, committing infanticide, and even accusing others of witchcraft—differed in the circumstances in which they appeared and the extremity of force used, but they were connected by Anglo-American women's common motivations during this period.

A confluence of social, cultural, and religious forces was at work in seventeenth-century Massachusetts. The push and pull of these elements determined how women conducted their lives. Pressure to conform to the ideals of Puritan womanhood and preserve their reputation in the eyes of the community and the authorities existed alongside women's imperative to protect the interests of their households and kin groups. The uncertainties of life and the ubiquity of violence in early New England encouraged some women to react aggressively, bolstered by a cultural tradition of female violence that lingered in the colonies. Yet in crossing the line to more overt forms of violence, women risked social ostracism, community censure, and, most seriously, official condemnation. The situations in which women chose to flout powerful social and cultural conventions and resort to overt violence—and colonial authorities' responses to these incidents—reveal the underlying, often unspoken priorities that shaped this society.

The Virtuous and Violent Women of Seventeenth-Century Massachusetts emerged out of a central preoccupation: how to rectify the Puritan image of virtuous womanhood with the actual women who appear in the historical record. History during this period is replete with stories of Anglo-American women who were assertive, unruly, and even violent. To understand how violence by these women was practically and morally possible and, at moments, even acceptable, I have placed women's actions within the context of their cultural world, their everyday struggles, and the hardships that plagued colonial American life. My research reveals a multifaceted, if not necessarily attractive, image of Anglo-American women's priorities and capacity for violence. Historians have made meaningful progress in challenging the idea of colonial women as either happy or unhappy "helpmeets," one peaceful, virtuous, and obedient, the other inherently disorderly and violent. One goal of this work is to do away with this dichotomy completely and examine these women simply as people responding to the challenges of their different situations and environments. "Violent" women could still be "virtuous" and vice versa.

Scholarship examining the southern colonies has engaged with women and their violent behavior, but studies on women in colonial New England have been slow to follow suit and generally do not situate violence as an important part of women's reality. When northern women have been portrayed as violent actors, their actions have been interpreted as chafing against the restraints of a repressive system. In glossing over Anglo-American women's violence as an aberration, we miss what can be learned by examining its cultural significance. My work reveals that even in its more dramatic forms, violence by colonial women in New England rarely functioned as social protest or a call for rebellion, regardless of how it was interpreted by authorities. Instead, most aggressive actions by women had conservative aims, dedicated to ensuring household security, property, or social standing.

My work has benefited from the insights and input of many. I am grateful to Edward M. Cook Jr., Catherine Brekus, and Janice Knight for their guidance and support throughout this endeavor. Each of them brought his or her unique expertise to the research. Meetings with Christine Stansell in the early stages of this project were inspiring and invaluable. The University of Chicago, the Mellon Foundation, and the Colonial Society of Massachusetts provided financial support for early versions of the project. Thomas Foster, Nina Dayton, Ann M. Little, and Mary Beth Norton were generous with their expertise and advice. The work of Laurel Ulrich has been an inspiration. I thank the staff of the Massachusetts Archives, the Haverhill Historical Society, the American Antiquarian Society, the Newberry Library, and the Peabody Institute of Salem for being welcoming and helpful. Lauren Fogle was kind enough to give my family a guided tour of Marblehead. Local historian Thomas Spitalere took me into Hannah Dustin's world in Haverhill. Among my colleagues at the University of Chicago, I particularly thank Sarah Weicksel and Elisa Jones, who provided encouragement and moral support. My greatest debt is to my family, who have been by my side from start to finish.

The Virtuous and Violent Women of Seventeenth-Century Massachusetts

INTRODUCTION

Sometime between the beginning of her imprisonment in the spring of 1691 and her execution for infanticide two years later, Elizabeth Emerson came under the guidance of Puritan minister Cotton Mather. How he found the time to minister to Emerson while pursuing those afflicted and implicated in the Salem witch trials is unknown. Perhaps at first it was convenience; she was incarcerated in Boston with some of the victims of the witchcraft hysteria. It was during his visits that Mather recorded spending "many and many a weary Hour . . . in the Prison," trying to "serve the Souls of those miserable Creatures" he had come to reach, including Emerson. Mather was able to elicit from the "Haughty and Stubborn" Emerson a confession of her crime—the murder of her newborn twins—and her sins. Mather recorded her confession that "when [the twins] were born, I was not unsensible, that at least, One of them was alive; but such a Wretch was I, as to use a Murderous Carriage towards them, in the place where I lay, on purpose to dispatch them out of the World."[1]

Emerson's execution did not conclude Mather's involvement with her family, however. Just four years later Mather would become reacquainted with Hannah Dustin, Elizabeth's eldest sister. At the end of King William's War in northern New England, Dustin had been taken captive by Abenaki Indians. To free herself, and in retribution for their murder of her infant daughter, Dustin slaughtered and scalped her Indian captors. Following her return home to Haverhill, Massachusetts, and a petition before the General Court for scalp bounty, Dustin and Mather renewed their relationship. Mather was intrigued by Dustin, a "Subject of such wonderful Deliverance . . . from captivity." In his eyes, Dustin had been transformed into a heroine like those from the Hebrew Bible, and she had brought the wrath of God down upon those who had attacked her.[2]

In Mather's hands, neither Emerson's death nor Dustin's redemption would bring an end to their fame and notoriety. On the day of Emerson's execution, Mather gave a moving sermon on her behalf. He published that sermon, and Emerson's confession, on several occasions throughout the end of the seventeenth century. Mather also published accounts of Dustin's captivity and escape three times between 1697 and 1702.[3] Elizabeth Emerson and Hannah Dustin would become examples to others: one a lesson about the price of sin and the other the promise of divine inspiration. Their actions made them infamous, but Elizabeth and Hannah were far from the only violent women in seventeenth-century New England. If we explore the deeper motivations behind their violence, we can discern a common trait they shared with many women of this time and place: a willingness to perform violent deeds for what they perceived to be the good of their household and kin group. Violence played a role in how the women of colonial New England struggled to maintain their corners of, and their places in, this distinctive environment. That role went unrecognized by colonial authorities, who sought to perpetuate an image of New England as a model of "meekness, gentleness, patience and liberality."[4] For the most part, historians have followed their lead.

My research traces a continuum of violence that touched almost all aspects of these women's lives, extending from within the household to society at large. It explores the shifting boundaries between acceptable and unacceptable violence for women and how they attempted to handle the demands of life in early New England within the confines of seventeenth-century expectations for their gender. This work also shows that even more serious acts of violence by Anglo-American women—in the course of the Indian Wars of the late seventeenth century, through infanticide, and even in the context of witchcraft accusations—were not necessarily intended to challenge structures of authority or patriarchy. While overt violence was more likely to bring them into the public eye, most of these actions sprang from women's desire for security, or their wish to protect property or standing for themselves and their families.

Through their actions many of these women demonstrated that they saw the people and property within their households as their responsibility and behaved accordingly. In most of the violent interactions in which Anglo-American women engaged, male authority figures either were not immediately present or else failed to act. This sense of personal ownership among women, especially married women, is intriguing. It suggests that women's actual control over their households was not necessarily in line with their legal status as dependents without the right to own or dispose of property. The predominance of wives as assailants in seventeenth-century New England indicates the extent to which household structure and obligations informed patterns of female violence. It was as mistresses of households that women most often entered disputes, maintaining order among servants, rescuing household goods, protecting property rights, or defending themselves or others. This differs from much of the violence committed by men, who were more likely than their female counterparts to commit violence in more "public" areas of colonial life, and outside their role as master of a household. Men also committed acts of sexual violence that were extremely rare for women.[5]

Overt violence was men's prerogative, and in this period masculine identities hinged on men's ability to defend their communities and control subordinates. My research shows, however, that the good wives of colonial New England could use moderate physical aggression in their roles as mothers, mistresses, and even neighbors without challenging societal expectations for their gender and maintaining the "dignity of anonymity."[6] Both household ideology and practical circumstances required wives to maintain the integrity of their households, with or without their husbands' participation. In New England, the uncertainty of life on the edge of wilderness, and the demonic threat that seemed to lurk on all sides, made this defense all the more crucial. Women using violence to ward off unwelcome intrusions—against property, reputation, or general safety—is a recurrent theme that runs through the acts of violence this book explores.

New England Puritans held up the biblical Bathsheba as a model of womanly virtue. Overlooking the more scandalous aspects of her story, ministers presented her as an industrious and productive housewife, a generous neighbor, and a trusted spouse and mother, a willing servant to her family and community.[7] She uses her skills and strength for the good of others. Bathsheba's strength in accomplishing her tasks is considerable: "She girdeth her loins with strength and strengtheneth her arms . . . Strength and honor are her clothing; and she shall rejoice in time to come." It is telling that this Puritan ideal was described as honorable, resourceful, and strong, not timid.

The Puritan Bathsheba, however, is content to live privately. "Her husband is known at the gates . . . among the elders," according to Cotton Mather, but Bathsheba is satisfied to look after her household. She seeks not to distinguish herself as an individual but to fulfill her duties as a wife, mother, daughter, neighbor, and church member. Mather described the pious women of New England as "Hidden."[8] While this is an exaggeration—women were interacting with neighbors and attending church meetings—in general, if a woman became conspicuous in her community, or, in rare circumstances, infamous in the colony, it was usually a signal that something in her life had gone wrong.

Whether violence by Anglo-American women could be acceptable to local, colonial, or provincial authorities depended on whether they judged the acts to be in service to larger societal order. Open unruliness, of course, was not tolerated and was seen as particularly disruptive when perpetrated by a woman, given the strictures against disobedience Puritan ministers thundered from their pulpits. Yet a mother beating a child behind closed doors, even brutally, was often deemed a necessary course of action to preserve household order.[9] An act like infanticide, however, reflected Puritans' concerns about the crime as a signal of both sexual wantonness and alienation from the community, and thus could never be rectified with community standards of behavior, regardless of the women's motivations behind it. Some more visible acts of violence could be acceptable, within specific contexts. In many instances, the context of an incident mattered more than the action itself. In the eyes of Essex County magistrates, attacking an Indian enemy in a time of war, or sending a witch to the gallows, for instance, could be regarded as beneficial to the colonial community at large, and thus worthy of praise. Magistrates judged violence against colonial officials, however, to be against the interests of the community in general, and thus disruptive and unacceptable.

A few notes about language and cultural meaning: In order to avoid underestimating the extent of physical violence in this society, my definition of "violence" is both broader and narrower than the way the term was understood in seventeenth-century New England. In early modern English societies, "violence" was used to refer not only to an unauthorized physical altercation but also to the vehemence or intensity of emotion, behavior, or language. The term itself was contested; it was used to delegitimize particular actions. In colonial New England, physical aggression was labeled "violence" only when it was seen as disruptive of or opposed to the public order. For instance, violence performed by the state or colonial authorities was rarely labeled as such, even if we would judge it to be violence today.[10] For the purposes of this book, I define "violence" as simply the deliberate exercise of harm against a person or property.

Although I refer to "Puritans" and "Puritanism" throughout the work, I do not mean to imply that New England Puritanism among the laypeople was necessarily a coherent body of thought. The clergy, however, were largely consistent in the belief system they presented, and a distinctive Puritan culture can be discerned in colonial New England which dominated the discourse of New Englanders. Finally, I use the terms "Anglo-American," "colonial Englishman/Englishwoman," and "settler" in this book relatively interchangeably. For my purposes, all of these terms refer to North Americans whose native language was English and whose culture or ethnic background was European in origin.[11]

Puritans' militant brand of reformed Protestantism contributed to a cultural milieu of tolerance for what we would today consider to be physical violence. This emerged most strongly in the context of anti-Indian violence during the Indian Wars and violence directed against accused witches in the seventeenth century, but acceptance of more commonplace violent behavior by women extended beyond those realms. While the Puritan leadership of seventeenth-century Massachusetts took a strong stance against unruliness, my research shows that authorities were loath to intervene in response to violent action alone, even when women were the perpetrators. Puritanism in the New World allowed such interpersonal violence to continue in the midst of rhetoric urging obedience and order because women's violent actions were frequently in service to these ideals. More pressing concerns—such as disorder, declension, dissent, sexual indiscretion, and slander—overshadowed Puritan apprehensions regarding women and physical violence. As examined in the final pages of this book, Puritan authorities' eagerness to use women's expressions of violence as literary weapons to reassert their own authority in the late seventeenth century confirms this.

Seventeenth-century Massachusetts was a routinely violent world. Hangings, whippings, brandings, and other forms of public corporal punishment took place in the village square. Communities relied on such practices to maintain order, and they established a baseline acceptability of violence that informed the rest of colonial life. The tasks to which most seventeenth-century colonial women dedicated their lives also brought them into intimate contact with many forms of violence. Anglo-American women, including mistresses of households, commonly slaughtered pigs and other livestock when preparing food. Pig slaughter practices in an English household in 1673 by a "cook-maid" inevitably mirror practices in New England during this period that were often undertaken by the mistress of a household, especially in frontier regions. The description is not for the faint of heart and suggests that the pig was alive during much of the slaughtering process:

> Making ready to slaughter a Pig, she put the hinder parts between her legs as the usual manner is, and taking the snout in her left hand with a long knife she stuck the Pig and cut the small end of the heart almost in two, letting it bleed as long as any bloud came forth, then throwing it into a Kettle of boyling water, the Pig swom twice round the kettle, when taking of it out of the dresser she . . . stript off the hair, and as she was cutting of the hinder pettito, the Pig lifts up his head with an open mouth . . . the belly was cut up, and the entrails drawn out, and the heart laid apon the board.[12]

Necessity dictated that women were familiar with bloodshed in the colonial period. The household functioned not only as a butcher shop but also as an old people's home, hospital, and welfare institution in early American life. Women took responsibility for the care of the very young, the aged, the injured and afflicted. Especially in more remote frontier areas, a housewife's abilities were essential for the survival of her family and that of her neighbors.[13]

Puritan influences did not fully stifle the underlying "Englishness" of colonial settlers and their persistent use of violence to navigate their lives. In using violence to aggressively protect family interests against threats from both authorities and enemies, women did not abandon their English roots. Their sisters across the Atlantic had played a central role in riots against land enclosures and for common rights in the early seventeenth century. These group demonstrations sometimes took a violent turn. As one contemporary commentator wrote, "Women are more disposed to be mutinous . . .

[and] in all public tumults they are foremost in violence and ferocity."[14] For Englishwomen, as for their New English counterparts, their concerns expressed through violence centered on the well-being of their families.

Historians have brought increased attention to women's lives in colonial New England but have not identified violence as a significant part of their world. John Demos broke new ground in the study of the colonial family, but violence plays into his work only in discussions of the severity of child rearing among Puritan parents. Gloria Main has offered a fuller picture of domestic and family life in early New England, for both English and Indian communities, but her account is even more peaceful than Demos's. Main argues that the demands of life in the New World, specifically the need for labor, tempered harsh English family dynamics. When scholars have examined violence, they have depicted it as an anomaly or only as a product of a flawed system of social relations. Helena Wall argues that the unruliness that plagued early New England sprang from the strain community policing and oversight put on personal relationships. My research pushes back against an interpretative model that defines men's violence as "normal," and thus women's violence as less important. In glossing over women's violence as an aberration (it was not), we miss what can be learned by examining its cultural significance.[15]

This book also explores the "gray areas" of violent behavior. The historian Laurel Thatcher Ulrich provides an illuminating typology of female violence, labeling it as either "social" (when it is authoritarian, defensive, disorderly, or demonstrative) or "antisocial"(when it signals an aggressor's "alienation from the community" in the form of murder). Ulrich's typology is very useful in labeling how New England authorities judged violence. Dividing violent actions into categories of "social" versus "antisocial" violence seems less useful for attempting to discern how women themselves understood their actions. While it is unreasonable to assume that historians can ever truly understand the intentions or motivations of the historical actors they study, it is reasonable to believe that women's standards for judging their behavior could differ from those of colonial authorities.[16] What was "anti-social" according to the colonial authorities was not necessarily so to the woman who committed the action, particularly for crimes like infanticide. My work investigates female violence on its own terms in the context of women's circumstances.

Anglo-American women's experiences of the New England Indian Wars as refugees, war widows, grieving mothers, and careworn good wives deserve more scholarly attention than they have received. A lively discussion of women as captives has emerged in recent years, and their stories have enriched our understandings of dynamics of race, gender, identity, and religion on colonial frontiers.[17] Yet as the economic and social effects of the wars spread throughout Massachusetts and New England, women on both sides bore loss and hardship, far from the frontiers on which the battles raged. Histories of the wars, with a few exceptions, have failed to explore their impact away from the areas of direct conflict, beyond discussions of demographic shifts and tax increases. Nor have women's experiences in these areas been given much attention. David Corlett has addressed the issue of refugees from King Philip's War and the economic strain they placed on more interior communities, and Douglass Leach and Kyle F. Zelner both discuss the impact of wars on individual communities, but none focuses significant attention on the impacts of the conflicts on women.[18] Anglo-American women's experiences of the wars reveal that the hardships extended from frontier to coast and crossed the thresholds of individual households.

In viewing women's acts of violence as connected to the functioning of the larger society and culture, as opposed to separate from it and nonessential to its operation, this volume benefits from the scholarship of Thavolia Glymph. As a scholar of gender and slavery in the American South, she has contributed work that is groundbreaking in holding (white) women accountable for their acts of violence. She argues that such actions cannot be dismissed as just "variations of capriciousness and hysteria" or a means for women to vent their anger at their own subordination within a system in which they had no control. This idea allowed white women to avoid the taint of the slave system while submerging their "human and historical agency."[19] Similarly, this book seeks to show colonial Englishwomen's complicity in a violent system.

There are revealing differences and similarities that appear from a cursory comparison of women's lives in the northern versus the southern colonies and their relationships with violence. The inconsistency between Puritan ideals and the stark reality of life in New England created a more fraught cultural dynamic in that region regarding women and violence then would have existed in colonies farther south. In the early seventeenth century, as Lois Green Carr and Lorena S. Walsh have famously shown, life in the Chesapeake would have seemed a far cry from the relatively stable Puritan communities of New England. High mortality rates and an extreme preponderance in numbers of men over women made family life either nonexistent or unstable for most colonists. Religious observance, Anglican as opposed to Congregationalist, also played a less central role in these societies.[20] In this context, women lacking male protectors, especially female indentured servants, would need to harness whatever means necessary to protect themselves in such a society, including violence. Church leaders preaching obedience would also have been rather thin on the ground in contrast to their ubiquitous presence in the northern colonies.

For wealthier southern women, expectations regarding their behavior became more culturally significant over time. As Glymph has shown, slave mistresses sometimes used extraordinarily violent means to "discipline" slaves, "often not the least bit shyly," but received little to no pushback for their behavior from either masters or authorities. In earlier periods of settlement, before the ideal of paternalist slaveholding could take root, open violence by women would have been even more acceptable than it eventually became. Under paternalism, mistresses were supposed to play the role of the "softer, female head of the household," who operated with compassion. Especially in the period just prior to the Civil War, outward expectations and ideas about female behavior for mistresses began to diverge from the realities that existed within their households. In a manner reminiscent of women in colonial New England, ideas about southern women began to play a larger role in defining their culture. The iconic image of the southern lady, the dedicated, caring mistress, became a crucial feature of pro-slavery ideology, even as white women continued to use violence behind closed doors.[21]

Scholarship on non-physical violence has also been beneficial to this volume. Jane Kamensky's work on the power of the spoken word in colonial New England provides a methodological model that is based firmly in the culture of that period and place and reveals the importance of reputation in that society, particularly for women. Kamensky charts various "speech offenses" and their punishments in seventeenth-century Massachusetts court records and uses these cases to draft an image of the uses of speech in everyday life. She explores the "economy of speaking in the seventeenth century," the weight placed on maintaining reputation, and the dangers of slander. She traces when speech would "flare up" in colonial life and become a problem and when speech could be dismissed an innocuous.[22] My research includes an analysis of seventeenth-century court records to explore what could be called a gendered "economy of violence" during that time: the exchanges of violence that shaped, and were shaped by, the society and culture of early New England.

Literature on gender and violence in English history provides theoretical contexts for exploring the meaning behind women's violence in colonial America. For instance, Natalie Zemon Davis has shown how women, as well as men, adopted the trope of the "unruly woman" in seventeenth-, eighteenth-, and nineteenth-century Europe when participating in riots and other forms of civil disobedience. Women told off priests and pastors, were central actors in grain and bread riots in town and country, and joined in tax revolts and other disturbances. Women, or men donning women's attire, were afforded a "complex license" for unruly action. As more subject to the sway of her "lower passions," a woman was not to be held accountable for her actions, nor could she be held fully responsible for them as subject to her husband under coverture. Davis locates this female trope within the world of early modern European village festival rituals and humoral theories of human biology and gender difference.[23] She does not emphasize the role of religion in these ideas about gender, especially in periods following the Middle Ages. For this trope to be explored in Puritan New England, the important roles of Puritan religious belief and pervasive Puritan culture need to be taken into account.

The New England Puritan version of the "unruly woman" that has appeared through my research is less riotous and less a subject of general amusement than her European counterpart. A few central elements of this European trope appear to have made the Atlantic crossing, however. First, most unruly women in old and New England were attempting to be sources of order and stability, regardless of how their actions were perceived by others. In New England in particular, the struggle against disorder for the sake of the "City on a Hill" was a deadly serious cosmic struggle against sin. Women, who made up the majority of church attendants almost from the beginning of settlement in the New World, seem to have seen themselves as part of that struggle. Women's involvement was central to the Puritan movement since its inception, and women continued to shape New England Puritanism by both working within the dictates of its leadership and expressing their dissenting opinions. When unruly women resorted to violence in this environment, they likely sought to make the world conform more closely to their vision of correct order, behavior, or belief.[24]

The Essex County witchcraft crisis offers an example of this phenomenon as well as a unique opportunity to explore how the trials dramatized a culture of violence in which women played a part. This book offers an original interpretation of this well-covered territory by placing witchcraft accusation within the context of women's everyday violence and their willingness to engage even in deadly violence under extreme circumstances. Scholars have shown how the trauma of Indian war impacted those involved in the Salem witch trials but have not presented that phenomenon as an extension of a larger pattern of female violence.[25] I argue that the witch trials of 1692 marked a shift in the gender of the official accusers and the seriousness of charges of witchcraft. Earlier witchcraft accusations emerged as part of relatively minor interfamily disputes and were put forward more frequently by men, with women offering testimony behind the scenes. After the upheavals of the late seventeenth century, women were encouraged to draw on these existing disputes by powerful male leaders in their communities and began to accuse one another formally of witchcraft. I interpret this as another instance of Anglo-American women using violent means to defend their households but also, in this case, as a means of defending community norms against those who appeared to violate them. How others then manipulated their actions had deadly consequences.

My work focuses primarily on Essex County, Massachusetts, which possessed a diversity of settlements in terms of size, development, wealth, and religiosity. This has enabled me to explore a wide swath of women's experiences and to decipher patterns in women's behavior relative to their position and circumstance. I have discovered that Anglo-American women were involved in an array of violent deeds, from attacking Indians to abusing magistrates, fighting with husbands, overcorrecting children and servants, and quarreling with neighbors. A minority in the criminal record, women nonetheless also committed acts of deadly violence against neighbors and intruders, as well as some of the most vulnerable members of their own families and communities.

While the wealthiest and most prominent women in the colony were rarely brought to court as violent offenders, for women of more common means and social standing, property ownership and attendance at meeting did not prevent them from committing violent actions. The richness of the source material available for Essex County was also a critical component. Sources that shed light on women's lives from this period can often be difficult to uncover.

Court records provide one of the few avenues through which historians can attempt to understand women's place in the functioning of this society. Therefore I rely on records and files from the Essex County Quarterly Court, the Massachusetts General Court, the Court of Assistants, the Superior Court of Judicature, and the Court of Oyer and Terminer as the frame on which I hang other historical documentation filling in personal and cultural contexts, such as letters, sermon literature, and narrative histories. Seventeenth-century legal realities make measuring rates of violence difficult, particularly household violence. The evolution of its treatment by the courts makes charting instances of abuse that appeared before the court problematic as a reflection of actual rates of violence. By the time the seventeenth century came to a close, courts in Massachusetts, as elsewhere in New England, had lost interest in prosecuting cases of household violence. Instances of household violence disappear almost completely from court records after 1691, a change far too abrupt to attribute to a drop in actual acts of violence. In addition, the criminal records of early New England tend to be both "incomplete and laconic." Physical violence between spouses, or directed against children and servants, was frequently handled—when handled at all—by local justices of the peace, whose records have failed to survive. When cases reached the courts, clerks were also casual in recording the victim's age and relationship to his or her assailant.[26]

While it is difficult to calculate an accurate quantitative measure of the rates of female violence in seventeenth-century Massachusetts, exploring why and how women appeared before the court reveals invaluable evidence of societal and personal standards of behavior. Changes in colonial laws, and how those laws were enforced, reflect how authorities' concerns evolved in the seventeenth century. Women's depositions in court can expose their underlying motivations and beliefs. As Kidada Williams explains in her work on testimonies by African Americans about post-emancipation racial violence, scholars' focus on charting statistics to discern the larger societal effects of violence has meant that the lived experience of violence can often be overlooked.[27] To try to capture women's experiences, I have utilized women's depositions as much as possible. These are some of the only evidence historians have of colonial women's voices in the historical record. Women who were literate sometimes left personal letters or journals, but these are rare. Those unable to write left almost no record of their lives outside of their interactions with the legal system. What women said about their own actions, and about their neighbors', sheds light on the priorities and codes of conduct that shaped their lives.

In order to explore the motivations behind and responses to female violence in the colonial period—in Anglo-American women's daily lives and in the context of war—this book has a chronological focus that spans most of the seventeenth and into the first few decades of the eighteenth century in New England. It begins during a period of relative calm for Essex County, the 1630s, which enables me to understand how women experienced and employed violence in the course of their everyday lives. King Philip's War (1675–1678) was a major event in the lives of New Englanders, male and female alike, and exploring women's expressions of violence during that conflict, and the continuing conflicts in the northern regions of New England—King William's War (1688–1697) and Queen Anne's War (1702–1713)—allows me to demonstrate the far-reaching implications of those wars. Trends in Puritan rhetoric as the seventeenth century came to a close and the Puritan leadership regrouped in the aftermath of war and political upheaval need to be examined from the perspective of the early decades of the 1700s.

CHAPTER I

☞ The Limits of Household Violence

Order and Disorder

As neighbors in seventeenth-century Salem, Martha Wolfe and Elizabeth Woodberry had a close and contentious relationship. The fields each woman's family used for grazing livestock shared a common boundary, on which Martha and Elizabeth kept a watchful eye from their houses nearby. One spring day in 1657, the women's concerns over encroachment on their families' property erupted into a violent quarrel. Regardless of the fact that both her husband and her son were in the field with her, Martha took it upon herself to defend their property when she accused Elizabeth of allowing her oxen to graze on the Wolfes' land. Martha then physically attacked her with a stick. Elizabeth fought back against the blows and scratches by pushing Martha, who fell over a bush. Martha then said that "she thought the Divell would take [Elizabeth] away for . . . lying" and accused her of going "to the meeting for nothing but to diceive others." In response to these attacks and insults, Elizabeth went to church authorities, repeated Martha's offensive words, and showed them the blood on her face. They declined to get involved, citing a lack of cooperating witnesses. Court magistrates presented and admonished both women for fighting after the incident had become public knowledge.[1]

This conflict offers a glimpse of how colonial Englishwomen used violence in seventeenth-century Massachusetts in the domestic arena. Men made up the majority of violent offenders brought before the courts, but women also appear as a visible, vocal minority in the criminal record. Women accounted for 18 percent of all the persons accused of all types of physical violence, or the immediate threat of violence, in the county-level courts in Essex County between 1636 and 1710. When instances of "household violence" are taken into account—violence between two or more people who interact in or near the household, such as husbands and wives, children and parents, masters and servants, and even neighbors—this number rises to approximately 25 percent. Given the close-knit nature of settlement in colonial New England, relationships with neighbors could sometimes be as intimate as those with family members. I therefore have expanded the definition of household violence to reflect this societal norm.

Women were brought before the court for fighting with or attacking their husbands, overcorrecting children and servants, and quarreling violently with neighbors during disputes over property or status. While both men and women were violent actors, what marked violence by women was its consistent application in the service of perceived family needs and interests. Just as Martha Wolfe defended her family's land from wandering livestock, most women's violence was focused on their primary domain: the household and surrounding areas. Court records show that men used violence in the household as well, but they were more likely than women to be involved in more general displays of aggression in the community, such as drunken tavern brawls and violent contests for masculine dominance. Women's violence was more targeted, aimed at maintaining familial order or preserving family property, safety, or status.[2]

The court record surrounding the dispute between the Wolfes and Woodberrys is also revealing of how colonial authorities responded to interpersonal violence between intimates by both men and women. Salem church authorities declined to get involved in the fight between Martha and Elizabeth, even after Elizabeth appeared before them bearing injuries from the altercation. While the Puritan leadership of seventeenth-century Massachusetts condemned violence between spouses and against children, servants, or neighbors, authorities were reluctant to actually intervene in household or inter-household affairs in response to violent actions alone. Some Puritan leaders like John Winthrop sought to make violence the monopoly of the state in this new land and discouraged extreme forms of violence in the household.[3] This was not due to a general aversion to violence; Puritanism was not a religion of the meek. Violence employed by women in the normal course of their everyday lives usually went overlooked and did not threaten a woman's dignified anonymity. But overtly quarrelsome households, they preached, were a danger to social order.[4] As in the case of

Wolfe and Woodberry, only after word had spread around the community did the court step in and try to resolve these issues. When it did intervene in cases of violence alone, the action it took was usually aimed at minimizing public disruption.

In seventeenth-century Essex County, it appears that violence was tolerated, and even expected, from both men and women in certain household circumstances. This is due in part to the fact that most of the early settlers of New England remained thoroughly "English." The long ocean voyage may have symbolized a spiritual rebirth for some, but it did not erode loyalties to English social customs, domestic habits, and established means of order and subordination. As in England, early Americans employed violence to enforce their standards of social order. The physical "correction" of wives, children, and servants was particularly common, just as it was not unusual for disputes between neighbors to erupt into violent disagreements.[5] Puritanism did not counteract these practices. As the altercation between Martha Wolfe and Elizabeth Woodberry shows, it was not just those outside the bosom of the church who participated in household violence. One, if not both, of the women regularly attended meeting. Religious conviction did not determine a person's willingness to use violence.

At a time when the rest of the world, including England, was immersed in revolt and internal strife, the Massachusetts Bay Colony was a relatively cohesive society for much of the seventeenth century. There were no massive demonstrations of violence or violent challenges to the power of the state until the end of the century. Puritans' emphasis on obedience, and their willingness to expel dissenters from their midst, were partially responsible for this stability. Still, Massachusetts was not the happy Eden of its founders' imaginings. Court records from the early years of the colony, from the Essex County Court to the colony-wide Court of Assistants and the General Court, are filled with brutal acts of violence, including murders, rapes, and assaults.[6] What ultimately helped maintain the social cohesion and stability of Massachusetts Bay was its reliance on the household and family as the foundations for society and, in a seeming paradox, the employment of violence therein. This occurred, if not with the tacit approval of the Puritan leadership, at least with the benefit of their blind eye.

The diffusion of authority in early New England reached unprecedented and perhaps unanticipated levels that went beyond the English model.

Without social welfare systems, police forces, or penitentiaries, the household filled the roles of all three and was the building block of social order. The patriarch of each household acted as its representative in the village or town, but such a system distributed authority within the household as well. It was primarily the mistress's responsibility to ensure that everyone in the household was fulfilling his or her duties. Both household ideology and practical circumstances required wives to maintain the integrity of their household and family, with or without their husband's participation.[7] In New England, the uncertainty of life on the edge of wilderness made women's engagement in household preservation and governance even more crucial. As a result, men did not possess a monopoly over household violence.

Cases of household violence by women and men in Essex County fail to follow patterns established by historians who chart a neatly progressive decline in violence in seventeenth-century New England. According to records in Essex County, the number of cases of household violence peaked in the 1640s, and again in the 1670s and 1680s, depending on the specific type of violence involved, and then dropped off almost completely as the eighteenth century approached. This pattern holds for both male and female perpetrators: the prosecutions for a specific type of violence peaked for men and women at the same time. The number of men brought before the Essex County Court in the seventeenth century for wife abuse peaks in the 1640s and then again in the 1670s–1680s. The number of women brought for husband abuse follows the same pattern, peaking in the 1640s and again in the 1670s–1680s. The numbers of both men and women accused of child abuse peaks in the 1660s and 1670s. The numbers of both men and women accused of violence against servants peaks in 1670s. Neighbor violence deviates from this parallel pattern slightly more than other forms. The number of women brought before the court peaks in the 1670s; the number of men peaks in the 1660s and remains constant through the 1670s.[8] This parallel pattern of violence does not fit the description of a society that disapproved of female physical violence per se or targeted it for prosecution. It also does not portray a society that was gradually moving away from more violent means of social control and interaction.

For both men and women, instances of household violence appear to have reached the attention of the court only when they were too dramatic, or too openly expressed, to be ignored. The cases that appeared in court records were therefore only the tip of a "violence iceberg." Silences in seventeenth-century court records reveal the acceptability of a wide array of violent behaviors between intimates, even for women. The legal system in seventeenth-century America was a "cultural performance" for the community in which social and cultural norms could be expressed and reinforced. As these cases illustrate, colonial courts chose to address instances of household violence when they encompassed other issues of greater concern to Puritan communities, such as sexual indiscretion or slander. Barring other complicating factors, most instances of violence remained beneath the authorities' notice.[9]

SPOUSAL VIOLENCE

The phenomenon of household violence in seventeenth-century Massachusetts was part of a larger continuum of violence that extended from the most mundane acts of physical aggression to the most sensational. As the foundation of life in colonial New England, marital relationships are the logical starting point for an examination of this continuum. The importance of marriage in seventeenth-century New England cannot be overstated. As much as the Puritan leadership of Massachusetts Bay wanted to keep at least the outward appearance of peace between spouses—the Massachusetts Body of Liberties outlawed "conjugal correction" in 1641—spousal violence remained a normal part of marital life in colonial New England. English practices of violent marital discipline and interaction proved impossible to abandon. Some New English husbands used violent means to "correct" their wives and maintain their authority. Some wives responded in kind, or lashed out at their husbands, usually for failing to live up to their expectations as a family patriarch, husband, and provider.[10] Seventeenth-century New Englanders saw marriage as a contract, and violence alone did not void that contract; violence was a natural, if regrettable, part of the marital relationship.[11]

Though willing to police other types of personal behavior, courts in seventeenth-century Essex County were hesitant to intervene in violent marital relationships. Court records reveal that cases usually failed to reach the courts unless physical violence between spouses reached outrageous levels—such as those verging on murder—or unless the instances of violence were particularly public and therefore undeniably disruptive to the community at large. Otherwise, for an instance of marital violence to receive court attention it usually had to involve another issue of more serious concern, such as adultery.

When the problem was limited to acts of violence, most neighbors and community members as well as court magistrates in seventeenth-century Massachusetts chose to avoid meddling in the married lives of their fellow village or town residents. This pattern in the Essex County Court records does not necessarily contradict the findings of other historians who have emphasized the almost unrestrained interference of neighbors and authorities in the family life of others in Puritan New England. In matters involving sexual conduct outside of marriage, for instance, communal policing appears to have been the norm. Because marital violence per se was not seen as a threat to marital stability, it was less subject to community comment. When cases of violence became too destructive and disruptive to ignore, however, the Puritan tendency toward communal vigilance eventually emerged. This was not a question of communal vigilance versus family privacy. Notions of privacy did not appeal to the English Puritans who migrated to the New World. They believed that neighbors and the church had a duty to regulate family life. Nonetheless, they also believed that separating married couples was justified only in very unusual circumstances. Violence alone was not considered unusual, and authorities went to great lengths to keep troubled marriages intact.[12]

The cases against Daniel Ela of Haverhill and Thomas Russell of Marblehead illustrate this reticence toward intervening in neighbors' violent marriages, as well as the Essex County Court's reluctant pursuit of spousal abuse cases. Daniel Ela was not averse to using violence to enforce familial obedience. The court officially frowned on such behavior only when violence as a tool of interpersonal social order was used to excess and became disorderly in itself. Ela was brought before the court in Ipswich in 1682 for the severe beating of his wife, Elizabeth, and for making threats against her life with both a knife and a cudgel. Following a beating, Elizabeth fled their house in a snowstorm looking for help, but her neighbor refused to assist her even after she warned, "If you do not entertaine mee and lett me abide in your house I will lie in the street in the snow & if I perish, my blood be upon your head." The neighbor chose instead to return her to her husband, who threatened him for "meddling" in his attempts to "order" his wife. Elizabeth fled to another neighbor. At that point the disruption was significant enough to reach the local authorities, who pressed charges against Daniel.[13] During court proceedings, so many neighbors attested to the abuse Elizabeth had received—the same neighbors who had chosen to watch her struggles from behind closed doors—that the court could not ignore the incident entirely and fined Daniel for his misbehavior.

Thomas Russell of Marblehead also inflicted persistent and intense violence on his wife, Mary, violence that was significant enough to gain the attention of authorities when combined with Thomas's other violent threats against neighbors. In 1680 Mary testified before the Essex County Court that on one occasion her husband came home late, beat her unmercifully, kicked her around the house, and struck her on the head. He had threatened to cut her throat or burn her, adding that if she complained, he would kill her. At least one neighbor testified that he had seen Mary bloody from her husband's abuse. Other residents of Marblehead testified that Thomas was a violent man and had frightened them many times at night by brandishing a gun or pistols "like a mad man." Regardless of his violent tendencies, however, the Essex County Court was willing to drop all charges against Thomas upon his promise of reform and Mary's petition attesting to their reconciliation. Since the time of her complaint against him, Thomas "hath carried it like a loueing husband to her," her petition stated.[14] This was enough for the court to drop the matter and move on to more pressing concerns.

Violence within seventeenth-century marriages was certainly not perpetrated exclusively by husbands against their wives. Both spouses were capable of inflicting serious harm. In most cases of wives abusing their husbands, the men appear to have failed to fulfill their role as household patriarch providing for the personal and financial security of their families, to which their wives responded with violence. Although these women's actions are reprehensible, the motivation behind them becomes clearer when they are placed in the context of a seventeenth-century household. As the prominent Puritan William Perkins explained in his 1609 treatise on domestic relationships, while it was a wife's duty to "submit" to her husband—at his side as a wife, as opposed to a servant—she must also be able to "depend on him in judgment and in will." When either piece of that dynamic failed to fall into place, violence seems to have been the result. For a household in colonial New England to function properly, the patriarch of that household needed to be both dependable and capable. If he could not appropriately head the household, he at least had to be out of the way, allowing his wife to take over the management of household affairs. From the outside, violence against a husband by his wife may have appeared to be the ultimate inversion of familial order. Indeed, according to Puritan teachings, a husband-beating wife affronted not only her spouse "but also God her Maker."[15] Clearly, however, there were instances in which women deemed that inversion necessary. This behavior would have sprung not from an anachronistic desire for individual power but from the need to respond to relationships and households in disarray. Surprisingly, even when these women appeared before them as violent perpetrators, courts were hesitant to intervene.

In the late 1640s, the Pray household was in chaos. Richard Pray frequently beat his wife, Mary, and verbally abused her, bragging about this ill-treatment in front of the family's houseguests. Richard would have failed to live up to William Secker's advice to the seventeenth-century husband for a successful marriage: to exercise authority over the household, "protect" his wife "from injuries," and "provide for her necessities," while showing "charity for [her] failings."[16] Several witnesses attested to seeing Richard attempt to beat Mary with a stick the size of a bedstaff and almost break her wrist by throwing a porridge dish at her hand. When asked about the abuse, Richard claimed that he would beat her "twenty times a day" in order to maintain control over his wife. All evidence from their relationship suggests that Richard's patriarchal control within the household had completely broken down and he had turned to violence in desperation. Mary Pray did not take her husband's abuse or personal failings lying down. She responded by making her husband's mistreatment well known throughout the community, rolling up the sleeve of her shift to display the "marks of ye blowes" that her husband had given her, which were "two great places black and blue." Mary also responded with violence of her own. At dinner one evening, she "threw a trenchr at him and also a bone," then directed her anger toward Richard's mother, whose presence was clearly an imposition. Witnesses testified that she would "say to her mothr in lawe get you [home] yow old hogge" and throw stones at her. Such a case seems like the type in which neighbors and courts would quickly intervene, but both delayed responding to the violent relationship. Eventually Richard was fined twenty shillings for beating his wife—the same amount he was fined for swearing and cursing—and another forty for contempt of court for denying the judges' authority over him. For her involvement, Mary was only admonished.[17]

Isabell Pudeator was another woman who did not quietly suffer her husband's shortcomings. The Pudeators of Salem seem to have been determined to destroy each other, and several of their neighbors witnessed their contentious relationship. Jacob was a less than ideal mate. He had been presented for "stricking & Hitting his wife," but the court lessened his sentence to a fine after being informed that there was "grate provocation" for the abuse. In 1676 Isabell was brought to court for disruptive behavior and for abusing her husband and his property. Neighbors testified that she was "a brawling and contentious woman & how yt she carieth both to her husband & her neighbors . . . neither as ye Law of god or man requireth." They had also heard her threaten to kill her husband by burning his house to the ground. She would have been better off if she had followed through on her threats. Four years later Isabell died, most likely poisoned by her husband with an excess of alcohol. Within a year, he married the woman who had acted as her nursemaid. Executed in September 1692 as a witch, Jacob's second wife, Ann Greenslit Pudeator, was one of the seven victims of the final hanging on Gallows Hill during the Salem witch trials. Regardless of the mysterious circumstances surrounding the end of his first marriage, the court's inaction seems to express relief that at least the Pudeators were no longer fighting in the street.[18]

Wives' abuse of their husbands in seventeenth-century Massachusetts was a persistent enough problem to justify amending the colonies' law code in 1650. The original language of the Body of Liberties outlawing conjugal correction in 1641 freed a wife from "bodily correction or stripes by her husband unlesse it be [given] in his owne defence upon her assalt." Nine years later, the Massachusetts General Court issued the following order, explicitly outlawing husband as well as wife abuse: "It is ordered by this Court & authority thereof, that no man shall strike his wife, nor any woman her husband, on pennalty of such fine not exceedinge ten pounds for one offence, or such corporall punishment as the Shire Court that hath examination thereof shall determine."[19] Although how equally this law was applied to both husbands and wives is uncertain, the fact that it was deemed necessary indicates that the Puritan founders were concerned about violence by wives.

Perhaps the colonial leadership should have thought to include prohibitions against husband abuse in their initial law code, given women's behavior in early seventeenth-century England, particularly in the context of the domestic household. During his travels around England in the autumn of 1599, Thomas Platter the Younger, the Swiss diarist and physician, commented that English "good wives often beat their men." According to Platter, wives were essentially allowed to do as they wished, and incidents of husband abuse were so frequent that they produced a familiar "rough music" in towns and villages. Platter's observations that England was a "woman's paradise" were no doubt exaggerated for literary and comedic effect, but the problem of the "unruly" early modern woman was well established. Scolds, or women who spoke out too aggressively and disrupted their communities, as well as women who beat or cuckolded their husbands, were the focus of both literary and legal disapproval during this period.[20]

Records from the Essex County Court attest that settlement in New England did not significantly alter these distasteful English social practices and means of navigating marital relationships. Some wives continued to respond to their unsatisfactory spouses with violence. These instances were more likely to reach the attention of the court than cases of wife abuse, given the inherent, if unintentional, challenge to male authority that accompanied them.[21] Still, the severity of the violence that was involved in most cases indicates that women came before the court only when a browbeaten husband could no longer hide the violence from neighbors and authorities. In 1641 Elizabeth Browne was brought to court for attempting to murder her husband, Hugh. A mariner from Salem, Hugh was probably gone at sea for extended periods of time, leaving Elizabeth to run the household and care for their children. Their reunions were not pleasant, and Elizabeth made it clear she felt her family was better off without him. Elizabeth was sentenced to be whipped for hitting Hugh over the head, throwing stones at him that cut his face, threatening to kill him, calling him "beast," and wishing him hanged and gone from her sight. Several neighbors witnessed these various altercations and testified that they had seen the couple "scuffling together" on numerous occasions.[22]

Generally, family violence received mild treatment by the courts unless connected with a more dire charge. For most cases of assault between family members, the most common sentence was a fine or a whipping or both. The wrongdoer was usually restored to his or her family after a short period of time. (At the same time, the Puritans passed laws to hang rebellious children and blasphemers.) Adultery by contrast, was an issue of particular concern for the courts, and they treated such behavior harshly. Adultery struck at the heart of orderly family life and undermined codes of sexual restraint. As a result, the offense was made a capital crime in Massachusetts and Connecticut legal codes even though it remained a misdemeanor in England.[23]

Courts treated adultery cases differently depending on the gender of the adultereer. As John Demos explains, "The essential element of [the] sin, was the women's infidelity to her husband." Following Mosaic law, Massachusetts courts defined adultery in terms of the married status of the woman. Adultery was considered to be intercourse between a married or espoused woman and a man who was not her husband, regardless of his marital status. A man's affair with an unmarried woman, whether he was married or unmarried, was considered fornication, which was a crime against public order but not a capital crime. This definition reveals the threat posed by female sexual incontinence. A woman's infidelity was a challenge to the man's right of property "in his wife," and illicit pregnancy posed a threat to the "orderly transmission of the social estate to the next generation."[24] Therefore, while violence between spouses, even when committed by women, was considered a regrettable event, female adultery was much more of a public threat.

The Penions' repeated encounters with the Essex County court system attest to the relative importance of punishment for adultery over violent deeds in the maintenance of societal order. As the historian Mary Beth Norton notes, the Penions' "two-generation record of twenty-six prosecutions over two decades in four colonies" remains unmatched. The patriarch and matriarch of the Penion clan, Nicholas and Elizabeth, were prosecuted and occasionally fined for fighting with each other and causing various degrees of injury. Neighbors witnessed their frequent altercations, and on one occasion Nicholas was presented for beating Elizabeth to the point of causing a miscarriage. Of all the Penions' misbehavior, however, it was Elizabeth's suspected adultery that truly brought down the wrath of the court. In 1648 the Massachusetts General Court tried her for adultery. Found "not legally guilty" of the capital crime, Elizabeth was nonetheless ordered "sevearly whipt twise" within one month for her "adulterous behavior."[25]

Cases of adultery had the power to inspire communal policing in ways that cases involving marital violence alone did not. It was not uncommon for communities to band together and punish the transgressors, with a focus on the woman in question, while violent marriages seem to have gone relatively unchallenged.[26] The Rows of Ipswich had just such a contentious marriage. William Row, a mariner, was known to beat his wife, Sarah, who responded to his provocations violently. Witnesses testified that Sarah threatened to "take [a] knife & cut his throat" and that "shee hated Will Like a Toade." These statements surfaced only in the course of Sarah's trial for adultery, however. Sarah was suspected of having an affair, and several townsmen warned her to stop. When she persisted in her overly familiar behavior, no fewer than thirty-five Ipswich neighbors went to court and testified about the moral outrage. The court appears to have shared the neighbors' sentiments but could not prove adultery. The erring couple was found guilty of "unlawful familiarity." The man was whipped and fined, but Sarah was sentenced to a more public shame. After a one-month sentence in a house of correction, the court ordered her to "stand all the time of the meeting" at the next lecture day at Ipswich "on a high place in open view of the congregation with a fair white paper written in fair capital letters for my whoresh carriage."[27]

In another instance of community policing, at least seven local witnesses came before the Salem commissioner in Ipswich in 1680 to attest to Mrs. Robert Lawrence's sexual misbehavior. During court proceedings, the violent way Mrs. Lawrence had treated her husband became a side note to the inappropriate company she kept. All witnesses agreed that Mrs. Lawrence had struck her husband with her fist and beat him while he was on the ground. More important, however, was the domestic upheaval that resulted from Mrs. Lawrence's keeping company with Samuel Gatchell and others in her home. Neighbors testified that he and several of his friends were at her house at all hours of the day and night, and one witness claimed to have seen Mrs. Lawrence and Samuel share a kiss. After testimony concerning her physical violence had ended, questions concerning her sexual indiscretions remained in the forefront. It is unclear from court records what Mrs. Lawrence was charged with, but the nature of the testimony indicates that it was her adultery, more than the abuse of her husband, that alarmed her neighbors and local court officials.[28]

VIOLENCE AGAINST CHILDREN

Patterns of violence directed at children in seventeenth-century Massachusetts were similar to those that informed violence in marital relationships. Violence toward children by both men and women was acceptable on a broad scale, and authorities usually did not question it unless it resulted in serious injury to the child or was administered by an inappropriate party, such as a servant or neighbor. In retaining these practices of harsh child "correction," colonists in New England followed established English patterns of discipline in which the right to use violence to regulate children's behavior went almost unquestioned. While historians have shown that images of early sixteenth- and seventeenth-century family life in England tend to be overly grim, they have not disputed that child rearing involved breaking children's will by force and maintaining a formal emotional and physical distance between children and their parents. The specific period, level of wealth, and extremity of religious observance appear as variables that had an important impact on child rearing. English settlers brought these standards of treatment of children with them when they reached the New World. Cotton Mather stated it simply: "Better whipt, than Damn'd."[29]

Indeed, the nature of Puritan religious belief, and the uncertainties of life in the New World, when combined with existing English practices of authoritative child rearing, almost guaranteed that children would encounter violence from an adult at some point in their development. Some devout Puritan fathers and mothers employed violence to "break the will" of their children and prepare their souls to humbly accept God's grace. New England's status as a "New Jerusalem" in the wilderness of the New World made the issue of a child's salvation desperately important not just to parents but to the community as a whole. While the state attempted to monopolize the most extreme forms of violence—power over life and death—mothers and fathers had not only the right but the obligation to administer physical correction when needed. The poet Anne Bradstreet eloquently expressed this sentiment: "Some children are so tough and morose a dispo[si]tion," she wrote, "that the plough of correction must make long furrows on their back, and the Harrow of discipline goe often over them, before they bee fit soile to sow the seed of morality, much lesse of grace in them."[30]

Records from the quarterly court of Essex County demonstrate the expectation that a certain level of physical violence, by either parent and within reasonable limits, was acceptable in child rearing. The court would not usually act against a biological parent unless the violence was particularly severe, the injuries were noticeable, or the punishment resulted in the death of the child. Undoubtedly there were unknown numbers of child abuse cases that simply went unnoticed, were brushed off as "correction," or were ignored. In the seventeenth-century colonies, as Norton observes, "beating one's children seems to have been taken for granted." The few cases brought against parents that actually appear in the court records "use such words as 'immoderate and cruel' or 'crewell, unnaturall, and extreame' to describe their conduct, thus implying that more 'natural' or 'moderate' correction would not have been censurable."[31]

In the spring of 1676, Michael Emerson was brought before the county court for kicking and severely beating his daughter Elizabeth with a flail swingle, a large wooden stick with a swinging arm designed for threshing grain. Details about the brutality of the abuse, and the extent of Elizabeth's injuries, are lost to history. But as he was one of only a few parents brought before a New England court for abusing a child, it seems fair to assume that both were significant. A flail swingle would have been capable of inflicting serious harm. Even the court, not prone to particularly dramatic language, described the abuse as "cruel and excessive." Nevertheless, the court dropped all charges against Emerson less than six months later. Elizabeth's brutal beating does not seem to have damaged her father's standing in the community any more than his contentious relationship with his neighbors did. He remained a respectable farmer and shoemaker in Haverhill and held the position of constable and occasional grand juryman.[32]

Court records reveal that both mothers and fathers perpetrated this level of physical violence against their children. Even in these extreme instances, however, there were other factors in play that helped inspire the courts' disapproval. In 1642 the Massachusetts Court of Assistants charged Anne Hett with the attempted murder of her child by drowning. While the situation surrounding the case is unclear, Hett's abuse of her child took place with the knowledge of at least two witnesses. The court came down hard on Hett, given her existing reputation for "scandalous speeches" against God and her "unruliness." As a result, she was sentenced to be "whipped, and kept to hard labor, & 'spare diet.'" Similarly, the court sentenced John Turner to be whipped and sent to prison in Boston for stabbing his daughter in the presence of at least one witness. Like Hett's "unruliness,"Turner's problems with alcohol ("being over-taken in drink") appear to have forced the court's hand in issuing its sentence.[33]

Another issue of apparently equal or greater concern for the Essex County Court than violence against children was the destruction of property in the course of that violence, particularly in the form of livestock. In 1649 the court punished both Ann Haggett and William Flint for abusing their children as well as a cow. In both cases the court listed the "victims" of the violence together, human and animal.[34]

By failing to prosecute less extreme cases of violence against children, New England courts protected the rights of mothers and fathers to correct their children's misbehavior. When the Essex County Court brought charges against Guy Baylye in 1652 for cruelly correcting his eldest son, the court was careful to point out that it had intervened only because of great danger to the son's health and life. Indeed, at times the courts actively encouraged the masters of households to control their children by whatever means necessary. The household power structure functioned as an arm of the state, with the masters of families operating as "semi-official constables," urged to impose corporal punishment. Authorities in New Haven ordered Nicholas Pinion of Essex County to whip his daughter Hannah in 1667/8 for her "wicked carriage" and "her bad Language as Cursing & other Corrupt base speeches."The court further protected fathers by prohibiting children from retaliating. James White Jr. was ordered to be whipped for threatening to strike back at his father during one such correction.[35]

While less frequently, courts sometimes ordered mothers to impose punishment on their children for misbehavior, making these women an extension of state authority alongside their husbands. Female children, in particular, were often their mother's responsibility. After being brought before the Essex County Court for great "disturbance and disorder in the meeting house," Elizabeth Hunt and Abigaill Burnam were remanded by the court, under family government, to the care of both parents, who were ordered to "correct" them for past offenses and to ensure they were better behaved in the future. By mentioning their mother explicitly during sentencing, the court encouraged her to be involved in punishing the girls.

In a more explicit example of the state not just supporting but actively ordering physical violence to be imposed by a mother on her children, the court in neighboring Suffolk County sentenced the son and daughter of John Chandler to be "severely whip't" by the parent of the same sex in "their own house in pursence of the constable" for their suspected incestuous activity.[36] Authorities saw violence by both mothers and fathers as a means to an end. What concerned the court was not family violence—since the court itself was perpetuating its use—but the maintenance of community order and social authority.

While parents were encouraged to "correct" their children, violence against children by male and female servants or neighbors was seen as a misappropriation of authority and therefore not generally tolerated. The vast majority of cases of violence against children that appeared before the Essex County Court fell under this category. These acts caught the attention of the court not for their violent nature alone but because they demonstrated the internal disorder of a household, or were particularly public and thus more disruptive to the community as a whole. Community order in colonial New England took precedence over almost all other considerations.[37] The suffering of the young victims of such violence therefore tended to fade into the background in these cases.

Violence by servants, specifically, against their employers' children was an indication that household governance had broken down more generally. Servants brought before the court for abusing the children of their masters were usually also prosecuted for other abuses of power, trust, and access in the household in which they worked. Hana Gray gained a degree of infamy in 1674 for beating her master's children, as well as for openly carrying on a sexual affair with at least one of her master's neighbors. She had also been seen riding her master's mare "astride: beare . . . in a rude maner." The court ordered that for her lasciviousness she was to stand at the meetinghouse in Salem on a lecture day with a sheet of paper on her head stating the offenses for which she had been charged. In a similar case, Margaret Lord was brought before the Essex County Court in 1678 for abusing her master's children and threatening them with further harm if they exposed her other "naughty doeings." Margaret had stolen extensively from her master and mistress—everything from food, beer, milk, and Indian corn to a necklace, gloves, linen, and silk. Witnesses also saw her wearing "a fine lace handerchief," stolen finery above her station.[38]

Female servants were not the only ones to be brought up on charges for abusing their masters' children. For male servants as well, violence against children was usually accompanied by other indications that the servant in question had stepped out of his place. Stephen Goodwin, a servant, was found guilty of threatening to kill the master's children and other servants, and of stealing and killing two hogs and breaking into the house of a neighbor and threatening that family with violence as well. The court forced Goodwin to pay treble damages for theft, sentenced him to be severely whipped, and ordered him to pay his master for the loss of a month's labor while he was in prison. He was escorted out of Essex County by several members of the court following his imprisonment. Five years later, in 1669, Daniel Musselleway was charged with abusing his master's daughter and maid. He was ordered to be whipped and imprisoned until he paid a fine, and was sentenced to work forty more days to complete his contracted period of labor.[39]

Authorities viewed violence against children by adult neighbors as more acceptable than violence by servants. Because of the small size and close-knit nature of village life in colonial New England, some communal parenting was to be expected. Neighbors in seventeenth-century New England played an important role in one another's lives, assisting in raising one another's children to be God-fearing, obedient members of the community. Everyone in the community was concerned about children's disruptions in the meetinghouse, for instance. Monitors armed with a "stick or wand" were elected to limit children's "unruly and uncouth behavior" during church services with the full acceptance of their parents. Neighbors often assisted neglected children, and the practice of "putting out" children to live and work in the household of a neighbor or relative was common.[40]

Violence used for the reasonable "correction" of children, like a swat by the monitor in the meetinghouse, was within the bounds of acceptable neighborly interference. There were limits to the practice of communal policing and child raising, however. Violence against children that was not in pursuit of productive ends, that was inflicted in anger or resulted in injury to the child or children in question, was beyond these bounds. Guido Baly was brought before the court in 1647 for striking his neighbor's child with a cudgel. The court emphasized the brutal nature of the attack and the child's serious injuries.[41]

Instances of violence against children that occurred during the course of public squabbles between neighboring families was also illustrative of a larger breakdown in social order and therefore became a subject of concern for the Essex County Court. In 1660 the court brought charges against Elner Jackson for threatening and abusing her neighbor Thomas Jones as well as his children. Jackson called the children "bastards" and pulled Thomas "by the hare of the head" and gave him "a boxe of the eare." The case was brought before the court after Goodman Jones insisted Jackson's apology be as public as the attacks had been. He wanted her to "give satisffaction" and admit her misdeeds in "publicke on the Lords Daie in the meeting house." She refused, and the case was taken to court instead. Similarly, children were caught up in a public feud between the Fairefields and Coys over debt and property lines in Ipswich in 1665. Walter Fairefield was fined for his and his wife's abuse of Coy's wife and children with blows and threatening words, as well as for breach of a debt. The attack on the children appeared to be in response to an attack on the Fairefields' horse after it was found on a portion of the Coys' land.[42] The Essex County Court intervened to try and ensure that the Coys' and Fairefields' tradition of name-calling and violent retribution would end with this second generation.

NEIGHBOR VIOLENCE

The type of violence that sometimes erupted between neighbors like the Coys and Fairefields, however problematic, was also not unusual in the context of seventeenth-century Massachusetts. Inter-neighbor confrontations—disputes that sometimes led to blows—fill the Essex County Court records. This is to be expected, given the nature of colonial communities. Neighbors were an almost constant presence in one another's lives and households, often freely entering one another's homes and property. Some neighbors were helpful and caring. Other relationships were unpleasant, distrustful, and violent. Both positive and negative relationships were played out in colonial courts. As an apparatus for negotiating social and economic agreements, the courthouse hosted affable exchanges. At the same time, many of the cases that appeared in New England courtrooms hardly portrayed an image of neighborly affection. Instead, "vendettas between groups of households . . . spiteful individuals stirring up scandal, and lots of dirty washing . . . hanging out in public" were sometimes the order of the day.[43]

Disputes over boundaries were a particular source of trouble in colonial New England. Boundaries between one man's land and his neighbor's, or often between adjacent townships, were an almost constant source of tension. Associated with these property disputes was usually another type of "trespass" as well. These infractions included debt or theft, or breach of contract or agreement. Because of the close-knit nature of neighbor relationships, many of these disputes appear to have been "experienced emotionally, by those directly involved, as a form of personal 'trespass.'"[44] Relationships between intimates gone sour sometimes erupted into violent arguments.

Married women in colonial Massachusetts could not technically own property; unless set aside in trust, any family property they possessed prior to marriage fell under the control of their husband. It appears, however, that many wives saw their familial holdings as their joint concern, and like their counterparts in early modern England, some entered into disputes with their neighbors to protect their family's interests. As Garthine Walker explains, it was predominantly as wives that women appeared before seventeenth-century English courts as violent assailants, rescuing household goods and defending property rights.[45] The same appears to have been true in seventeenth-century New England, as the Essex County Court records reflect. Women were brought before the court for entering into violent disputes with neighbors over the use or misuse of property and space. These altercations reached the attention of the court when outside witnesses or groups became involved and arguments between neighbors devolved into some form of public disorder, frequently involving personal insult.

In 1656 and 1658, Bettres and William Canterbery and Goodwife Rowden were brought before the Essex County Court for disagreements over livestock boundaries that had turned into violent confrontations. On one occasion, several witnesses stated that upon finding the Rowdens' pig on their property eating their peas, William Canterbery went to complain to Goodwife Rowden about the offending swine. Rowden responded by throwing stones of two or three pounds' weight at Canterbery with such force that if he had not fallen out of their path, they "myght haue spoyld" him. This was the most public incident to date, but it was not the first time Goodwife Rowden's behavior had proved violent. Rebecca Canterbery testified that when her father was working on his own farm, she had seen Goodwife Rowden throw stones at him with the intention of hitting him.

She also noted that Rowden would chase their cattle with her dogs, or hit them with sticks, whenever they were let out of their yard. The Canterberys themselves were not opposed to using violence against their troublesome neighbor, however. A few years earlier, Bettres Canterbery had confronted Rowden carrying a stick and calling her a "lousie slutt" with "but one Shift," adding that "all the clothes she had were upon her back." Witnesses then heard "a great crie" from Rowden, as if in response to a beating, and saw that she displayed the "print of blows." The Canterberys were charged with both "provoking speeches" and "a strong suspicion" of assault on Goodwife Rowden. John Rowden was fined for his wife's offenses and bound for her good behavior.[46]

In 1667 Margaret Bennett testified before the Essex County Court that several neighbor women had attacked her as she attempted to prevent them from trespassing on her land. According to her statement, when Margaret told the other women to go around her property, for "she would not have them . . . make a highway through her lot," two of the women, Frances Gilligan and Martha Beale, struck her in the face, knocked her down, and "fetched blood on her," calling her an "old whore." What Margaret's testimony failed to mention was that she had not politely requested that the women bypass her land but instead, with her adult son watching, had come armed with a "scragged clubb," threatening to "knock out [their] brains." During the conflict she seriously injured one of the trespassers, who died not long after.[47] When the parties charged each other with battery, the court sided with Margaret. Her protection of her family's property justified the violence that ensued, even for a woman.

Disputes over space and its appropriate use took place outside the context of land as well and involved encroachment on personal boundaries and markers of status. The Essex County Court brought in several women and girls for fighting over seating in the meetinghouse, quarrels that turned into physical confrontations. Seating in the meetinghouse was not something people in seventeenth-century Massachusetts took lightly. When attending meeting, men and women were assigned specific places according to their standing in the community. Seated on the opposite side of the aisle from the men, wives and daughters were placed in the same position and order as their husbands and fathers, with widows given a spot in relation to the standing of their late spouse. These arguments, therefore, were about more than finding a place to sit, but were confrontations about one's place in the community. Women, it seems, were willing to physically, and sometimes violently, assert the status of their family. Given such a public location as the meetinghouse during church services, the court could not help but step in to restore order.

Goodwives Wolfe and Stackhouse of Salem were involved in one such power play in the meetinghouse that led to a physical confrontation. In 1673, on the Lord's day, Goodwife Stackhouse was sitting on a bench in the meetinghouse when Goodwife Wolfe came in to take her seat. Stackhouse, for unknown reasons, refused to move over to allow Wolfe to take her assigned seat next to her. Instead of sitting somewhere else, somewhere not reflective of her standing in Salem, Wolfe chose first to stand in front of Stackhouse and later to sit on her knees. One witness attested to being "ashamed to see them . . . contend for the uperhand." By the time Stackhouse finally agreed to move down, she was apparently injured, and was so "sick" she had to be helped out of the meetinghouse. Wolfe was fined for her undeniably disruptive behavior in front of the entire church community.[48]

In another argument over seating and station, the Burnhams and Hunts of Ipswich took their dispute to more intense levels of physical aggression. Both Abigail Burnham and Elizabeth Hunt were found "culpable of disturbance and disorder in the meeting house" for shoving each other, pushing each other's chairs, and fighting for space. Elizabeth was apparently kneeling in her chair when Abigail came into the meeting and pushed her. Elizabeth "rose up and spacke to her teling her it ware enough: enough att this time for shame." Elizabeth then shoved Abigail down on her knees. As girls who were still under family governance, Elizabeth and Abigail were remanded to their parents for punishment. This was probably a wasted effort for Elizabeth, however, given the prominent role her mother played in their continuing conflicts. When not encouraging her daughter's behavior, literally pushing her daughter's chair against Abigail's, Elizabeth Hunt Sr. was herself pushing the girl and elbowing her to "the "defacing of her linnon." Goodwife Burnham was more prone to verbal acts of aggression, telling the Hunt family's servant sitting with them that she had no right to be there.[49]

In the course of its work to maintain community order, bad language and name-calling appeared to be as much of a concern for the Essex County Court as acts of violence, even for women. As Jane Kamensky observes, the importance and power of the spoken word in early New England should not be underestimated. "Taken together, the dislocations of colonialism, the dictates of Puritan belief, and the mundane realities of village life" created an environment in which the spoken word came to hold "special powers and special dangers." Massachusetts courts were filled with presentments for speech crimes, including blasphemy, witchcraft, contempt of authority, defamation, and swearing. People's words, Puritans believed, held the power to hurt in ways that even a physical blow did not. Nobody in New England, Kamensky argues, would have believed the old adage "sticks and stones will break my bones, but names will never hurt me." Instead, the New England version of this saying held that "a soft tongue breaketh the bone." Cotton Mather quoted scripture, stating, "I will take heed unto my ways that I sin not with my Tongue; I will keep my Mouth with a Bridle." For women in particular, pressure to govern their use of language was intense.[50]

Records from the Essex County Court attest to the relative importance of speech offenses versus violent acts for women. In many cases in which a woman was brought up on charges of violence as well as inappropriate speech, the verbal transgressions appear to have taken precedence, at least according to the listing of the offenses in question and the detail devoted to explaining them in the court records. For instance, when Anis Chubb and Elizabeth Vinsent of Manchester physically assaulted another young woman, they were presented before the court in 1656 for "giving railing speeches & foule language & fighting." Similarly, Elizabeth Poe and Martha Henley were fined by the court in 1675 for "scolding & rude cariage & speeches & hiting" each other. When Mary Grant was presented before the Essex County Court for her violence and speech offenses against Elizabeth Mill in 1680, the court records detail her verbal attacks but leave her violent deeds mostly to the reader's imagination. Mary called Elizabeth a "a crooked-back slut and a thief." Her "upbraiding her for her deformity of body and other provoking words" appear to have been more reprehensible, and therefore more deserving of attention, than the assault on Elizabeth.[51]

Cases of defamation and slander took on a special significance in early New England because Puritan settlers in that region had an extreme fear of public exposure and humiliation. The seriousness with which colonial communities treated instances of slander and defamation, as opposed to their relatively lenient treatment of violence, is also evident in a case from Haverhill in 1682. One evening the widow Sarah Stickney arrived at the Haynes' house, where John Atkinson and his wife were visiting, and accused John of being the father of her child. Goody Atkinson denied the charge, saying, "You lo Impuent whore to Lay ye Child or bastard to my husband." Sarah responded with "like uprobias, reprochfull reviling speeches" and refused to leave. It was then that Goody Atkinson attacked, "slapt her hand in her face . . . and spit att her." The court never punished Goody Atkinson for the physical attack, but Sarah Stickney was charged with slander for her accusations of sexual misconduct. Though Sarah received a physical blow, petitions to the court by both John Atkinson and his wife argued that it was they who had been "much wronged" by the "false information of the sayd Sarah Stickney."[52]

VIOLENCE AGAINST SERVANTS

Perhaps more than any other type of household violence, servant abuse in seventeenth-century Massachusetts illustrates the daily violence that people lived with, expected, and perpetuated. Masters and mistresses physically "corrected" both male and female servants. The men and women dispensing this correction were allowed considerable leeway in how they chose to keep their servants in line. Even Cotton Mather, who was known for arguing against the beating of children, expressed the harsh standard for correction of servants that served as a community and cultural norm when he argued that the punishment of a disobedient servant should be so "moderate with Humanity, that he may not be thereby Killed or Maimed." Handbooks for constables and justices of the peace affirmed that almost all forms of correction for unruly servants were acceptable, up to the point of serious injury or death. Court officials and the populace as jurors judged when a master or mistress crossed the line from properly exercising the prerogative of authority to the "wrongful beating [of] another." As masters themselves, they ensured that this standard remained difficult to reach.[53]

This liberal standard for correction contradicted the written law of the land in Massachusetts. The Body of Liberties frowned upon the use of physical violence against servants, even permitting them to flee from abusive masters "with no penalty." In these cases, as in other instances of household violence, practices and traditions from the old country overshadowed the stated wishes of Puritan authorities and the enactment of the Body of Liberties in real life. Following the English pattern, courts rarely questioned the physical disciplining of servants. The master possessed the right of correction over his servants, and he "was permitted, even expected, to use the rod or the whip in a moderate fashion." He was not alone in this, however. Just as a wife was considered subject to her husband, servants in a household were subject to her. Mistresses had the power to correct servants with "words of reproof" and "stripes if needful." As in England, women's "authority to inflict discipline on others was delimited by the household."[54]

Women's domestic authority—their position as holders of natural or civil authority or power—legitimated their use of force in these instances, and in New England in particular, it reached new levels. Women's authority over female servants went almost unquestioned, and Essex County Court records indicate that most violence by mistresses was indeed directed at female servants. Yet their ability to discipline servants was not entirely limited along the lines of gender. The insecurity of life in unsettled regions of the colonial wilderness, and men's necessary absences from the family farm, meant that women frequently took on the role of "deputy husband." Although a good wife "never wore the breeches," she did often take charge of the house, the children, and all the servants.[55]

On the one hand, as reflected in the court records, authorities saw violence by women as acceptable when it was used in the course of exercising their significant authority as mistress of the household. On the other hand, violence by either male or female servants against an employer was almost never allowed. Given power disparities between masters and mistresses and their servants, court records do not illustrate the same give-and-take of violence between these groups that existed between husbands and wives, for instance. Servants who acted against their employers were always punished when these cases reached the courts, usually with a whipping or some other sort of severe reprisal.[56] More commonly these incidents were handled within the household, and charges of overcorrection of servants were ignored.

Most personal assaults on servants were, of course, never recorded because the victim feared prosecution, accepted such violence as a normal part of life, or preferred not to publicize the incident. Only the most "unusual" cases tended to reach the attention of the Essex County Court, for example, when the violence was considered extremely brutal, when the abuse disrupted community life, when an unusual form of punishment was used, when it involved sexual indiscretions, or when a servant was assaulted by someone other than the master or mistress. As in other instances of household violence, therefore, the examples of violence against servants that appear in the seventeenth-century court records are just a small sample of a much more extensive practice.[57]

The 1681 case brought by Joane Suifland, an Irish indentured servant, against her master and mistress, Thomas and Naomi Maule, illustrates the court's unwillingness to prosecute even the most heinous examples of such violence. Suifland appeared before the court and testified that during her service to the Maule family, both the master and mistress had "many Tymes unreasonably beate" her with a "hors whip," sometimes in excess of thirty or forty blows at a time, even before her "cloathes haue bin on." She feared that the family would kill her before long and requested that "shee may be released from so cruell & barberous a servitude & putt to some other where she may be more Christian like dealt with." Several witnesses attested to seeing Suifland bloodied and bruised, and others had seen Naomi Maule beating the maid and kicking her out of doors, threatening her with further violence. Thomas Maule, known as a "greate lyar & a contentious person amongst his neighbors," was also known to beat his servant. None of this swayed the court. While Thomas Maule was presented and fined for profaning the Sabbath during that same court visit, his and Goody Maule's repeated abuse of their maidservant was unworthy of even an admonishment.[58]

The unspoken assumption in cases of servant abuse was that the servant in question deserved whatever punishment he or she received, regardless of the servant's claims of excessive violence. For example, in 1677 the court charged Sarah Taylor with quitting her service in a disorderly way and spreading rumors that her mistress had severely beaten her. As far as the court record shows, no effort was made to investigate Sarah's claims of abuse. The court instead found Sarah guilty of telling contrary tales and claimed that she must have had some evil counselors, which was the main source of the trouble. They found no standing for legal conviction on her charges of cruel correction, but instead ordered that the servant's mother monitor her behavior and ensure that she refrain from entering the company of two other women, who were ostensibly a source of the mischief. In a moment of leniency, the court allowed Sarah to be placed with another godly family for work, in recognition of the extreme poverty of her family.[59]

Assumptions about servant misbehavior, and the normalcy of violence in ensuring servants' obedience, are evident in the case brought by Thomas Bettis against his master, John Simmons. Simmons had tied his servant to the foot of a bed in winter, regardless of the freezing temperatures and the servant's sparse clothing, in addition to beating him with a stick until the "blood ran down all . . . to [his] feet." One of Bettis's fellow servants was called to testify in March 1681 in court concerning the incidents, and his responses to the vicious beating of his fellow servant are entirely lacking in empathy. He indicated that the beatings were justified by the servant's "rude" behavior. The court agreed and ordered Bettis to return to his master and compensate him for "the damage sustained by his running away" by serving Simmons for another six months.[60] Neither the master, other servants in the household, nor the court found the employment of such violence objectionable.

Differences in economic status and social standing between servants and masters meant that servants usually had little recourse for relief, even in instances of excessive abuse. Martha Stacy's parents attempted to petition the court in 1680 concerning injuries she had sustained while a servant to Joseph Cocker and his wife of Newbury. The petition forced the court to investigate the claims, and they found several neighbors who would attest to the servant's ill-usage at the hands of her master and mistress. Neighbors had even urged the Cockers to return Martha to her parents rather than continue to abuse her, but they replied that because her parents were poor, they were unconcerned about what became of her. Mrs. Cocker, in particular, was seen beating Martha on several occasions, and when asked about her maid's injuries, she claimed that Martha had gotten drunk and fallen down. The end result of the case is unclear, but there is no evidence that the court charged either of the Cockers with any crime or punished them despite public knowledge of their abuse of Martha. This may be explained in part by the fact that Mrs. Cocker was the daughter of Captain William Hawthorne of Salem, an eminent member of the community who had held a position as an Assistant of the town and was commissioned captain of Salem Company.[61]

While public knowledge of violence against a servant was not usually enough to ensure that a master or mistress would be punished, it was an impetus for the court to acknowledge that instances of abuse were taking place. In 1682 the court took notice of abuse suffered by a servant boy in the home of Benjamin and Elizabeth Jones after the community began to discuss it openly. A witness testified that she had seen the Joneses whip the little boy, beat him on the head, and kick him. When confronted by neighbors about the abuse, Elizabeth replied that the more people talked of the situation, the worse it would be for the child. In this case, concern for the appearance of community order appeared to trump a master's prerogative. The Joneses were ordered to pay twenty shillings, and the boy was taken away from them. In 1673, when Jacob Garland was beaten by his master, John Mason, at the home of a neighbor, the outcome was less positive. After drawing him over the threshold and hitting his head against the paving stones, Mason escaped any punishment, but the court ordered the servant, Jacob, to pay a ten shilling fine, presumably for being found in the wrong place.[62]

The burden of proof for cases of servant abuse fell squarely on the servant's shoulders and usually remained unattainable even when the violence took place in the public eye and involved persons with as unsavory a reputation as the Coreys of Salem. Mary Corey was brought before the Essex County Court in 1678 after two witnesses saw her beating a servant with a walking stick. The charge was brought among other complaints against the Coreys for public drunkenness, cursing, swearing, and abusive speech toward their neighbors. The court fined Mary for several of these offenses but dismissed the charges of servant abuse because they were not proved within the year. The court apparently did not take into account the Coreys' history of abusing servants. In 1675 Jacob Goodale, a servant for the Coreys, died from injuries sustained from a beating. Giles Corey himself admitted to having beaten Jacob, and witnesses described the almost one hundred blows he inflicted on the servant "with a stout stick." Rather than being convicted of murder, Corey was only heavily fined.[63]

Cases of "unusual" punishment were more likely to reach the attention of the court than those that fell within "normal" bounds. Acceptable punishment included most beating and bruising that fell short of permanent injury or disfigurement. Silences in Essex County Court records attest that many forms of violence were "usual" and therefore to be expected in the course of maintaining order with regard to a servant. Correction that involved a kick, slap, or punch would usually not even result in admonishment, if it reached the court at all. Correction that was considered degrading, however, was more of an issue. In 1682 the court reprimanded Phillip Fowler and ordered him to pay costs for hanging up his servant Richard Parker by the heels. The court reinforced Fowler's justification in giving correction to his servant, which the boy deserved, but disapproved of the manner of punishment. Hanging by the heels as butchers do with animals for slaughter was too humiliating. Fowler was cautioned against using this method of correction again.[64]

The case against Samuel Bishop in 1682 illustrates the court's discomfort with unusual forms of correction as well as its concern with sexual immorality. The case also reveals a mistress's role in, and opinion about, the appropriate punishment of servants. After a complaint from Tobiah Taylor, a servant to the Bishops, about the strange and cruel punishment that had been inflicted on him by his master, a grand juryman investigated the incident. Taylor claimed that Bishop had tied and whipped him, hanging him by the hands with his legs tied straddling a bench so he could not move. When the grand juryman and a magistrate went to Bishop's house, Bishop admitted he had punished the man. Bishop's wife sprang to her husband's defense, arguing that Taylor was a troublesome servant and had received punishment for being "very disobedient going out at night and not coming home in any season contrary to my husbands knowledge," smoking "his pipe of tobacco after he was in bed wch was very dangerous and hazarded our lifes and all," and "prophaning the sabbath," and for his "familarity" with a female maidservant in the middle of the night. Her husband's actions, she maintained, were within the bounds of propriety, for he had only "clapt" Taylor "with his hand," which "broke no bones & fetch no blood." Her husband had also encouraged her, she said, to "get a Rod" and whip the maidservant "for fit as I saw." The court accepted Goody Bishop's explanation of the incident as well as her definition of reasonable correction by both master and mistress. The case does not appear to have gone any further.[65]

The violent physical correction of a servant was not enough to bring John Jackson and his wife before the Essex County Court in 1660. When the accusations turned sexual in nature, however, the court took notice. Mary Soames was a less than ideal servant. When told to do her work, Soames had said to Goody Jackson, "Doe it youer selfe." In response, Goody Jackson gave her "a nick upon ye arm," and the maid cried out until Jackson told her to hold her tongue. Goody Jackson then "gave hir blow with the bake of her hand." The court took issue with none of this until Soames accused John of sexual molestation. Apparently he had come into her chamber and tried to force himself on her. The fourth time this occurred, Soames was able to escape by biting his nose. Jackson was presented for fornication and bound to appear at the next lecture day at Ipswich. Witnesses testified that they feared Goodwife Jackson would either kill or do deadly injury to Soames because of her accusations. Instead of ordering Goody Jackson to control her own behavior, however, the court ordered the constable to look after the maid.[66]

As these cases attest, the acceptability of violence against servants in seventeenth-century Massachusetts was determined less by the act of violence itself than by the party perpetrating that violence. Masters and mistresses were expected to use violence against servants in order to maintain authority within their households. Violence against servants by other people, however, was unacceptable. Beating another man's or woman's servant was frowned upon by the court and the community, but not out of distaste for violence itself. An individual's proper superiors could use physical punishment, but no one else.[67] Assaulting someone else's servant in effect deprived another master or mistress of his or her right to be that person's superior, and therefore the employer's right to utilize that servant's labor. As a result, cases of violence against servants that reached the court were often either brought by or directly benefiting masters in an effort to preserve that right.

The court actions brought against Charles Hill in 1666 and Walter Fairefield in 1682 illustrate how much the court respected a master's access to a servant's labor and wanted to preserve it. Hill was brought before the court for striking and wounding the servant of Nicholas Maning. Hill was seen walking away from the servant, who lay bleeding in the lane. As a result, the court sentenced Hill to be whipped, ordered him to pay a fine to the injured servant, and sentenced him to pay the costs of medical treatment. He was also ordered to reimburse Maning for the servant's lost labor. Similarly, when Thomas Fiske brought a case against Walter Fairefield in the Essex County Court for abusing and striking his servant, who was then unable to perform his work, the court found for Fiske. After the court discovered that the servant had lied regarding the weapon used and had exaggerated the extent of his injuries, however, it repealed the sentence. Fairefield, the accused abuser, was only reimbursed for costs.[68]

The Essex County Court upheld a mistress's right to a servant's labor, as well as her authority to dispense correction in the form of physical violence, even through a proxy. Elizabeth Woodbery's presentment for striking the Hubbards' maid Elisabeth in 1664 illustrates both tendencies. Woodbery admitted that she struck the servant but claimed she was acting in the place of Goody Hubbard, her cousin. The Hubbards defended her by arguing that they had asked Woodbery to supervise Elisabeth in their absence, knowing the servant was untrustworthy. She was "bad, unruly, sulen, careless and destructive & disobedient . . . Haveing occasion to be from home, & not dareing to leave such an one with or childe and house alone wee desired the aforesed Eliz Woodbery . . . to be over her & in place of vs." They added that Woodbery "did noe more then she had or authority for & that her mistresse if prsent would have don the same." They expressed confusion about why the case had reached the court at all: "We do much wonder that there should be so much made of it, when as we conceive, had it been a breach of law for or couzin to have strook her, wch it is not, she doeing of it by or power & representing us."[69] The Hubbards believed that they had full power to correct their servant as they saw fit, and that it was the place of Goody Hubbard, or someone acting in her stead, to dispense the punishment.

The examples of household violence presented in this chapter—between spouses, against children, directed at neighbors, and used against servants—demonstrate the pervasive violence that, as it went almost unquestioned, seeped into the very foundations of colonial New England life. An examination of Essex County Court records brings into focus an important seventeenth-century reality, and one that historians have been far too apt to overlook: both men and women encountered and perpetuated a culture of household violence that extended from cradle to grave. Like men, women both experienced violence and committed acts of violence for their own ends. Women, however, consistently directed their violence toward maintaining familial order or preserving family property, safety, or status. Because this violence was woven into the social and cultural fabric of English settlements in early Massachusetts, it became a pervasive force that dictated the limits of what was acceptable in human interaction.

Neither the colonial courts nor Puritan authorities effectively counteracted, or even necessarily contradicted, these ideas about the utility of violence. Instead, as the court records demonstrate, they tended to reinforce the notion that physical violence itself was usually unremarkable and part of the normal functioning of a marriage, household, and community. This is surprising, especially for women, given the Puritan lip service against domestic violence that appears in the Body of Liberties as well as ministers' strictures on feminine obedience. While some forms of female violence were met with disapproval—those that involved extremely disruptive, public behavior, for instance—the courts' treatment of many instances of household violence reveals that they did not generally disapprove of physical violence by women. Indeed, within reasonable bounds, it appears to have been relatively unimportant, especially when compared with concerns about women's sexual and speech offenses. While concerns about female violence varied significantly according to the context in which that violence took place, alarm was more uniformly expressed about female adultery, blasphemy, and defamation.

As explored in this chapter, the ability of women to use violent means to try to ensure the proper functioning of their households remained relatively unhindered by Massachusetts authorities throughout the seventeenth century. As we will see in the following chapters, however, authorities' willingness to tolerate women's violent behavior on behalf of the interests of their families or kin groups depended, in large part, on whether those interests forwarded the needs of society as a whole. The motivations behind a range of women's violent actions may have remained largely the same, but how the community and authorities interpreted those actions differed greatly.

CHAPTER 2

☞ From "that wicked house"

Women and Infanticide

In the spring and summer of 1691, the Emerson family of Haverhill, Massachusetts, was the object of unwanted public scrutiny. The Court of Assistants had called Michael and Hannah Emerson before them to answer questions regarding their daughter Elizabeth's alleged infanticide of her newborn twins. Unmarried, Elizabeth was accused of "being instigated by ye Devil" to "feloniously kill & murther" her bastard infants, sewing up their bodies in a "small Bagg or cloath," and concealing them "in sd Emmersons house." When examining her parents, the court questioner asked with incredulity how neither her father nor her mother had been aware that their daughter was pregnant, that she had given birth, or killed her children. "Did you not know or suspect That yor daughter Eliza was at times w Child?" the court demanded of her mother. "Did you know nothing at the time or afterward of her delivery?" the examiner probed her father. The Emersons denied any knowledge of the incident. Elizabeth's responses were the same. She had kept her pregnancy from her family, given birth silently and without their knowledge, and concealed the death of her infants on her own. Elizabeth continued to insist on her family's innocence until the end of her life on a Boston scaffold on June 8, 1693.[1]

Elizabeth and her family had received unwanted attention before, during her trial for fornication in 1686. Elizabeth had given birth to an illegitimate daughter that year. Her parents had been brought before the court, along with Elizabeth's older sister, to testify concerning her alleged misdeeds. Elizabeth claimed that her pregnancy was the result of a rape by their neighbor Timothy Swan. The community was skeptical. During her "travail," or the most painful part of labor in childbirth, several neighbor women called

Elizabeth's account of the attack into question. Elizabeth claimed that she could not scream or fight "because his arm was cross her throat" and did not spread word of the attack because "she did think it would be a disgrace to her." The neighbor women found Elizabeth's answers unconvincing. So did the Essex County Court, which failed to charge Swan with rape but fined Elizabeth for fornication. There is no record that Swan was similarly fined, although he was required to provide maintenance for the child, which he consistently failed to do. Even Elizabeth's claims of rape could not preserve her or her family from the public shame of sexual indiscretion and the stain of immorality. During the trial, the taint of Elizabeth's deed was already upon her and her household. Denying that his son was the father of Elizabeth's illegitimate child, Robert Swan Sr. maintained that Timothy would never have associated with Elizabeth or gone "into that wicked house."[2]

In Puritan New England, female worth was measured in large part by a woman's reputation; it determined her status and her prospects, but it was tenuous to preserve. Pursuing pleasure, such as socializing outside the home to the neglect of domestic duties, could draw community notice and censure. The consequences of sexual immorality for women could be dire. Colonial courts and communities imposed more severe punishments on women than on their male partners, and out-of-wedlock pregnancies provided inescapable evidence of a woman's guilt. A woman could salvage her reputation if she married her partner, but those who could not had almost no hope of restoring their place in society. Moreover, women's families and households also faced public shame, humiliation, and contempt from their communities. The consequences of a loss of reputation, including the chance to make advantageous alliances, could impact the entire household. Many of the women brought to court for sexual offenses were servants, but that did not necessarily mean that they did not have families in the area. An analysis of the financial status of female fornication defendants in Essex County indicates that while some female servants were poor or orphaned or both, or were recent immigrants, other women with documented work histories had prosperous parents living in the same community.[3]

For some women, hiding the evidence of their ruin through infanticide can be viewed as a terrible but pragmatic choice. When Elizabeth Emerson murdered her newborn twins, she was of course attempting to hide evidence of her sexual indiscretion for her own purposes. As with most women, she would have preferred to live in dignified anonymity. Elizabeth also knew, however, the consequences of her pregnancy for her family and tried to spare them further public shame. Paradoxically, women like Elizabeth broke Puritan mandates against concealment and taking life in order to try to ensure that they and their household would remain a part of that society, their status unremarkable.

Infanticide was not unique to the women of New England, although the act seems to have been more fraught with meaning and more heavily prosecuted in those Puritan-dominated colonies. Englishwomen in the mother country appeared in court for committing infanticide, prompted by a lack of reliable contraceptive methods, poverty, and fear of public disgrace for unwanted pregnancies. Indictments and convictions for the crime increased dramatically in England after 1624, when a new law made the concealment of the death of an illegitimate child sufficient evidence for convicting the mother of infanticide. This law resolved problems with proving whether a child had been born dead or died of neglect, violence, or natural causes. The statute presumed that a woman's child was born alive. If she maintained that the infant was stillborn, it was her responsibility to prove it "by One witness at least."[4]

For most of the seventeenth century, New England courts did not need a formal statute to prosecute and execute women for infanticide without solid evidence of their guilt. The 1624 English concealment standard was not formally adopted into colonial legal codes until the end of the seventeenth century, but it served as the standard of evidence for colonial courts from the beginning. From 1646, the first recorded infanticide case in New England, juries convicted women for infanticide in the same proportion as English juries after 1624. During the seventeenth century, only thirty-two women in New England were charged with infanticide, but in a region with a low homicide rate, this number takes on a greater significance. Four out of every seventeen homicide cases were for the crime, and most women were convicted and executed. Puritans' harsh treatment of infanticide cases deviated from their general tendency toward magisterial discretion and leniency in felony cases, compared to the rigid "bloody code" of English common law. This response reflected Puritans' particular concerns about the crime as a sign of both sexual wantonness and alienation from the community. The Puritan leadership warned that women who hid their illicit acts and concealed the consequences of those unions had essentially excommunicated themselves. Cotton Mather called these women "forlorn Outcasts" who "stood just upon the Edges" of society and faced an "awful Eternity."[5]

Historians have followed ministers' and magistrates' lead in defining infanticide as a profound separation from the community. For instance, Laurel Thatcher Ulrich describes infanticide, along with other deadly acts, as a type of "anti-social violence." Infanticide, she argues, "signaled a [woman's] rejection of the entire social and human order" in Puritan New England.[6] Certainly conviction for infanticide placed a woman outside the social order, by way of the noose, but depicting infanticide as inherently antisocial or as a rejection of the community misses the profoundly "social" aspects of such a crime, especially in the unique environment of colonial New England. I argue that infanticide itself—while a deplorable deviation from acceptable standards of behavior by any measure—was not inherently antisocial. When we take evidence into account that indicates women committed infanticide in order to preserve their reputation, and thus remain a part of society, it becomes increasingly difficult to classify the crime as antisocial. During a period in colonial New England in which sexual morality was policed and prosecuted with unprecedented intensity, women who committed infanticide sought to remain part of the very social order that condemned them.

This is a new interpretation of why colonial Englishwomen committed infanticide, further complicating categories of "social" versus "antisocial" violence for colonial women. In doing so, it examines the profound role that both household reputation and practical circumstances played in these women's crimes. This is not intended to normalize infanticide in Puritan New England. It is impossible to know how many instances of infanticide were successfully concealed, but by all accounts it was universally denounced. The public portrayed women accused of infanticide as disgraced perpetrators of unimaginable acts. Acknowledging that infanticides did occur, however, and why, reveals the extent to which violence infused even the most personal aspects of women's lives. By examining the impact of fornication, adultery, and bastardy prosecutions on women and their households, as well as evidence from infanticide cases, we can also see that women in seventeenth-century Massachusetts committed infanticide as part of a conservative desire to avoid disgrace and social rejection for themselves and their household.

My research also reveals that women rarely acted alone. Other members of their household either assisted them directly or signaled their tacit approval by choosing to look the other way.

When examined in the context of other forms of violence perpetrated by women in seventeenth-century Massachusetts—most of which, I argue, were aimed at preserving family property, safety, or status—infanticide is both a marked departure from the norm as well as an extreme example of it. While violence alone was not aberrant for women, deadly violence by women was uncommon. On the surface, such a crime also signaled the destruction of the family order. It was anti-maternal violence at the expense of not just the family but all humankind, directed at its most vulnerable members. For Puritans as Calvinists, this would seem to fulfill the promise of the worst of human nature: inherent selfishness and depravity allowed to flourish uncontrolled.[7] In those instances, however, in which the reputation and standing of an entire household or family seemed at stake, infanticide begins to resemble other forms of female violence during this period. It could be interpreted as an extreme, terrible, and desperate sacrifice for the continued respectability and prosperity of those with whom a woman lived and worked and loved.

THE COSTS OF SEXUAL MISBEHAVIOR

The communal nature of life in colonial New England meant that personal privacy within a household was almost nonexistent. It is unlikely that other members of a household would fail to notice a pregnant woman within its walls. It would have been more possible to conceal an unwanted pregnancy from the community at large in seventeenth-century Massachusetts than within an individual household, but avoiding the neighbors' watchful eye would still have been a significant challenge. While everyday acts of violence frequently went unnoticed and unchallenged, the same was not true for sexual misbehavior. Ordinary inhabitants of Puritan communities, as well as political and religious leaders, were on the lookout for out-of-wedlock pregnancies or even overlong dalliances between unmarried people in the community. The Essex County Court focused significant attention on prosecuting sexual misconduct cases. Between 1636 and 1718, the court presided over 818 fornication cases alone, and devoted particular time to cases that involved extramarital pregnancy.[8]

Some historians have argued that the large number of cases involving sexual misbehavior indicates that such cases were routine affairs, conducted in rote forms and rarely the focus of the real energy of the colonial courts or communities.[9] On the contrary, as Else Hambleton argues, such fornication convictions and judicial assignments of child support "brought public awareness to private sexual behaviors the community considered shameful." She continues: "Puritans thought of themselves as parts of a larger, Godly, community. The exposure of sexual activity that violated community standards . . . by a society that expected conformance to community values, was a source of great shame and an experience to be avoided."[10] Courts described sexual misdeeds in their records using terms like "incontinence" and "filthiness." Testimony from community members reflects the same views on extramarital sex. When testifying at a fornication trial in 1674, the well-regarded and elderly Goodwife Reading remarked that any who engaged in sexual activity outside of marriage were "whoremongers and adulterers God would judge." Certainly Hester Jackson was not alone in feeling "undone" after an illicit sexual encounter. God had "left her to temptation," and her shame was severe.[11]

Likewise, Puritan ministers had strong words for those who would misbehave, warning of the consequences not only for themselves but also for those associated with them. Cotton Mather called sex outside of marriage "an Odious Fornication, which is a further Step, of that Uncleanness whereunto the Raging Lusts of men do carry them." He warned that those "Unwedded Persons" who chose to "prostitute themselves" with the sins of the flesh "Shall not Inherit the Kingdom." Increase Mather, preaching on the topic of fornication, railed against the devastation that would be wrought by such deeds on those who committed them as well as their family members. According to Samuel Sewall's recollections, Mather had shown that even respectable people "might fall into such scandalous Sins as might bring temporal Wrath and ruin upon themselves and upon their posterity." The "temporal wrath and ruin" Sewall spoke of was why both men and women were so anxious to avoid fornication prosecutions. The inherent shame affected not only the persons involved and those immediately around them but also their descendants. When Cotton Mather's own son Increase was accused of getting a "Harlot big with Bastard," Mather lamented his child's misstep: "Oh! Dreadful Case! Oh, sorrow beyond any that I have met withal! What shall I do not for the, foolish Youth! What for my afflicted and abased Family?" Puritan Massachusetts was a society based on a culture of honor and shame. It mattered deeply what the neighbors thought.[12]

This image of colonial New England runs counter to scholarship that has attempted to downplay the importance of sexual misbehavior in Puritan communities. These studies, however, do not take into account that women shouldered greater blame and punishment in the aftermath of unmarried sexual acts, or that most sexual encounters occurred in situations of dramatic power imbalances. Sex that resulted in unwanted pregnancies frequently was not between consenting young people, or those who had previously arranged to marry, but between men and women of different social and economic status. While scholars have shown that premarital pregnancy became more common throughout the seventeenth century, and courts were increasingly tolerant toward couples with "early births," the same did not hold true for single women convicted of engaging in sex. As punishments for premarital pregnancy gradually disappeared, courts continued to prosecute single women for fornication in disproportionate numbers. For women unable to marry their partners, there is little evidence of a sexually tolerant culture in seventeenth-century New England.[13]

Extramarital sexual contact in colonial New England communities was treated as a serious issue, and those who committed it lived with a very rational fear of discovery. Colonial courts imposed punishments of public shame and humiliation on those found guilty of sexual crimes. Abby Chandler has argued that by "taking part in the community ritual of the sexual crime trial, defendants were punished while serving as an example to other transgressors."[14] For these punishments to serve as a deterrent to others, they needed to be both harsh and humiliating. For most of the seventeenth century, Massachusetts courts commonly sentenced those convicted of fornication to a public whipping. A whipping was ten stripes, a severe whipping between fifteen and forty. Whippings were usually conducted in public, with the victim stripped to the waist and tied to a post located in front of the meetinghouse. The central location, and exposure of the victim, were no accident.[15] One can only imagine the spectacle of a lone figure, tied to the whipping post, back exposed, while fellow community members gathered to witness her brutal punishment and shame. Family members must have flinched with every jeer from the crowd and lash of the whip. Women bore the brunt of these punishments for sexual misdeeds. With pregnancy as undeniable evidence of sexual misbehavior, at least for single women, they could not escape punishment for their crimes.

THE SHAME OF FORNICATION

When Mary Dane of Ipswich, unmarried, sixteen, and pregnant, was convicted of fornication by the Essex County Court in 1654, she was sentenced to be publicly whipped. The fact that John Dane, Mary's father, was one of the most respected men in the community and that Mary had no previous record of misbehavior failed to preserve her from public punishment. At the same time, Jeffrey Sknelling, the man convicted of fornication with Mary, was only bound for good behavior. Sknelling's previous fine for "divers lies" and "suspicion of filthiness" in 1650 apparently did not influence the court's decision to release him without requiring a whipping, a fine, or child support payments. The court did not explain its reasoning for such unequal treatment, but it was not unprecedented in seventeenth-century Massachusetts. Essex County Court judges had the discretion to release men accused of fornication—or named as fathers of children by their female partners—with lenient sentences, or no punishment whatsoever.[16] It appears a judge exercised that right of discretion in this case and laid the blame solely at Mary's feet.

In 1659 William Bingley and Elizabeth Pressye (Preston) of Newbury, both indentured servants in the Pearce household, were charged with fornication. In an unusual move, the judge ordered William to be whipped, probably because of his status as an indentured servant. He was also ordered to pay forty shillings to his master Pearce for Elizabeth's "laying in" from her resulting pregnancy. Elizabeth, however, was to face a more severe physical punishment than her partner: she was sentenced to be "severely whipped" and to remain in her indenture with her master until the court released her from service.[17]

When Mary Sheffield was brought before the Essex County Court twice for fornication, first in 1658 and again in 1662, she was whipped both times, the second time severely. During her first presentment, Mary refused to name the father of her child and faced punishment alone. When she was brought back to court in 1662 for the same offense, she reluctantly named her employer, Esaiah Wood, as her partner in fornication and the father of her second child. She had been "enticed into the barn by him the night he lay with her," but afterwards when she became pregnant, he refused to acknowledge the child as his own and face the "shame" of his sin in front of his wife and father. Even when witnesses in court attested to his general proclivity for "lascivious acts," he declared all accusations false and refused to confess. While Mary faced a severe whipping for fornication, Wood was ordered only to pay child support for their son.[18]

An amendment to the Massachusetts Bay Colony fornication law in 1668 cemented the gender imbalances in punishment that had been growing in the colony. Whereas there had been a "slight overprosecution" of women for sexual crimes in the 1640s, by the 1660s punishment for fornication was heavily skewed toward women.[19] Concerns about financially supporting children born out of wedlock led the court to exclude men from prosecution for fornication in favor of an assignment of paternity instead. Paternity required a lesser standard of evidence to convict than fornication—just a woman naming the father of her child during her "travail." The man accused could not be convicted of fornication, barring confession or the testimony of witnesses, but would be considered the "reputed father" of the child and made to pay support. Assigning paternity in this manner helped ease the costs to colonial taxpayers of supporting illegitimate children but also ensured that men would receive no public punishment for their crimes alongside their female partner. Even with this lesser standard of evidence, however, men would sometimes walk away from fornication cases with no repercussions.[20]

In addition to corporal punishment, part of the shaming ritual for women charged in fornication cases involved public name-calling by colonial courts. Criminal court judges shamed women convicted of fornication as a matter of public record and a moral lesson to the community. When Alice Williams, the daughter of a gentleman, was facing charges for fornication in 1643, the court referred to her as a "slutt" before imposing a fine and sentencing her to be whipped. Edward Flint, the father of her child and a married man, was only fined.[21] Judges and juries also openly discussed the sexual history of female defendants accused of fornication. In December 1710, for example,

Elizabeth Dunwell was given "ten stripes on the naked back" for having a third bastard child. She named the father, but because no witness confirmed the charge, the reputed father was dismissed without punishment. During sentencing, the court noted "that this is the third bastard child which she hath had and so become a common strumpet or little better."[22] This type of public reprimand and punishment was particularly powerful in the culture of early New England, where speech, language, and reputation were immensely important. Denigrating those who transgressed was designed to reinforce respect for community values and domestic norms, thus promoting social cohesion.[23]

These types of punishments, however, were not necessary to reinforce community values against extramarital sex, which were well entrenched during this period. At the same time, it seems unlikely that those who were willing to engage in sexual misadventures would be dissuaded from doing so because of these punishments. This is particularly true because men, who usually acted as sexual aggressors, were also not the ones to bear the brunt of punishment or shame.

What these punishments succeeded in doing was to encourage women to conceal their unwanted pregnancies and to dispose of the evidence through infanticide. Women had far more to lose, and most were left with few options. Certainly some women were resourceful and insubordinate enough to find a way to deal with the problem of an unwanted pregnancy through abortifacients, or a woman might force or bribe her partner to marry her in the aftermath. Those without resources at their disposal faced a terrible dilemma.[24] They could bear bastard children, face their punishment and shame, and try to move on with their lives, though they must have known that their name would be tarnished in the eyes of their community and their household would be the subject of gossip and speculation.

During her slow march to the gallows in 1701, a Newbury servant woman named Esther Rogers confessed her reasons for twice committing infanticide. She had concealed her pregnancies and births to avoid the public stigma of illegitimacy. Describing her first pregnancy, she stated, "After I perceived I was with Child, I meditated how to prevent coming to Publick Shame." In the absence of other viable alternatives, Esther fell victim to "Satan presently setting in with his Temptation" and "resolved to Murder the Child." She gave birth to a child in the upstairs room of her master's home and "stopt the breath of it" before hiding it. The "Darkness of the Night following" allowed for a "Private Burial in the Garden." A year later she fell again into that "horrible Pit" of "Carnal Pollution." This time she delivered her unwanted child outdoors by a pond, "covered it over with Dirt and Snow," and returned to the house before her family would notice her absence. This time, however, her growing belly had aroused community members' suspicions. Several neighbors followed her tracks in the snow the following day and discovered the dead infant.[25]

Esther emphasized in her narrative that "not a person living" in her master's house was aware of what she had done on either occasion. Born in Kittery, Maine, she was apprenticed to the well-respected and God-fearing Woodbridges of Newbury when she was thirteen. The Woodbridges had treated Esther as a member of the family, given her a Christian education, taught her to read, and schooled her in John Cotton's catechism *Spiritual Milk for Babes.* In her "Declaration and Confession" she describes the Woodbridge house as a place of stability and godly living, and it stands to reason that she sought to conceal her pregnancies not only for her own reputation but also to avoid scandal for the household as well. The fact that the father of both of her illegitimate children was a "Negro man belonging to that House" probably added extra incentive to hide evidence of the affair. After the death of her first child, she was haunted by "Awakening, Frights, and Convictions," and, fearing she would fall into sin again, she left the Woodbridge house several times to spare herself and the family further risk of shame. In his sermon given before her execution, John Rogers made clear the stain that had fallen on Esther and those with whom she associated. "Can a man touch Pitch, and not be defiled forth with?" he demanded from the pulpit. The Woodbridges had failed to maintain a godly household and thus allowed sin to darken their home.[26]

THE PRICE OF ADULTERY

Public punishments for adultery were even more dramatic and shaming than those for fornication. Adultery, defined as sex with a married woman (the marital status of the man in question was not relevant to the crime), struck at the heart of Puritan communities by disrupting households and family dynamics. By definition, adultery had to involve at least one female culprit, making a far higher proportion of female to male defendants (one to one) than in all but two other crimes: witchcraft and infanticide. A misdemeanor in England, adultery was a capital offense under Massachusetts and Connecticut legal codes, technically punishable by execution.[27] Although only one couple was actually executed for adultery in colonial New England—juries usually tailored their findings to "suspicion of adultery" or "lying together" to avoid dispensing the death penalty—the threat of death hung over those discovered committing the crime. Offenders were frequently sentenced to stand on the gallows with a "roape about the neck" to symbolize how close they had come to death.[28]

Standard punishments for adultery included elaborate public displays designed to shame the offenders. Suspected of adultery, in 1677 Darby Bryan was sentenced by the Court of Assistants to stand on the gallows "wth a roape about neck" and "then taken doune & tyed to a Carts Tayle . . . stripped from the Girdle vpwards on his naked body to be whipped thence to the prison wth thirty nine stripes well layd on." Abigaile Johnson, in whose bed Bryan had been discovered, was sentenced "in like manner . . . to suffer in all respects." Whipping "at a cart's tail" involved being tied to the back of a cart, stripped to the waist, and flogged while being dragged through town, enabling everyone in the community to witness the sentence being carried out and the perpetrators' shame. In 1683 Joshua Rice and Elizabeth Crockett were found guilty of "lasivious Gross & foule actions tending to Adultery" and given the same sentence, with the specification that the rope hung about their necks also be draped over the gallows. Similarly, Thomas Davis of Charlestown, being found "not Guilty legally according to Indictment but found . . . Guilty of very suspitious acts leading to Adultery," was sentenced to stand on the gallows and to be whipped "at a cart's tail."[29]

Courts reserved their most condemnatory language for women found guilty of adultery. Elisabeth Broune, the wife of William Broune, and Thomas Davis's partner in the adulterous activity, was given the same sentence Davis received but was subjected to a special indictment for "Prostituting hir body . . . to Comitt Adultery." At least according to the Court of Assistants, both parties involved in adultery had failed to have "the feare of God" before their eyes, and both had been "Instigated by the divil," but Elizabeth had offered her body to Davis, not the other way around. When

Philip Darland and Mary Knights were found guilty of "of vile filthy and abominably libidinous Actions," both were sentenced to be "Conveyed to ye place of execution & ther caused to stand on hower with a Rope about [the] neck Cast ouer the Gallowes" and to be "fastned to the Carts tayle & whipt seuerely." When Mary's sentence was read, however, the jury made sure to include the word "whorish" in their verdict. The "Jury brought in their virdict as aboue in all Respects adding the word whorish to ye Actions," the court recorder specified.[30]

Community members mobilized to police those suspected of extramarital sex, particularly adultery. Even in the rough maritime community of Marblehead, neighbors would not abide rumors of the Beales' sexual misadventures. Martha had been previously married, but the union had been annulled. Twenty-two years after marrying William Beale, Martha's earlier marriage continued to plague the couple. A neighbor was forced to pay a fine and publicly apologize for defaming Martha by calling her "an adulteress" who "made the church cover for her rogery . . . to the dishonor of God the church and court." Blame for Martha's supposed transgressions did not fall on her shoulders alone. Later that year, a group of townspeople wielding clubs attacked the Beales' home. The crowd taunted William, shouting: "Come out, you cuckoldly cut: we are come to beat thee. Thou livest in adultery."[31] Similarly, when Sarah Roe of Ipswich was spotted being overly familiar with her neighbor Joseph Leigh while her husband was away at sea, at least thirty-five of their neighbors came forward to testify to their moral outrage. Both Joseph and Sarah were found guilty of "unlawful familiarity." Joseph was severely whipped and fined. Sarah was sent to the House of Correction for a month and ordered to appear in the meetinghouse on lecture day bearing a sign reading "for my baudish carriage."[32]

In January 1698, Sarah Smith of Deerfield faced a dilemma. After her husband, Martin, had been captured in an Indian raid three years previously, she had taken comfort in the arms of a neighbor, Joseph Colson. Sarah was technically still married because Martin's fate was uncertain. As Sarah's relationship with Joseph progressed, her "Godly father in law" offered her "continual Counsils and Warnings" to stop the affair for the sake of herself as well as their family. It was her failure to heed this familial advice, as Cotton Mather recounts in his narrative of her story, that "laid the Foundation for her Destruction." Sarah soon discovered she was pregnant with Joseph's child. He offered her money to conceal the child and begged her not to name him as the father. Sarah had few options. She knew that having the child virtually guaranteed conviction for adultery. Given the consequences for such a crime—repeated severe whippings and public shaming on the gallows, let alone irreparable damage to her reputation in the community—Sarah chose instead to try to erase the evidence of her crime, first attempting to abort the pregnancy without success. Eventually she gave birth to the baby alone, and "with intent to conceale her Lewdnesse," strangled it and attempted to hide the body. Neighbors who knew she was "ill" later found the child and reported her to the authorities. Sarah was executed for infanticide later that year.[33]

In his execution sermon for Smith, titled "Warnings to the Unclean," minister John Williams looked out on the Deerfield assembly and admonished his audience for their lack of vigilance throughout Smith's affair and resulting pregnancy. "I would fain have clarity . . . I fear there are several [in this assembly] that have Murdered in their hearts, and some who have been guilty of interpretative Murder, for hiding and concealing the Uncleanness for which this poor Condemned One was guilty," he thundered from the pulpit. Williams suggested that Sarah's neighbors knew of her affair, and possibly even her pregnancy, and were thus complicit in the lie and passive accomplices in infanticide. Others who failed to come forward after Sarah was no longer showing signs of pregnancy, were also responsible. Sarah's father-in-law, for one, was aware of her extramarital relationship and could not have been ignorant of her growing belly, or its sudden disappearance. Sarah herself admitted in an interrogation that she confided her pregnancy to her friend Mary Lyes, who advised her to "conceale it." For Williams, at least, the entire community was implicated in Smith's deed. Ironically, the one party that Williams did not blame in his sermon was the actual father of Smith's child, Joseph Colson. When Smith named Colson as the father, he denied any involvement. Without evidence or a confession, there was little authorities could do, and Colson was not charged with any crime.[34]

In addition to the penalties already described, those convicted of adultery faced the additional possibility of banishment. As the ultimate social exclusion, banishment would not have been a pleasant prospect for men, but it would have been particularly difficult for women and damaging to the households of which they were an integral part.[35] Margaret Seale was sentenced to be severely whipped and banished upon pain of death for committing adultery in 1637. A few years later, when Thomas Owen and Sarah Hale were brought before the Court of Assistants for having a relationship outside of her marriage, both were charged with "adulteros practises" and sentenced to "bee sent to the gallos wth a roape about [their] neck, & to sit upon the lather an houre the roapes end throwen over the gallos." Following punishment, Owen was returned to prison. Hale, by contrast, after being "censured for her miscarriage" and punished, was also banished.[36] When, after a four-year absence, Ruth Reed returned from England in 1673 to her husband in Massachusetts with a toddler, she was charged for attempting to foist an illegitimate child on her husband. Saying that she had offended all by "most Impudently returning to these parts Imposing the sajd child on hir husband Wm Read," the court stated that if she did not vacate the colony within two months, she would be forced to stand on a stool in the marketplace on a lecture day with a sign reading "thvs i stand for my advlteros and whorish carriage" and whipped thirty-nine stripes.[37]

Ruth Briggs, a married woman, concealed evidence of her adultery by committing infanticide and was executed for her crimes in 1668. Originally from Essex County, Massachusetts, Ruth was the eldest daughter of the troublesome but close-knit Pinion family of Lynn. Her parents' discordant relationship had brought them before the Essex County Court on several occasions, but the couple had remained together and raised five children. Ruth married and had a daughter, but her first husband died just a few years later, and she returned to her father's household when the family relocated to New Haven. Ruth remarried in 1665, to a Peter Briggs, but was convicted of adultery with a man from the local ironworks. As a result, the Connecticut Court of Assistants banished her from the colony. Ruth was found again in her father's household a few years later. The court charged her father with harboring a public enemy, asking why "he entertained Ruth Brigȝ soe Contrary to the mind of the towne & of authority," and ordered Ruth removed. In a show of mercy, the court delayed her ousting on account of the cold winter weather. Ruth, however, had since become pregnant again outside her marriage. She at first attempted to miscarry using an herbal draught but failed to end her pregnancy. She later gave birth to the infant in secret and buried it in a nearby swamp, but not before her physical condition had aroused the suspicion of community matrons. They discovered her dead infant, and Ruth was sent to Hartford for trial before the Court of Assistants. She was executed for adultery and infanticide.[38]

The timing of Ruth's infanticide suggests that she attempted to conceal her illicit pregnancy in order to remain in her father's household in New Haven. The court's leniency in delaying her exit from the colony and allowing her to remain with her family until the spring thaw had perhaps planted a seed of hope that she could continue among them if she avoided further sinful and illegal behavior. When Ruth discovered that she was pregnant again, and the husband she had abandoned was nowhere in sight, she knew that her pregnancy would be de facto evidence of her adulterous behavior and ensure her immediate banishment from the colony. Her own future, and the fate of her daughter from her previous marriage, would be questionable at best if they were forced to live without the protection of an established household. The Pinion clan was a problematic but tightly knit, and Ruth relied on them for protection until the end of her life. From her jail cell in Hartford, as she waited for her trial to begin, she wrote a letter to her relatives apologizing for her past conduct and expressing gratitude for their efforts on her behalf, her "very life depending on [their] witness." There is no record that the father of her illegitimate child received any punishment for his role in her crimes.[39]

THE IMPORTANCE OF SEXUAL REPUTATION

While men stood a chance of absolving themselves of charges for adultery, fornication, and bastardy in early New England, too often women's "swelling stomachs and closely witnessed births" gave them away.[40] Once blighted by sexual indiscretion, women could never be fully absolved of their guilt. They could be reintegrated into the community after charges of fornication, following a public confession and penitence, but Puritan communities offered little support or compassion to unwed mothers. One did not have to be tossed out of the community or excommunicated to suffer from a loss of reputation. In large part, a woman's worth was measured by her sexual reputation in Puritan colonies. In colonial Massachusetts as elsewhere in the region, women lacked property rights, with very few exceptions. It was crucial to the future of their families for men to be assured that their property would pass to their legitimate male heirs. For women, chastity prior to marriage, and a good sexual reputation after marriage, were vital to protect the status of households.[41]

The case of Susannah Martin versus William Sargent Jr. illustrates the importance of sexual reputation and how a lingering stain of sexual uncleanness could follow a woman and her family even after her marriage. George Martin, Susannah's husband, brought Sargent to court on charges of slander in 1669. Sargent had been spreading rumors around the Essex County town of Salisbury that Susannah had become pregnant years before while working as a servant in the house of Captain Wiggins. According to Sargent's story, Susannah had given birth to a bastard child in Wiggins's stable. When a man entered and saw what had happened, she attacked him, grabbing him by the collar and threatening to kill him if he told anyone. Susannah denied the entire story, and her husband won the case for slander and a small sum in damages. While the court found the slander case in the Martins' favor, rumors about their family continued to swirl. Speculation that George Martin Jr. was a bastard also reached the court and had to be silenced by the Martins yet again. The family's place in the community never seemed fully settled. For instance, George objected to their seat placement in the meetinghouse, arguing it was unsuitable for their station.[42]

Had Susannah's previous sexual misadventures come to light earlier in her life, it is unlikely that she would have been able to marry a prosperous blacksmith like George Martin. In Puritan communities, marriageability depended on a good sexual reputation. Chastity, femininity, and marriageability went hand in hand. Marriage was essentially the only path available for women, besides servitude, to leave their father's household or attempt to improve their station. For a woman who bore an illegitimate child in early Massachusetts, marriage was difficult. According to Hambleton, only 20 percent of women who bore illegitimate children between 1640 and 1685 "made a subsequent marriage free from the taint of sexual scandal." There was almost no incentive for men to marry a pregnant lover, especially if the woman was of lower social and economic status. Puritan fathers were permitted wide discretion in when and how they distributed property to their sons, giving them a degree of control over their offspring's choice of spouse. Many sons remained economically dependent for years, delaying marriage until a relatively late age. More immediately, marrying a pregnant woman was a legal admission of guilt for fornication and bastardy in New England courts.[43] Most disgraced women, like Mary Sheffield of Ipswich who was convicted twice for fornication in 1659 and 1662, remained single until death. After being abandoned by the father of her child, who said he "would not abide the shame thereof," she all but disappeared into her employer's household. The only remaining record of her life is an inventory of her meager possessions by her employer after her death.[44]

Other women, like Hester Jackson of Scituate, lost most of their value to their households after becoming pregnant out of wedlock and being convicted of fornication. Hester was seventeen when she was sent home to her father, unemployed and pregnant, in 1663. She claimed the father of her illegitimate child was her employer's son Joseph Gilliam. The man who had "tempted her to Harlot," as her father stated, would not marry Hester, and there is no record that she was able to make another match. Her father regarded Hester as "unclean" and worthy of punishment. "If such uncleanness be not punished . . . sin will abound," he said, "and the world fill'd with a generation of bastard Which god forbid." Even Hester regarded herself as "undone." Joseph "did tempt me often, and at last the Lord left to the temptation, so I was undone by him," she lamented in court. If Hester was attempting to improve her social and economic status by trying to win her employer's son as a husband, her gamble failed. Hers was a common tale in early New England. Most women who calculated the odds that pregnancy would gain them a wealthy husband faced the harsh reality that men rarely married their lower-class lovers.[45]

Marriage was basic to women's survival in early New England, and intermarriage outside one's immediate circle was a crucial means by which colonial families formed alliances and kin networks. For Puritans and non-Puritans alike, people's identities, their standard of living, and their status in their communities depended largely on their relations. Social and commercial networks frequently developed through kin relationships. The loss of sexual reputation severely impaired a woman's ability to make a match and marked a significant missed opportunity for both women and their families to form advantageous connections. Those women who were able to marry following a conviction for fornication or bastardy often either married within an existing kin network or secured a husband of lower status than they would have expected to find had they remained "public virgins."

Even in these lower-status matches, women with a previous conviction for fornication were unlikely to be welcomed with open arms by the other women of the family.[46]

After being publicly labeled a "slutt" by the Court of Assistants, Alice Williams was unable to make a suitable match with a man of unsullied reputation. A gentleman's daughter, Alice should have been able to secure a husband of equal standing, but her prosecution for fornication appears to have limited her options. Eventually Alice married her former lover and master, who was divorced and more than twice her age. Alice's dalliance with a married man had essentially taken her off the marriage market for anyone but her disgraced partner in fornication.[47] Similarly, Mary Dane, from one of the most respected families in Ipswich, was whipped for fornication in 1654. The father of her child chose not to marry her, and this incident seems to have left her with few options in marriage partners. Mary went on to marry a man within her family circle, her stepbrother by marriage. Mary's public indiscretion dashed any hopes the family may have had of improving their situation through marriage. Elizabeth Sessions's pregnancy out of wedlock in 1690 drew the attention of the Essex County Court and brought her charges and punishment for fornication and bastardy. Her marriage to Richard Carrier, whose family had a questionable reputation in Andover, signaled that the Sessions family had moved to the margins of respectable society.[48]

The infanticide case of Sarah Threeneedles illustrates the importance of sexual reputation, marriage, and family for women in early Massachusetts. A covenanted church member, Sarah nonetheless ignored the godly council of her ministers and parents by engaging in a sexual affair with Thomas Savage Jr., a shopkeeper in Boston. This "undutiful Carriage towards her parents" resulted in an out-of-wedlock pregnancy. After the father of the child refused to marry her, Sarah lamented that "he had ruin'd her" by their sexual indiscretion and their unwanted child. Rather than bear the child and face disgrace for herself and her family, Sarah took desperate steps to hide the evidence. She secretly gave birth to her bastard child before dawn in an open pasture and left it to die from exposure. During her trial for infanticide, Sarah made her motivations clear. If only Savage had married her, she would not have killed their child. If he had even held out the hope of marriage, she would have stayed her hand, and things would not have "come to this."[49] As a couple, the two would have faced court and community censure for engaging in premarital sexual contact but would have been reintegrated into the community. After being abandoned, Sarah decided that killing her child, and the possibility of getting caught, were preferable to facing ruin and the end of her chance for a respectable marriage and family.

HOUSEHOLD INVOLVEMENT IN INFANTICIDE

Colonial courts and the community called the respectability of an entire household into question during the course of a public trial for the sexual misconduct of one of its members, but the head of the household in particular was often a focus of court proceedings. Such cases "centered as much on the involved heads of household as the trial participants themselves," Abby Chandler argues. One's standing in a Puritan community depended on the public perception of character, and the ability to maintain a godly home. Keeping control over one's dependents was integral to the self-definition and standing of a household master or mistress.[50] In the aftermath of an out-of-wedlock pregnancy, the wealthiest heads of households could bribe or cajole the father of a pregnant woman's child to agree to marriage, thus preserving her reputation, at least in part. When this was not possible, and unwed mothers were brought to trial for fornication or bastardy, heads of households often appeared before the courts to attempt to redeem their own involvement in the incident and restore some of their damaged family reputation.[51]

Mary Osgood was living with her grandfather William Osgood in Salisbury in 1686 when she became pregnant out of wedlock by a local man named Joseph Barnard. Mary's pregnancy ensured her conviction for fornication, but her grandfather still spared no expense in the course of her trial, paying for at least six depositions regarding the nature of his granddaughter's relationship with the father of her child and Barnard's own previous assurances of his honorable intentions. William himself testified that Barnard was "a suitor to her & had bin a great while." The Osgoods' neighbor Mary Whittier also stated to the court, "As I did aprehend he intended to make her his wife." William's logic in presenting an elaborate paternity case makes sense only as an attempt to redeem his household's reputation and his own status as its head. The amount of child support he could have collected through such a trial would not account for the cost of the trial itself. Instead, the case allowed William Osgood to make it clear that he had inquired about Barnard's intentions toward his granddaughter, and that both he and his granddaughter had been misled by a manipulative suitor. He hoped that by presenting the circumstances of Mary's pregnancy in this manner, he could show that the family had no wish to flout Puritan law and thus preserve the Osgood name and Mary's chances for a successful marriage later on. His efforts seem to have been worthwhile: Mary was able to marry Philip Favor less than two years later and start a household of her own.[52]

Similarly, the case of Susannah Andrews, orchestrated by her father, Joseph, demonstrates the importance heads of households placed on the public redemption of a household's sexual morality and their own culpability for its damaged reputation. After his daughter became pregnant in 1707, Joseph Andrews pursued the father of her child, his nephew Ezekiel Andrews, through the court system. He paid to file a formal complaint against Ezekiel to force him to appear in court for a paternity hearing. Before the court, Joseph testified that Ezekiel was a frequent guest in their home and gave every appearance of being a suitor for his daughter. He also publicly claimed that he knew of no other suitors pursuing her. Andrews paid to present other witnesses before the court to testify concerning the intimate relationship between his daughter and nephew. Jane Andrews, his daughter-in-law, stated in court that she had seen "Ezekill Andross gott out of the bed from my Sister Susannah Andross." Unlike in the Osgood case, however, Joseph Andrews could not present any real evidence that Ezekiel actually intended marriage. The closest statement he could summon was that Ezekiel had stated he would "provide" for his daughter if their relationship progressed, and that she "shal not trouble you" if a child was the result.[53] In the end, Joseph's efforts to salvage his daughter's reputation as well as that of himself and his household were ineffectual. All he succeeded in doing was bringing greater attention to his family—for almost all of the depositions and testimonies on either side in the trial were from the Andrews clan—and his daughter was never able to marry and leave her father's household.

The Martha Proctor versus Thomas Choat paternity case from 1705 illustrates the lengths to which heads of households would go to preserve their reputation. When Martha became pregnant out of wedlock, it was her mother, Deborah Proctor, who addressed the issue in court as her daughter's representative in the fornication and paternity proceedings. Deborah's husband, Benjamin, had died the year before, leaving the Proctors with few financial resources besides their land on Hog Island in Narragansett Bay. As a widow, Deborah could not afford to pay for numerous depositions attesting to her family's good character. As a means of getting around this obstacle, Deborah submitted a "Declaration of the Case" to the court, describing the circumstances through which her daughter had been "ensnared," the identity of the accused father—Thomas Choat, their married neighbor—as well as the persecution her family had suffered from the Choat family since Martha's pregnancy had come to light. Thomas Choat, by contrast, as a financially stable head of a household, came to court armed with ten depositions in support of his claims of innocence, and filed a preemptive complaint against the Proctors to prevent them from smearing his good name. Deborah's efforts to clear her family could not hold up against Choat's legal onslaught, and he was acquitted on account of a lack of evidence. Martha was convicted of fornication and bastardy. After the trial, she disappears from the historical record. It is logical to conclude, therefore, that she was unable to marry and may have remained in her brother's household as an unpaid servant.[54]

As these cases attest, both male and female heads of household took sexual misbehavior very seriously, particularly when the woman was a relative, and when possible, they sought to shield their household from the stain of sexual impropriety. While infanticide has generally been viewed as a solitary crime, the nature of life in a colonial household would have made concealing a pregnancy from a woman's immediate relatives, with whom she often shared a bed and other living quarters, nearly impossible.[55] Colonial courts would handle cases after an unmarried woman's pregnancy came to light. If the neighbors and local magistrates had not yet discovered a woman's illicit pregnancy, however, some family members might seek to assist in hiding her shameful state from the court and community through infanticide. Given the stakes involved, some mothers and fathers chose to actively help during the birth and concealment of an unwanted infant, while others offered their tacit approval by choosing to ignore the situation. It is impossible to know how many pregnancies were hidden in this manner, but concealing pregnancy and childbirth would certainly have been easier for a woman who had her family members' assistance. Unwanted pregnancies could be kept from public notice, especially pregnancies that came to term in late winter or early spring, when expectant mothers could either stay indoors and out of the public eye or wear concealing layers of clothing.[56]

The Court of Assistants convicted John and Esther Andrews as accessories to murder when their daughter Susanna was tried for infanticide in 1695. Although Susanna shared a bed with her mother, she testified that neither her father nor her mother had any knowledge of her pregnancy, and that "being alone," she was "delivered of two living bastard Children," whom she then murdered and left in a field near her family home. The court suspected her parents' involvement in her crime, though they could not prove that John or Esther was actually present at the time of the twins' birth. John adamantly denied that he "knew any thing concerning his Daughter Susanah being with Child" or that she had given birth to two infants and disposed of the evidence. He withstood "much presing upon him" by local magistrates to admit his knowledge and involvement. Other witnesses proved to be his and his wife's undoing, however. After hearing testimony from Elizabeth Kenedy and Susanna Ransom, who worked in the Andrews household, the court found that John and Esther did take an active role in concealing the crime. They "did countenance comfort . . . and succour the sd Susanna and did hide and conceal the sd Murder, and did Secretly bury the sd Infants," according to the indictment. All three Andrewses—Susanna, Esther, and John—were sentenced to hang.[57]

Michael and Hannah Emerson of Haverhill avoided being sentenced to death alongside their daughter Elizabeth for infanticide in 1693, but the court questioned them as accessories to the crime. Most of the inquiries from the court centered on the location in which Elizabeth admitted to having given birth—"upon a trundell bed att the feet of her fathers bed in the same room where her father and mother were in bed"—and the fact that her newborn twins appear to have been carefully sewn up into a sack before they were concealed in a chest and then buried in the yard. Court questioners seem to have been skeptical that neither Michael nor Hannah, who were supposedly asleep next to her during the course of Elizabeth's labor, would have noticed their daughter giving birth to twins. They asked Elizabeth why she did not "call for help," to which she responded that "there was no body to call but my father & mother & I was afraid to call my Mother for fear of killing her." This exchange did not put the matter to rest. The court continued to ask Michael and Hannah how they could have been unaware of the pregnancy or births. Hannah admitted to noticing that Elizabeth was "big," but nothing else. The court also did not believe that Elizabeth—who appeared very "ill in her Look," according to witnesses following the birth of her children—could have managed to sew the infants into the sack and dispose of them herself. They asked her mother why she did "Sew them upon a cloth for burial," which she denied. Elizabeth's and her parents' denials were suspect, for it would indeed have been a feat for her to conceal the pregnancy and births and then carry out the burial on her parents' property without their help. In the end, however, the court did not have enough evidence to execute them along with their daughter.[58]

Her mother may have assisted Elizabeth in concealing evidence of her sexual immorality to avoid the censure of the female community of Haverhill. During the birth of Elizabeth's first illegitimate child, neighbor women who attended the birth treated all the Emerson women with open contempt. Johanah Hasteltine, Johanah Corlis, Lidia Ladd, and Mary Neff gave a revealing deposition for the fornication case against Elizabeth in 1686. According to their account, they questioned Elizabeth during her travail about her claims that Timothy Swan had raped her and that the attack had resulted in her pregnancy. The women could not understand why Elizabeth did not effectively fight him off, "Scratch him, or kick him" or "make the Towne ring of it." It was Hannah Emerson who answered for her daughter during the interrogation, reminding them first that Swan's arm was across her daughter's throat and second that Elizabeth had kept quiet out of a desire to avoid disgrace. When Goodwife Hasteltine asserted that Swan must have "ly wth her more times" consensually, because "it was impossible . . . for a maid to be wth child at the first, being forced," Hannah refuted the accusation. "Why might not she be with child?" she retorted defensively. When Goodwife Corlis asked Elizabeth if someone had "not counselled her to lay [her pregnancy] to Tim Swan," Elizabeth's sister Hannah Dustin felt the need to defend herself. "I am clear for some said I was her Counsellor," Dustin stated, adding that "she had nothing lay on her Conscience upon that accot."[59] It is apparent from the women's treatment of not only Elizabeth but also Hannah Emerson and Hannah Dustin that the entire family had been denounced for immorality.

The Haverhill women's behavior is not surprising in the context of Puritan New England. Women who bore children out of wedlock faced official punishments by colonial courts, but they also encountered unofficial punishment in the form of community contempt, particularly from other women who had managed to maintain their respectability through the trials of adolescence and the process of courtship and marriage. As Hambleton writes, "Their successes enabled them to view the women who bore illegitimate children as contemptible failures and provided the women's community with the moral authority to police the behaviors of single women." Midwives and female neighbors often did the work of the law and community by bringing to light illicit sexual activity. In most cases in which an unmarried woman became pregnant, it was other women who first became suspicious and sought to investigate a single woman's unexplained illness or changing figure. During a single mother's travail and in the aftermath of childbirth, this community of women acted less like nurturing caretakers than as "quasi-judicial, inquisitorial figures," collecting evidence for colonial courts and paternity suits.[60] The women's abrasive and thorough questioning during the birth of Emerson's illegitimate child is representative of the role such women adopted regarding out-of-wedlock pregnancies.

It was from the women in her community that Margaret West actively concealed her stepdaughter Elizabeth Atwood's pregnancy and tried to hide the birth and death of Elizabeth's bastard child in 1725. Whispers swirled around Ipswich that the young woman had been ill for most of the winter. When neighbors stopped by the West household, Elizabeth was lying in bed and Margaret was upset. "Old mrs. West looked on her Daughter & hung her hands and Cryed," reported Elizabeth Dressor. Dressor was suspicious that Elizabeth was pregnant, and when she mentioned that she "seems to be like a woman in travel [*sic*]," both daughter and stepmother denied the accusation. Margaret replied, "No . . . how you talk so?" and insisted that Elizabeth had "never known a man on such account, no never in her life," before ushering Dressor out of the house. Dressor returned later in the day with another neighbor, Mrs. Jewitt, to find the bedclothes in disarray and Elizabeth weak and "in a miserable condition." Yet "Eliza Atwood said Her never had a Child if itt was the Last Breath She had to draw," they reported, "& her mother said no she never had a child if itt was ye last word she had to speak."[61]

The women began to tell a different tale after Jewitt found Elizabeth's chamber pot "filled with . . . bloody matter and bloody cloaths," which had been "taken away by mrs West who caried it and put under the stayars."

Elizabeth finally confessed that she had given birth standing up and the baby had fallen on its head. She was not sure if the infant was alive or dead at the time. Her stepmother claimed that she had entered the room after Elizabeth had wrapped the baby in a handkerchief and hidden it between the bedstead and the wall, before their neighbors entered her chamber. She pleaded ignorance about Elizabeth's actions, even after concealing the bloody childbirth linens. The court imprisoned and investigated Mrs. West "upon Suspicion of being abettor or Aider" in the crime but eventually released her. Elizabeth was unapologetic until the end. She wore her shabbiest clothes to the gallows, knowing that by tradition the hangman kept the clothing of the person he executed. When asked why she laughed as she walked to her death, she said, "'I am laughing to think what sorry suits the hangman will get from me." Her one regret seemed to be that her stepmother had been forced to endure so much on her behalf. During her trial, she stated that she "did not Expect things would be as they ware." Instead, she had assumed that her stepmother would not be implicated in her crime but would only "be Examined and sent home again."[62]

Female relatives' sexual misbehavior was not the only source of potential shame and loss for a household. Pregnancies among unwed female servants also reflected poorly on other members of a household, particularly masters and mistresses. Household structure, if functioning correctly, was designed to bring order and godliness to colonial New England society. That a member of a household had engaged in illicit sexual activity was a signal that such order had severely broken down, that the web of mutual obligations between husbands and wives, parents and children, and masters and servants had not been effective in controlling an individual's behavior.[63] Just as a household provided its members with a legal, financial, political, and social identity via the household head, the behavior of its dependents helped determine how a community viewed a household and those within it. This held true for relatives and non-relatives alike.

When their servant Amy Munn became pregnant out of wedlock in 1699, there is no record that her employers, Mr. and Mrs. Wadsworth of Farmington, Connecticut followed legal prescriptions to report her condition to the local magistrate to begin both fornication and paternity proceedings. Amy's pregnancy remained a secret until the day she went into labor, when once again the Wadsworths failed to make her pregnancy known to their community through the usual preparations for childbirth, which included calling the local midwife as well as other neighbor women to attend the birth. Instead, Amy gave birth with only her master in the room. As the court later stated, such secrecy allowed her to "offer violence to the child in the Birth . . . In pursueance of her resolution to make away with the child." She "neglected all means and helps for preserving the life of the child," and apparently so did Mr. Wadsworth. He, at least, absented himself from the room so Amy could finish the deed and ensure the child was completely "destroyed," cutting its throat with a "sharp edged instrument." Despite the Wadsworths' complicity, the court prosecutor laid the full blame at Amy's feet. "And to add to her wickedness she endeavoured to make [the Wadsworths] accessaries to this Horrible crime," he stated, by persuading "Mr. Wadsworth and his wife to conceale this murther." Regardless of the evidence of the crime and the Wadsworths' role in it, all were acquitted of infanticide. Munn was found guilty of fornication and willful neglect of her child, while the Wadsworths were not found guilty of any crime. Although they did not explicitly state their reasons for concealing Amy's pregnancy and the birth of her illegitimate child, the integrity of their household must have been a major factor.[64]

When their "spanish indian slave" Marea became pregnant in 1676, Stephen and Hannah French of Weymouth took steps to preserve the moral integrity of their household against the stain of her behavior. The Frenches would have been held responsible for Marea's actions as their slave, at least in the eyes of the community. They attempted to limit their neighbors' knowledge of Marea's "travail" by sending her to give birth on the Indian side of town. This was not an act of kindness on their part. Marea knew no one in the Indian community and did not speak their language. A local Indian sachem reported to Hannah that Marea had said a "grat many Indians me much Shamed" for coming among them in her condition. Without any support, Marea gave birth alone. She claimed that the baby was stillborn, but neighbors soon grew suspicious. One neighbor gossiped that Marea had killed it and the child had been "throwed out to the hogges and they had eat some of it." His gossip sparked others in the community to investigate the disappearance of Marea's baby, but they found no child, only evidence that she had recently given birth. After Marea was indicted for infanticide, the Frenches again took steps to preserve their reputation. There was no point in denying that Marea had fornicated while under their authority, but they had not harbored a murderer. Several members of the Frenches' network of kin testified that the afterbirth found on the scene was "much corupted & wasted in the womb togethr with the Child," indicating that the child was indeed born dead. Marea was found not guilty, and the Frenches could salvage at least part of their sullied reputation.[65]

The women of the Parker household of Boston went to great lengths to protect their family's reputation after a free African servant in their employ, Zipporah Done, became pregnant out of wedlock in 1663. The father of her child was almost certainly Jonathan Parker, nephew of her master, Richard Parker. Jonathan had a history of sexual violence. He had gained notoriety for attacking a newly married neighbor in her home when her husband was gone by climbing in through the window and into her bed. She screamed, and he was caught by the town watch. He was removed to London quickly by wealthy relatives before he could face authorities. As a resident in the Parker household, he would have had easy access to Zipporah, and the timing of Zipporah's pregnancy suggests she had become pregnant before he left the colony.[66]

Zipporah was visibly pregnant by the time two well-respected African women of the community approached the Parkers' housekeeper, a Mrs. Sands. They asked her why Zipporah had not been taken to the magistrates to report the pregnancy, name the father, and pursue steps to obtain support for the child, the proper procedure in such a case. The housekeeper asserted "hir mrs sayd [Zipporah] was not wth child." The family continued to deny her pregnancy when another African woman came to inquire after Zipporah's health, hearing she was "ill abed." Mrs. Manning, the Parkers' daughter, turned her away, claiming that Zipporah was "well on her leggs." A few days later, before Mrs. Parker could send her off to Barbados, Zipporah gave birth to a son.[67] Mrs. Parker, Mrs. Manning, and Mrs. Sands did not have a midwife attend, insisting that Zipporah's birth pangs were a "fitt of the Collick" and that the birth was "not Coming to its prime." When Zipporah's child arrived, they claimed it was stillborn. Mrs. Parker pinned the tiny corpse in a linen cloth to bury in the Parkers' field the following day. The women agreed to keep the news secret from their patriarch, Richard Parker, for fear his oath as an officer of the Massachusetts Bay Colony Council would compel him to reveal the incident although "providence had ordered it to be secret."[68]

The Parker women's attempts to conceal the birth and death of the child—and save their family's reputation—were not successful. An unknown neighbor lodged a complaint about Zipporah's suspicious condition. A search uncovered the corpse of a full-term light-skinned infant in the general location where Zipporah confessed her child was buried. This discovery contradicted statements the Parker women had made that the child was "sixe weekes before the time" and "blackish" in their attempts to point suspicion away from Jonathan as the father. The inquest judged that the death was not natural, given that the infant's head had been cut off. Removing the head would have served a dual purpose of obscuring both paternity and cause of death from suffocation or strangulation. It is possible that one of the Parker women took this desperate, brutal step. In the end, the court could not prove that Zipporah had murdered her child, or even that the headless child in the field was hers, and she was charged only with fornication. Her master and mistress refused to post bond for her release, forcing her to petition the court and beg for leniency. The Parker women were admonished by the First Church of Boston for "Concealing the sin of fornication in their negro servant" in front of the "publick Congregation."[69]

For a family like the Parkers, who were among the upper echelons of Massachusetts political society, their motivation for concealing the birth and death of a bastard child in their household was to preserve their family's reputation and the image of their household. Some women certainly committed infanticide for selfish reasons, embodying the sinfulness Puritan ministers expounded upon in their execution sermons on the evils of infanticide. The sermons made it clear that these women had committed the ultimate act of selfishness and were solely culpable for the death of their unwanted children.[70] As we have seen in the cases presented in this chapter, however, this view of the women who committed infanticide is far too simplistic. Self-interest and selfish concerns were frequently not the only motivations for such actions; household and family interests also played a role. Family members even sometimes played a part.

By the late seventeenth century, the concerns of Massachusetts ministers and magistrates about community cohesiveness had reached a fever pitch. In the wake of the Indian Wars of that period, Cotton Mather spoke in an execution sermon as if an entire generation of youth had been struck down by war as well as by sin. "How many Scores of Young men have sometimes been lost from one Little Town, within two of three Years, by the Disastrous Plagues and Wars that have been upon us!" he lamented. "Tis Wickedness, and especially, tis Uncleanness; That is the Knife which cutts the Throats of Millions in every generation." In another execution sermon he told his audience that "Several Bastard Children have been Murdered in this Place: But there has not unto this Day been any Detection of the Murderers." Mather's listeners took it upon themselves to police their neighbors' ungoverned sexuality and deceit in order to return their community to God's favor. Women were the focus of the crackdown. Increased scrutiny brought an unprecedented number of prosecutions for infanticide in New England in the 1690s. Only one woman of the ten accused of committing the crime was acquitted during that decade.[71]

It is ironic that authorities' efforts to ensure social stability were focused on women who, ultimately, were not trying to rip apart their community but instead sought to remain respectably within the fold. Frequently it was their desire to be part of society—their reputation intact and their family respectability preserved—that led them to commit such horrible crimes. The courts, of course, did not take such motivations into account when they sentenced these women to death. In a final irony, the moral crackdown designed to preserve the Puritans' future actually increased the body count—in the numbers of infants murdered by desperate women as well as the number of mothers executed for their crimes.

CHAPTER 3

☞ Almost Inconceivable Foes

Anglo-American Women and Indian War

In the aftermath of King Philip's War, frustrations over continued Indian threats led a group of Anglo-American women to commit an act of unimaginable brutality. By 1677 the war had interrupted New England fishing and seaborne trade, damaging the coastal economy. Wabanaki Indian groups were also targeting fishing as part of their continuing frontier strategy in the northern theater of the war. By midsummer, Indian pirates had captured more than twenty vessels off the northern New England coast, thirteen manned by sailors from Marblehead. The crew aboard one of these ketches managed to retake their vessel and direct it to Marblehead harbor with two Indian pirates in custody. They intended to take their former captors to the authorities to collect a reward or sell the prisoners into slavery and recoup some of their financial losses. A group of colonial Englishwomen ensured that the Indian prisoners never reached Boston.[1]

On Sabbath day, when the fishermen and their captives arrived on shore, they met townspeople emerging from the meetinghouse. Word had spread that another Marblehead ship had been taken, and most assumed that all the sailors had been killed. According to the influential Puritan leader Increase Mather, who recorded the incident in his diary, the women were especially angry that the Indian prisoners had been allowed to live, and in "a boisterous rage," they "set upon & killed them." According to another witness, mariner Robert Roule, the women grabbed the captives by the hair and, using their hands, stones, and wooden billets—whatever was lying nearby—they "made an end of the Indians." The constable of the town did not intervene to put an end to the assault. As they murdered the men, the women were "crying out" that "if [the Indians] had been carried to Boston they would have been set at liberty." Although the Indians probably would have been charged with piracy, a hanging offense under Massachusetts law, the women did not trust the magistrates in Boston to sentence the Indians to death.[2]

The incident stands out as one of the more brutal moments in the clashes between Anglo-American and Native American peoples that marked late seventeenth-century New England. Yet the violence that these women directed toward their Indian enemies—and their contempt for colonial authority—did not emerge out of nowhere on the shores of Marblehead harbor. These women were either members of the community, and thus dependent on the coastal economy, or refugees who had fled to the southeast to escape destruction on the frontier. In either case, by attacking the Indians and expressing their antipathy for colonial authority, the women were looking after the interests of their families by confronting perceived threats.[3] The Marblehead attack was not a random incident or an expression of uncontrolled female rage but a dramatic example of women using violence to preserve their way of life, this time with horrific results. The attack itself was extraordinary, but these women were not alone in either their aggressive inclinations or the sentiments that inspired them.

The devastation of King Philip's War (1675–1678), King William's War (1688–1697), and Queen Anne's War (1702–1713) added unprecedented urgency to colonial Englishwomen's desire to protect the interests of their families. The wars pushed Anglo-American women, like those in Marblehead, to disobey cultural conventions demanding respect for authority and opposing overt violence by women and to direct their hostility openly against those most evidently to blame for their suffering. No longer would some wives and mothers quietly "bear Adversity" or "suppress Resentments, under the greatest Provocations," as the Puritan divine Cotton Mather advised their sex. The tragedies of the wars also instilled doubt in the validity of colonial authority and caused some women to challenge the limits of appropriate behavior in their communities. The violence and loss caused by the wars left a void, and when remaking their lives in its wake, some Anglo-American women were willing to step out of their place. During King Philip's War and its aftermath, women in Essex County, Massachusetts, began attacking two almost inconceivable foes: colonial officials and native peoples. Constables, tax collectors, and tithingmen became the targets of female ire once women could no longer bear the personal and financial costs of the conflicts. And then later, as raids continued in northern regions of the colony during King William's and Queen Anne's Wars, stories emerged of Englishwomen attacking and defending themselves against Indians as the most obvious source of their suffering.[4]

The violence that Anglo-American women exhibited during the Indian Wars was a step beyond the everyday forms of violence in women's lives in colonial New England. Whether women were prosecuted for trespassing into more open expressions of violence depended more on the identity of their victims than on the brutality of their actions. For instance, historians have overstated witnesses' moral outrage over the 1677 killings in Marblehead. Authorities appear to have been less concerned about the loss of life than about women taking control out of official hands. Increase Mather was troubled that the women had "very barbarously" murdered the Indian captives, but he was more focused on the ramifications for English-Indian relations. "Doubtless if the Indians hear of it," he wrote, "the [English] captives among them will be served accordingly." In the end, the General Court reached a stalemate: the murder of Indian pirates, even as brutal as this, was not worthy of further action, and the women's transgression did not constitute enough of a threat to colonial authority to pursue.[5]

Historians have also mislabeled the Marblehead incident as "random" or an expression of female rage gone awry in order to understand what they consider to be these women's inexplicable actions.[6] This interpretation takes the incident out of context, missing similarities between these murders and other anti-Indian violence by Englishwomen during this period. It also overlooks parallels to women's resistance to colonial officials during the Indian Wars. By not leaving it to the magistrates to handle the Indians, the women were simultaneously demonstrating against the perceived lenience of the magistrates in Boston and expressing their anger toward Indians. Like other women who used violence against colonial officials and Indians during the Indian Wars, they acted without male protection, confronting both real and perceived threats.

Aggressive protection of family interests against threats from both authorities and enemies was not unique to the women of colonial New England. The necessity for women's violence also increased during the English civil wars. Englishwomen's concerns, like those of their New English counterparts, centered on the well-being of their families. Puritan strictures on the importance of female obedience seem to have dampened women's participation in mass demonstrations of violence in early New England. The incident in Marblehead, where the impact of Puritan teachings on the rough maritime community was relatively weak, was a rare event. At the same time, however, militant strains of New England Puritanism offered mixed messages regarding violence, and the Hebrew Bible often equated religious devotion with violent action against enemies by both men and women.[7] Instances of women's violence that appear in the historical record from this period have been shaped by the push and pull of these forces.

Whether overt violence by women could be acceptable in seventeenth-century Massachusetts depended on how it was judged by local, colonial, or provincial authorities. Attacking an Indian enemy could be regarded as beneficial to the colonial community. While such an action was usually held to be outside a woman's purview, it could still be acceptable if it was beneficial for Anglo-American peoples living under threat of attack. These incidents also had the benefit of appearing conflict-specific: they were acts of desperation rather than examples of women's natural inclinations. In addition, Indian peoples particularly in the later seventeenth century, were rarely sympathetic victims. Juries frequently refused to convict white colonists of murdering Indians, regardless of the evidence. Violence against colonial officials by women, however, was always judged to be against the interests of the community and particularly disruptive. Prosecuting women who had attacked officials helped publicly reassert hierarchies of gender and social and political power. Courthouses were designed to reinforce the social order, with judges on a raised bench and wealthy men in front-row seats. Women attended court only when called for prosecution or to testify.[8]

While the targets of women's violence during these conflicts came from populations on opposing ends of the societal spectrum, women's aggression against both groups sprang from the same motivation: the desire to protect their households and kin groups. The hardships of war reinforced this motivation. Because of King Philip's, King William's, and Queen Anne's Wars, many women lost property, a sense of security, and, most important, loved ones. Sources from Essex County indicate that some women during this period were unwilling to submit peacefully to these sacrifices imposed on them by the wars, by colonial authorities, or by their Indian enemies.

IMPACT OF THE INDIAN WARS

Before we examine specific instances of Anglo-American women's violent behavior during the Indian Wars, it is crucial to understand the impact of these conflicts on them. Fewer women than men were causalities of fighting, but as widows and refugees, women scrambled to find ways to survive; as wives, mothers, and household managers, they dealt with the personal, social, and economic strains of the conflicts. Women could not bring back family members who had been killed or reverse the economic strains brought on by the wars, but they could take steps to preserve or rebuild their households.

In terms of the proportion of the population who were killed, the Indian Wars were among the deadliest conflicts in American history. During King Philip's War, losses to colonial communities as well as to the Wampanoag and their northeastern Wabanaki allies were devastating. Nothing could have prepared the English colonists for the losses they would experience in the wars or the sense of uncertainty that accompanied them. The Puritan community viewed the wars as "a bloody punishment for its people for sins committed" and searched for someone to blame. Many Anglo-American men, women, and children were killed or carried into captivity; others died of starvation and exposure as a result of Indian raids. Violent death "seemed to emerge without warning from the forests, then disappear . . . whence it had come." Raids brought the horrors of war to the colonists' very doorstep. Colonists struck back, killing thousands of Native Americans to avenge their losses. As James K. Folsom and Richard Slotkin explain, because New England society was relatively so small, made up of tiny towns and hamlets, "virtually every community and every family" was affected by the extensive losses. Even those communities that did not directly experience the devastation of war included members who had lost relatives to the conflicts, and news of the wars spread quickly throughout New England.[9]

For the settlers of Massachusetts Bay, out of a total population of approximately thirty thousand, one in every sixteen men of military age was killed or died as a result of King Philip's War alone. Increase Mather, in his *Earnest Exhortation to the Inhabitants of New-England* (1676), remarked on the number of widows and fatherless children left as a result of the fighting and urged his listeners to heed it as a sign of God's punishment. Mather wrote: "Is it nothing that so many have been cut off by a bloody and barbarous Sword? Is it nothing that Widdows and Fatherless have been multiplyed among us? . . . Shall not such solemn strokes at last awaken us?" For every married man killed in the Indian Wars, there was a widow who would have to find a way to subsist without her husband, or become a burden on her town or colony.[10]

Widows began to appear regularly before the courts during King Philip's War to settle their affairs after a husband had died "fighting the indians." The first mention of "the war" in the Essex County Court records appears in September 1675 with several cases of men being slain in the war without leaving a will. The number of intestate probate cases steadily increased, and cases of men killed in the wars would continue to appear. Widows who possessed some property were sometimes left to act as executrixes of their husbands' estates. For those less fortunate, the loss of a husband could impoverish a woman and her family. Some women undoubtedly turned to their extended families for assistance. Others pleaded for help more publicly. Mary Knight reached out to the court in June 1676, desperate for assistance after her husband was killed in the conflict. Mary was "very poore & herself & children . . . in great want." The court ordered the committee of militia of Beverly and the selectmen of Manchester to "forthwith take care that the said mary & her children may be releived & not suffer for want." Desperate women inundated the General Court, as well as the governor and magistrates, with similar petitions for relief and assistance into the 1680s. The majority of these petitions were successful, and the General Court usually offered at least a few pounds for the widow and her family.[11]

A new generation of widows came forward for help during King William's War and Queen Anne's War. Though fewer than during King Philip's War, a steady stream of women brought petitions for relief and for compensation as war widows before the General Court, governor, and magistrates between 1692 and 1711. At the same time, militia leaders published bills to encourage men to volunteer to fight the Indians, assuring potential soldiers that their families would be taken care of if "God forbid . . . any of ours should fall." So "that our Encouragement be given tham," one bill from 1704 provided that "ye sum of three pounds be given to each surviving souldier enganged in that service" and "five pounds be allowed to ye widow of each of ye slaine." This was a costly but necessary strategy to ensure that married men would continue to enlist to fight in the Indian Wars on the frontiers.[12]

In order to support all aspects of the war effort, colonies imposed additional financial and social burdens on New England communities. Some of the major hardships that resulted from King Philip's War, and continued as fighting on the northern frontiers of New England failed to abate, resulted from the economic and social strains of the conflicts. Difficulties caused by the wars spread throughout the region, far from where the battles raged. The destruction of property and the cost of conducting the war amounted to £21 per household, a sum that was more than the annual salary of the secretary or deputy governor of Connecticut at the time. Colonies in turn placed a heavy load of taxes on the people. In five sessions between July 1675 and October 1676, the General Court of Massachusetts ordered thirty-five "rates," or as-needed collections of property tax, to fight King Philip's War.[13]

Colonial officials were less able to enforce wartime tax increases in frontier areas of New England. Haverhill residents, for example, could not keep up with rising costs. Samuel Ayer, constable of Haverhill, wrote a letter to the General Court asking for leniency in paying their taxes owed. The town was in "a poor condition" and unable to collect additional taxes from its citizens. "There are many that Have not corn to pay their Rates, manei more which have not mony," he wrote. "I know not what to take." Colonial authorities chose to focus instead on areas with greater wealth that they could logistically control. For Massachusetts Bay, this placed a heavier financial burden on the towns closest to Boston. Chronic inflation was also a problem throughout the conflicts of the late seventeenth century, which added to the difficulty of supporting and maintaining a household. At the same time, safe towns in the interior took in refugees by the hundreds and struggled to sustain the added cost of their survival. The towns had to cope with increased taxation and this flood of refugees and widows as many of their able-bodied men were drafted for military service or killed in combat. This placed a strain on communities and raised questions of fairness. Petitions for "Relief of Service" submitted by men illustrate these difficulties. John Leverrett, for instance, with the council of Caleb Church of Watertown behind him, petitioned to be exempt from militia duty in order to run the local mill. Women's petitions seeking to keep men at home are even more revealing. Hannah Stanley of Malden begged the council to release her husband from service to manage their farm, which was "lying to spoil for want of tending" as she tried to raise their family of four young children. Like many colonial Englishwomen during this period, Hannah was overwhelmed by the demands of running a household, maintaining a farm, and bringing up children in her husband's absence. Her personal struggles eventually took precedence over the fight against the Indian threat, and she asked for him to return home.[14]

Petitions for relief and reimbursement that appear in court records show that many women during the Indian Wars felt they had given enough in support of the conflicts. Some widows petitioned for relief from taxes, given losses they had already sustained. Obedience Curtis, whose husband was slain in the wars, wrote that she was "indebted to the Country for the rates" imposed on her estate but simply could not pay them. Elizabeth Johnson petitioned for relief from taxes at least twice after her husband was killed in the wars.

Other women sought compensation for their contributions to the war effort by other means. Sarah Tuckerman wanted repayment for curing her son of wounds suffered in King Philip's War. Since his injury, she wrote, they had been surviving "by her hard labour," and the government was "duty bound" to pay her. Elizabeth Bent, war widow and mother of seven, sought to be repaid for the expense of quartering "severall Souldiers" during the war as well as for two horses that had been impressed for service. Similarly, when soldiers arrived in Lancaster "when an attaque was made upon it by ye enemy," Mary Garder did not appreciate the damage the soldiers' horses did to her field. She petitioned for compensation for that damage, as well as the expense of "entertaining" soldiers afterward. Hanah Wascarr petitioned for the return of a barrel of gunpowder or its equivalent. The powder had been taken "by Authoritie . . . for use, in the late Warrs." Hanah apparently did not consider it a donation to the cause.[15]

VIOLENCE AGAINST COLONIAL OFFICIALS

Public morale all over New England showed signs of deteriorating under the burdens of war. In the midst of this, colonial governments quarreled so bitterly among themselves over the culpability and handling of the wars that they added to the difficulty. Colonists distrusted the government under normal circumstances, and colonial governments' failures further jeopardized their legitimacy.[16] The impact of these additional burdens—and a loss of confidence in colonial authorities—appeared in the form of physical attacks by Anglo-American women on colonial officials in Essex County starting in the late 1670s. Attacks by women on men in positions of authority had been almost unheard of before King Philip's War. Instances of women directing their aggression against tax collectors, constables, and tithingmen to protect their personal and household interests began to appear only after the conflict began.

During King Philip's War, the wife of Petter Harling of Marblehead was prosecuted and fined for abusing military officers in the execution of their duties. The officers had come to her home to collect a fine against her husband for neglect of militia training and also to make sure the home was "provided with armes" as the law required. Goodwife Harling first refused to show them her husband's weapons, he being out, and then refused to pay the fine in the form of specie or property, threatening, "If you touch any goods of mine I will knoke out your Braines." She also pushed one of the officers, who called for assistance, restraining her while the others took a pewter dish as payment. As the men made a hasty retreat, Goody Harling's words rang in their ears: she would "haue [their] Hearts Blood," and she would "doe The Clerke a mischeefe" before long. In court, the officers provided a detailed account of what had transpired and described her "many Railling words" and disorderly behavior.[17]

During that same period, Margaret Giffard of Lynn threatened the constable and a deputy marshal, bodily preventing them from seizing household goods in payment of debt to the state. The Giffards had been plagued by financial problems related to John Giffard's position as agent for the Iron Works Company in Lynn and had moved to upper Saugus to distance themselves from the trouble. Only during King Philip's War, however—after Indians had killed her son at Saco—did Margaret resort to physical violence to avoid payment. When men entered her residence and began collecting items of brass, iron, and pewter, as well as a gun, Goody Giffard was not willing to let her property go without a fight. She tried to detain the constable by force, grabbing his black staff—the symbol of his position in the community—in the process. She insisted that the family owed nothing else and "vowed they should have no goods there." Witnesses recounted the incident in court as part of the Giffards' lawsuit for unjust removal of goods. Their lawsuit was unsuccessful and the Giffards were ordered to pay all costs.[18]

Similarly, the threat of increased taxation inspired violence from Elizabeth Dodg of Ipswich in 1680. Goody Dodg did not respect the authority of colonial officials to impose any further on her family and was willing to attack them to defend her property. Thomas Hobs came to the Dodges' house and began discussing possible rate collection and the attachment of several items of their property, including a sled and a large kettle, in payment for increased taxes. Perhaps hardened by her first husband's death at sea in 1672 and the extended absences of her second husband, Captain John Dodg, while he was off fighting in King Philip's War, Elizabeth responded that if men "did com thither" to collect for rates, "she would mak the blood run about there eares." When Hobs commented that if the constable commanded him to collect her taxes, he would not be afraid to come, she "caught" him by the hair and struck him in the face. Goody Dodg was also not intimidated by the constable. She stated that if she could get hold of his staff, she would use it to beat him around the ears. When three selectmen arrived later to make good on their collection threat, Elizabeth fought to keep her property, striking one man on the hat or the side of the head. Angered, three of the officials dragged her down and one struck her on the neck with his fist. When a nearby witness exclaimed, "Rescue the woman, what will you let her be Cilld!" neighbors rushed over to restrain the men. Their reprisal was so severe that the court seems to have decided she had been punished enough.[19]

In a region that had lost so many to the Indian Wars, some women used violent means to protect their husbands, sons, and friends from being imposed upon further by the authorities. Hana Mason was sentenced by the court in Salem to be fined or whipped for attempting to strike a tithingman in 1677. Hana was the wife of John Mason, a former soldier who had been stationed at Wrentham, which had been hit hard during King Philip's War. When Henry West came to the Mason household to investigate a fight that had occurred there, Goody Mason was unwilling to allow him to question anyone in her household. She reached into her fireplace and seized an andiron and tried to strike him with it, calling him "thou West, thou Harry, thou Deuill." When the andiron was taken away from her, she picked up a chair and threatened West with it as well. Goody Mason was accused of being intoxicated during the episode, which may explain her violent, bold response to West's intrusion. Drunk or sober, however, she was clearly hostile to colonial authority. There were at least three men at the gathering, but Hana was most angry at the tithingman for his attempts to enter her household, and she was the only person willing to use violence against him.[20]

In 1679 Mary Mould threatened the constable with a firebrand and punched his assistant in the face when they came to serve a warrant against her husband, Thomas. Mary had brought land and some property to her marriage to Thomas Mould, but he had squandered them away over the years. Thomas was now charged was stealing wood from their neighbors' fences, ostensibly to use as firewood. Mary had grown accustomed to poverty as well as hardship. Her brother had fought in King Philip's War but had been paid a pittance for his service. He had survived the experience, only to be killed in a later raid on Haverhill. When the constable and his assistant came to confront her husband, Goody Mould was in no mood to cooperate. Both the constable and his companion "Receved severall bloes" from Goodwife Mould, according to the appearance of the constable's coat, and the other man's face, in the aftermath. When a warrant was taken out against her as a result of the attacks, Mary refused to appear before the court.[21]

Ann Fox was prosecuted in 1681 for abuse of a deputy marshal. A nurse, Fox had probably been called upon to help in the recovery of soldiers returning from King Philip's War. The horrors of war had been multiplied by a smallpox epidemic. In 1681 Fox was working as a nurse in Salem. When a deputy marshal arrived and inquired after Robert Cannon, a mariner wanted for debt, Ann was anything but helpful to the authorities. Cannon tried to flee, and the marshal pursued him into the dwelling. When the men arrived in the "sick chamber" upstairs, Fox pulled the marshal "by the hair," and he fell backward over a stool. Cannon delivered two or three blows and escaped. It appears that Fox was attempting to stop the fight from disturbing her patients as the men "did heave one the other about the Roome & upon the sicke people & Children" during the commotion. She did more than just restrain the official, however; she attacked him. Also, she never attempted to seize Cannon although he was being just as disruptive. Abraham Adams, the owner of the property, was ordered to pay a fine on her behalf for not controlling his subordinate.[22]

In the wake of King Philip's War, Elenor Hollingsworth struck a constable and threatened him with an axe in order to allow her son William Hollingsworth Jr. to escape arrest. William had failed to fulfill an agreement he had made to man and "victual" a ship bound for Virginia. Goody Hollingsworth was an elderly woman by the mid-1680s, but she was still the proprietor of the Blue Anchor in Salem, a tavern she had been running since her husband's death in 1677 in the war. The Blue Anchor welcomed a variety of patrons, including passengers from the Marblehead ferry, as well as fishermen and mariners. Elenor had managed to keep these dissident elements in her tavern in check and to earn a living with the help of her son, even in a time of war. She was not going to allow William to be taken away. When she saw the constable and deputy accosting her son, she came out into the yard, threatened to "stafe out" their brains, and hit the constable at least four blows. Old Goodwife Hollingsworth was publicly admonished and ordered to pay court costs.[23]

These women's responses to authority were part of a general dissatisfaction with colonial officials and their demands in the context of the Indian Wars. This disenchantment crossed socioeconomic boundaries. Women from different walks of life perpetrated violence against colonial officials during this time, from those on the edge of subsistence to women of standing and property. Of course, most women who had other options usually did not choose to respond to such situations with violence. Those who could seek relief from their burdens in other ways, such as through petitioning, probably did so. Petitioning of this kind was not an option for most women, however. The women who attacked colonial officials during this period were only peripherally affected by the demands of the Indian Wars, and therefore unable to petition for relief from the increasing burdens the conflicts imposed.

These women share several other characteristics. They lived in eastern settlements like Salem, Ipswich, Lynn, and Marblehead, and while they remained out of the line of direct attack in the wars, and were therefore not preoccupied with imminent daily threats to their survival, they were not exempt from the hardships of war. These women's interior communities bore the brunt of the economic strains of the conflicts, contributed men to fight in militias, and supported growing numbers of refugees from the frontier. Women also did not seek out public officials to attack. Most violent actions by women occurred in their own households against those who intruded and imposed on them, their family members, or friends.[24]

That most attacks by women on colonial officials took place within the household is partially due to the practical realities of women's lives: women were more likely than men to be at home when colonial officials came calling. The vehemence with which many of them defended household members, possessions, and even guests, however, suggests a sense of personal ownership over these people and items that went beyond women's legal status as dependents. The predominance of wives as assailants in these cases indicates that their position as mistress of the household, and the obligations that entailed, informed patterns of female violence. If men were unable, or unwilling, to defend their household from further intrusion by colonial authorities, these women did not hesitate to do it in their stead. Several incidents of violence by women involve protecting domestic items from confiscation, such as dishes, cooking utensils, and other domestic tools for which the men of the household would have little use. When colonial officials attempted to seize these objects in payment for debts or taxes, some women took upon themselves the responsibility of obstructing them.

While attacks by women on colonial officials in the seventeenth century appear almost exclusively during the Indian Wars, the numbers of acts of violence by Anglo-American men toward colonial officials was more consistent throughout that period, with at least two per year.[25] If the fluctuation in the numbers of women brought to court for violence against officials were due only to court officials' increased concern with attacks on their authority, I suspect that the numbers of men appearing in court for this type of misbehavior would fluctuate also. I postulate that there was not a parallel increase in violence against colonial officials among men because men had other outlets for their frustrations that women did not, such as bringing their concerns to colonial officials during other interactions or venting at the local tavern. It is also likely that in these periods of increased financial difficulty for the colony, officials were more likely to visit households to collect back taxes or debt, bringing them into more frequent contact with women in general.

Essex County Court records list no attacks on colonial officials by Anglo-American women after the upheaval of King Philip's War had ceased and before King William's War would embroil the colony in conflict in the late 1680s. Sir Edmund Andros's tenure at the helm of New England politics was a period of political upheaval in New England, but the early days of his governorship were a time of relative peace with neighboring Indian tribes. In addition, the direct financial burden on Massachusetts communities was less heavy than it had been previously. Under Joseph Dudley's interim leadership from 1684 to 1686, many Massachusetts residents simply chose not to pay taxes. Andros's revenue acts under the Dominion of New England were highly unpopular because they were imposed without benefit of an assembly. The acts, however, actually dispersed the tax burden more equally to Maine, New Hampshire, Connecticut, Plymouth, and Rhode

Island, lowering the burden on Massachusetts to less than it had been during the years of King Philip's War.[26]

Andros's disdain for colony and town sovereignty made his regime increasingly unpopular, however, and political animosity against it began to build. He and the council passed a law in 1688 limiting town meetings to one a year, depriving local leaders of control over their affairs through this long-standing institution of New England government. Men in Essex County committed acts of violence against colonial officials during this time, but their actions had a political bent.[27] Women would not become involved in violent actions against colonial authorities again until King William's War. The war dredged up concerns about Andros's Catholic sympathies and dragged New England communities back into deadly conflict with neighboring Indian tribes and their French allies as part of the contest between England and France for control of North America. While less deadly than King Philip's War, King William's War was extremely destructive in terms of life and property. It was marked by frequent armed conflict with a variety of northern Indian groups, whose involvement was ever changing and complex.[28]

Andros was accused not only of instigating King William's War but also of being secretly in league with French and Indian forces. It was hinted that Andros, a peer from the Isle of Jersey, was "of a French extract, so in the French interests" and therefore had "Sinister designs . . . as to our Troubles with the Indians." These suspicions seemed confirmed after Andros released several Indian prisoners taken during an attack on Saco. His hopes for a reciprocal captive exchange never came to pass, and as far as many colonists were concerned, he had succeeded only in freeing "Cruell mordrous Rogs." In the wake of Andros's failed diplomatic attempts, news of his friendly relationship with the Indians—and his supposed conspiracy to destroy the colonies—circulated widely. Mary Graves of Sudbury testified to hearing Solomon Thomas, an Indian, speak about the governor's Catholic beliefs and true allegiance to the Indian cause. Others also came forward with stories of Andros's treachery.[29]

Andros's strategy of impressing men for frontier anti-Indian expeditions during King William's War achieved few military successes, but causalities were high. This sank his popularity even further. In a "Declaration of the Gentlemen, Merchants, and Inhabitants of Boston," Cotton Mather detailed the widely held belief that Andros's strategy of amassing troops to the northeast was excessive, wasteful, and even purposefully ineffective. "Tho' 'tis judged that our Indian Enemies are not above 100 in number, yet an Army of One Thousand English hath been raised for the Conquering of them . . . not one Indian hath been kill'd but more English are supposed to have died though sickness and hardship thane we have adversaries their alive," he wrote. Soldiers under the command of Andros's officers also told stories of severe mistreatment. The officers showed disdain for their untrained Massachusetts recruits. Captain Lockhart was one officer known to call his soldiers "Damn'd Sons of Whores" and beat them with his fists or his half pike. He abused one soldier so badly that witnesses were convinced it was the "cause of his death." Soldiers also testified concerning a general lack of supplies and being forced to labor while ill.[30]

The prolonged service of their husbands, sons, and fathers under such conditions—under a cloud of suspicion about a secret Catholic threat in their midst—was more than some Massachusetts women could take. In April 1689, when colonists learned that King James II had been deposed in the Glorious Revolution, a crowd stormed the fort of Boston and demanded that Andros be ousted from power. Reports from the event describe the gathering as a mix of the everyday inhabitants of Boston and surrounding towns rather than militiamen, suggesting that there were women among the crowd. People filled the streets, and as "the drums began to beat," they started "hasting and running, some with and some for arms." John Riggs, an ensign under Andros, reported that "by the time this reached the Governor's ears there were at least a thousand people in arms, seizing and carrying to prison all whom they suspected to oppose or disapprove their designs." Rumors swirled that before he was apprehended and imprisoned by leaders of the uprising, Andros attempted to flee by donning women's clothes to escape into the crowd.[31] Such a rumor was designed to humiliate the fallen leader, but if Andros tried to blend in among the mob by wearing female attire, it also supports the assumption that women participated in the uprising.

LIFE ON A FRONTIER AT WAR

Confidence and trust in colonial authorities only deteriorated further during King William's War as Indian forces ravaged frontier settlements.

Anglo-American women living on the northern frontiers of New England witnessed the ineffectiveness of garrisons and colonial militia forces to keep their enemies at bay. Town fortifications could protect the lives of some in a community under attack, but they were not designed to defend the towns in their entirety. Not every settler could reach the safety of a garrison in time to avoid being injured, taken captive, or killed. Indian raids produced extensive damage to public and private property outside of fortified areas, including to homes, agricultural fields, and grain stores. Colonial governments could not afford to reimburse these heavy losses or provide military and material support.

The vulnerability of frontier fortifications, and the apparent mismanagement of the war, encouraged the Indians to undertake further attacks on colonial settlements. After her return from Abenaki captivity, Ester Waldron Elkins Lee, daughter of the prominent Waldron family of Dover, New Hampshire, testified that the Indians with whom she had been living for a time in 1689 were emboldened by the weaknesses of English settlements. They reported moving around them with ease and were unimpressed by the protective strategies put in place. As they told Ester, "since ye came into oure Bay ye heave some of ym beene under everie of our Garrisons and know wt wee are in Number and all our circumstances." Undaunted, the Indians amassed a large force of "upwards of two hundred fiftie" Indians to continue their attacks on the frontier. The disorganization of colonial authorities in conducting the war heartened them further. The Indians say they "are much encouraged by some Gentlemen in Boston for ye managing ye warr," Ester reported after her return home.[32]

Several colonies attempted to utilize raiding parties to prevent attacks on towns. This offensive strategy was a less expensive option than building substantial fortifications, but militia forces in the field were notoriously unsuccessful. Frontier towns reached out for assistance in times of threat, usually to no avail. Colonial forces could not police vast wilderness frontiers with towns separated by up to twenty or thirty miles. By the time relief forces arrived, the attackers would have long since retreated into the wilderness. Nathaniel Saltonstall of Haverhill wrote several letters to the Massachusetts leadership regarding threats to the town during King Philip's and King William's Wars and asking for soldiers to remain on the ground there. The residents were in "need of present & settled assistance," he wrote.

"Mischief is done us; for before ye can be wth us ye enimie is hidden or gone, & nothing to be done but for ye men to return, unless ye would stay as men in service." At the same time that Saltonstall was asking for help, however, he was also turning down requests for assistance from neighboring towns. "I am not in a capacity to help" at Salisbury, he wrote, "but want men for o[u]r necessary defence." Saltonstall himself was accused of being "very negligent of his Duty as Coll" in allowing "his majesties subjects" to be "killed & captivated" in Indian raids.[33]

Historians disagree about the reasons behind the poor performance of colonial forces in the wars and the fairness of evaluating those forces by the professional military standards of the day. Public perception of their effectiveness at the time, however, is a more important measure for our purposes. Confidence in colonial and provincial militias was not high. Mary Pray's letters to Captain James Oliver reflect these doubts. Living and running a tavern on the front lines of conflict in Essex County, Pray was extremely critical of the authorities' inability to protect her community. She was incredulous over the failure of the militias to "destroy the savages" and stop the Indians' advance. "We here are al amased to see . . . that no cours is taken with these vilans," she wrote. After placing their trust in a "fals peac" with the Indians, authorities left the colonists exposed to attacks as the war continued westward. Upon hearing that the governor intended to send a company of militia, Pray wished that "the Lord grant they may not be deluded to spaer them by flatery." She wanted the "murderous wretches" wiped from the face of the earth but doubted the militia's ability to accomplish the task.[34]

After Andros was ousted from power, neither the situation for settlers on the frontier nor confidence in provincial authorities improved. As news spread that the governor had been deposed and arrested, militiamen pressed to serve under him deserted frontier forts and garrisons en masse. The new government of Massachusetts reduced the number of garrisons Andros had put in place and recalled any officers suspected of Catholic sympathies, leaving frontier settlements even more exposed to Indian attack. The result was disastrous. English residents of Schenectady and Salmon Falls, Maine, were massacred in February and March 1690. Colonial leaders like Samuel Sewall blamed the losses on settlers' "own carelessness and want of vigilance" while continuing ineffective, even disastrous offensive missions into New

France. A false peace treaty with the Eastern Abenaki in 1694 resulted in the devastating attack on the English settlement at Oyster River in New Hampshire later that year.[35]

The General Court only increased personal losses in the wars by ordering residents of communities under attack to stand fast or lose their property and by forbidding poor relief for refugees. Colonial governments wanted to preserve their frontier towns to act as a buffer for their interior settlements. Hence, General Courts informed the inhabitants that any family that left home without permission from the governor or Assembly would risk forfeiture of their property. An "Act to Prevent the deserting of the Frontier of this Province" was issued by the General Court of Massachusetts Bay in 1699, listing frontier communities as "outposts" not to be "broken up or voluntarily deserted" in a time of war. The "maintaining and defending of the Frontier" was considered to be "of very great import," and it would "greatly prejudice his Majesties' Interest & encourage an Enemy if any of the outposts should be quitted or exposed by lessening the Strength thereof," regardless of the threat to the town residents.[36] This left frontier settlers in an impossible bind: lose their lives if they stayed or their livelihoods if they fled. The provincial government had essentially abandoned its settlers on the frontier while forcing them to act as a human barrier to attacks on the interior.

VIOLENCE AGAINST NATIVE AMERICANS

In the face of such an impossible situation, some of the Anglo-American women who stayed behind took it upon themselves to protect their families and the interests of their kin groups through violence. Most often this was directed against the most immediate source of their distress: the Indians they encountered. The exploits of Susanna Eastman Wood Swan of Haverhill demonstrate the lengths to which some women were willing to go to protect their kin. Mrs. Swan knew well the costs of living on the frontier. Indians had killed her first husband and daughter, and she had been taken captive by Abenaki Indians during King Philip's War in 1676. Upon her return, Susanna married and had a child, only for her husband and child to be killed in the raid on Haverhill in 1697, when she was again taken captive. When she was able to return to Haverhill and remarry in 1699, Mrs. Swan was determined to protect her family and prevent being taken again. Whenever her husband, Captain John Swan, was away fighting the Indians, Susanna hung balls of carpet rags in the upper windows of her home and had her children move them about with the yardstick and beat a drum when the Indians were in sight, giving the impression of greater numbers within. When Indians attacked her home in 1708, Susanna first attempted to bar the door. When her attackers managed to break it down and tried to crowd inside, Mrs. Swan seized the spit off her fire and drove it through the body of the man in front. According to local legend, this sent the invaders into retreat, saving Susanna, her children, and her family's property from harm.[37]

When fighting for their lives, Anglo-American women on the frontier must have recalled horrific raids they had either lived through themselves or heard about from their fellow settlers. No family wanted to re-create the Wakelys' fate in their Falmouth settlement in the mid-1670s. It was a late summer evening when Lieutenant George Ingersoll heard gunfire in the distance in the direction of the Wakely farm and noticed "great smoke up in the River." He sounded the alarm but could not assemble enough men to investigate safely. The next day, with reinforcements, Ingersoll followed the smoke to what had been the Wakelys' home. The carnage that Ingersoll found was horrifying. "An house burnt down, and six persons killed," he reported. An older couple was "halfe in, and halfe out of the house neer halfe burnt." Thomas Wakely had been "shot through the body . . . his head dashed in pieces." His pregnant wife and two of their children had been similarly killed, their bodies mangled. Several family members were missing, including an eleven-year-old girl.[38]

In the wake of incidents like these, some Anglo-American women were willing to use whatever means necessary to ensure their survival. A few were praised for their actions, particularly those who acted in defense of homes or were taken captive. When Indians attacked, gendered expectations for Anglo-American women's appropriate behavior were altered momentarily in the face of the coming onslaught. In a few histories of the wars, some women were praised for their "Amazonian" courage in fighting like men when forced among the savages.[39] The reality of life for women during these periods of war made societal acclaim or condemnation irrelevant, however.

Their actions had more practical motivations. Most of their stories have undoubtedly been lost to history. The uncertainties of life on the frontier, the fragmentary nature of colonial recordkeeping during the late seventeenth century, and the deadly hand-to-hand nature of fighting during the Indian Wars suggest that numerous instances of Anglo-American women using violence against Native American men and women were never recorded.

The everyday militarism of early New England also would have made anti-Indian violence less remarkable, whether by men or women. From the earliest days of English settlement, New England was a military culture. The first emigrants came prepared for military confrontations with the "savage and brutish" natives in this new land. Puritan pilgrims brought muskets, pikes, armor and artillery pieces, and a supply of powder and ammunition when they crossed the Atlantic. The Hebrew Bible held particular fascination for New England Puritans, who looked to its battles and warriors as examples in their own struggle against the Indians for their biblical Israel. They were preoccupied with security and military issues, as records from this early stage of settlement demonstrate. During the early 1630s, the Court of Assistants required every settlement to take measures for its defense, including mandating militia service and ensuring that all settlers were equipped with a musket, powder, bullets, and match. Legislation "ordered that evy Towne within this Pattent shall . . . take espetiall care that ewy pson within their Townes (except magistrates & ministers) as well servts as others, be furnished with good & sufficient armes." Weekly drills were mandatory for all militia units. In 1645 the Court passed a law requiring that not just grown men but all youth from ten to sixteen years of age be "instructed upon ye usual training days, in ye exercise of armes, as small guns, halfe pikes, bowes and arrowes, &c."[40] These laws ensured that every household contained guns and other weapons, and most inhabitants would have at least been familiar with them, if not proficient in their use.

Households on the frontier frequently doubled as military garrisons. Some garrisons were created from public buildings such as meetinghouses, but most were fortified private dwellings. This meant that many Anglo-American settlers lived and worked in the midst of military installations. A few garrisons were built out of brick, but most were fortified log houses, vulnerable to fire and other destructive forces.[41] These dwellings would have been well stocked with weapons and others supplies in case of an attack.

In the event of Indian raids, women did what they could to defend their garrison homes, firing muskets and wielding whatever weapons were at hand.

A few stories of their bravery have survived to the present day. The women of Wells, Maine, famously fired muskets during King William's War when the townsmen were outnumbered by attackers. Donning men's hats and "loosening their hair that they might appear like men," women in a small garrison in Oyster River defended their post against a war party in 1706. The women, "seeing nothing but death before them . . . fired so briskly that the enemy, apprehending that the people were alarmed fled."[42] These stories are remarkable not because these women attempted to defend themselves but because they were successful in their efforts.

If given a choice, most Anglo-American women would have preferred either to flee with their children or allow men to handle the fighting, as Laurel Thatcher Ulrich explains. In the midst of a frontier war, however, this was frequently not possible. Indian forces had perfected the element of surprise in their military strategy. English towns and settlements took vigorous measures to try and detect an imminent attack, including employing signals for alarms and dispatching continual watches and scouts. Still, Indian attacks too often took them by surprise. Enemy forces made their attacks slowly and cautiously, approaching with stealth and camouflaging themselves behind objects until they came near enough to strike. At times they would fall upon the inhabitants before daybreak, when most were unprepared to defend themselves. Those living in settlements that came under attack had few options. Some chose neither to run nor to surrender.[43]

The case of Mary Loggia demonstrates women's willingness to defend themselves in wartime. A Salem resident, Mary was not on the front lines of fighting in King Philip's War but had been left alone, with the help of a "Youth" named John King, while her husband was off at sea. In the middle of the night in May 1677, a man known as Joseph Indian crept into her house. Mary later recalled that she had awakened to see a figure in the room. It "gott upon my bed," she said, and when she tried to speak to the figure, "Hee gaue mee noe Answer, which made mee Sitt up in the bed to see what the Matter was, or whoe itt should bee." In the moonlight, Mary noticed the intruder was an Indian and shouted for help. She called out to John and "told him theere was An Indian upon my bed desireing him presently to Arise & call some body to Kill him." Before reinforcements could arrive, however, Mary had "gotten a hould of [Joseph Indian] by the haire of the head & was beating him" with her fist. The intruder freed himself and jumped out the window. John King's recollection of the event confirmed that Mary was not content simply to scare her Indian attacker away but was determined to try to inflict serious harm upon him.[44]

For breaking into Mary Loggia's home and attempting to assault her, Joseph Indian was sentenced to be "whipt," a relatively lenient punishment for such a crime against an Englishwoman. The court's sentence demonstrates colonial governments' attempts to distinguish between enemy and non-enemy Indians, and their efforts to treat non-enemies in their midst fairly. Official colonial policy was to punish all offenders in assault cases strictly but equally. The principle of fairness behind the colonial Indian policy was based not on the idea that the Indian nations of New England were equal to the English, or that the Indians themselves were equal individuals, but instead on the "just rule of a civilized nation over a backward, savage tribe; the superior over the inferior; the strong over the weak; the wise over the ignorant." Colonial policies for most of the seventeenth century reflected leaders' practical desires to avoid exacerbating conflicts with Indians. Just as Increase Mather feared retribution against English captives for the 1677 murders of Indians in Marblehead, other colonial leaders wished to avoid giving Indian tribes any further excuse for violence.[45]

Most settlers in colonial New England do not appear to have shared these officials' concerns, however. Juries, always made up of adult white men, were reluctant to convict other white men or women of any charge more serious than manslaughter for murdering an Indian, commonly citing "extenuating circumstances" in order to reduce the charges. Particularly during King Philip's War, and again in King William's and Queen Anne's Wars, many settlers equated "Indian" with "enemy." Initially, English colonists viewed Indians as a heathen nuisance to be ignored, destroyed, displaced, or converted. The Indian Wars marked a turning point in which the "savage" became a threat as well as a destructive force sent by God. Mary Rowlandson, who was taken captive by a group of Narragansett Indians during King Philip's War, illustrated this view in her captivity narrative. For Rowlandson, Native Americans were "a scourge to the whole Land."[46]

The idea of Indians as less than human took greater hold as the seventeenth century progressed. After the execution of captured Indians in 1676,

Judge Samuel Sewall and several physicians conducted a dissection of one of them. Reaching into the abdomen of the corpse and "taking the heart in his hand," one physician "affirmed it to be the stomack." While made in jest, the remark was a comment on the notorious "heartlessness" of the Indian. This pervasive notion helped justify violence against Native Americans, and colonists indiscriminately lashed out against any Indian who dared enter an English settlement. Women were not necessarily a civilizing influence on the frontier in this respect, nor does it seem that they were expected to be. Like colonist Mary Pray, who had reveled in the idea of wiping the Indians from the face of the earth, at least one woman jumped for joy when militia-men returned to Fort Amsterdam with a number of severed Indian heads. Another began to celebrate by kicking the heads around the compound.[47]

One need only read Captain John Underhill's account of the Puritans' war against the Pequot people in the late 1630s to understand the brutality English settlers had imposed on the native tribes of the region from the earliest years of settlement. In response to the deaths of two English soldiers, and the Pequot leaders' refusal to name the parties involved, English forces descended on Pequot villages. Although the native people had fled, soldiers "burnt their houses, cut downe their corne, destroyed some of their dogges" that remained.[48] When the Pequots responded by shooting arrows and torturing an English sailor they had captured, Captain Underhill and his forces attacked a Pequot fort. Surrounding the fort with three hundred men, the soldiers sent "a volley of shottee" upon it. Praising God for the accuracy of "souldiers so unexpert in the use of armes," the English ignored the "dolefull cry" of the men, women, and children within. After setting the fort on fire and watching people burn to death inside, the soldiers killed anyone who attempted to flee. "Our souldiers received and entertained with the point of the sword, downe fell men, women, and children," reported Underhill. "There were about foure hundred soules in this Fort, and not above five escaped out of our hands." To justify their actions, Underhill stated that "sometimes the Scripture declareth women and children must perish with their parents." Thus, "we had sufficient light from the word of God for our proceedings."[49]

In this context, it is apparent that the Puritans would not have demanded that anyone in colonial New England, including women, refrain from violence against Indians on religious grounds. Cotton Mather depicted

Hannah Dustin and Mary Neff as heroines from the Hebrew Bible after they slaughtered and scalped the Indians who took them captive in 1697. In his description, they were valiantly protecting the Puritan enterprise from a heathen other. Mather asserts that the women intentionally "took up a resolution to imitate the action of Jael on Sisera." If this was the case, identification with a strong and violent female figure like Jael, who murdered an enemy of the Israelites with a tent stake through the temple, would only have strengthened the women's resolve to murder their captors and anyone else nearby whom they saw as a threat. In Puritan New England, Hannah and Mary would probably have been familiar with the figure of Jael, who appears prominently in the Song of Deborah in the book of Judges. Jael was considered "blessed above women" for her deed. In Dustin's letter petitioning for church membership at the end of her life, she cites her religious belief as a source of strength and inspiration during her captivity.[50]

While Hannah and Mary may have identified with a figure like Jael, and even, perhaps, modeled themselves on her, they also had more immediate and tangible inspiration for their violent actions. As Anglo-American women, defined by their place in familial relationships, they were guided, too, by pragmatic desires to avenge their loved ones, protect themselves, and ensure the continued economic survival of their kin. Both women had been profoundly and personally affected by the Indian Wars, in terms of the loss of loved ones and family property, as well as the sense of insecurity that must have plagued them throughout their lives on the frontier of New England.

The outbreak of King William's War in the fall of 1688 struck close to home for Thomas and Hannah Dustin, their family, and their Haverhill neighbors. When fighting broke out on the frontier, Governor Andros declared war on the eastern Abenaki and led a force of seven hundred provincial soldiers into Maine. Hannah's cousin Joseph Emerson was impressed into service as a soldier for the expedition. By the time Andros's forces reached Pemaquid, the Indians had retreated for the winter. Andros ordered his men to remain in Maine to build forts, however, causing many of them to die from exposure and harsh treatment. Though Joseph survived the experience, the hardships of war would soon follow him back to Haverhill. His brother Thomas was killed during an Indian raid on the town in 1696, along with his wife and three children. Their son Thomas Jr. was carried into captivity and never recovered.[51]

Several of Hannah's relatives were living at Oyster River during the devastating Abenaki attack on that settlement. Before daybreak on the morning of July 18, 1694, 230 Indians and twenty French Canadians burst without warning onto the sleeping village. According to a local history, "before the sun was two hour high, forty-five of its people, tomahawked and scalped, lay in grotesque heaps among the smoldering timbers of their homes." Three garrisons and thirteen farmhouses were burned to the ground, and forty-nine people were taken captive. Among the captives was Judith Emerson, the wife of Hannah's brother Samuel. Judith was also a cousin to Hannah Dustin's midwife Mary Neff.[52]

In the spring of 1697, Hannah Dustin and Mary Neff were themselves taken captive. In addition to what they had already suffered at Indian hands, the brutal murder of Hannah's newborn daughter at the beginning of her captivity—an infant Mary had helped bring into the world as a midwife—would have been a loss beyond description. Their Indian captors threw the infant against a tree, killing her, and then left her body on the ground without a Christian burial before forcing Hannah and Mary to march into the wilderness. In his later retelling of Dustin's story, Cotton Mather was careful to portray Hannah as a grieving mother, filled with a righteous anger to destroy her child's murderers. According to Mather's version of events, her subsequent murder of ten Indians, including women and children, was justified in the aftermath of such a tragedy.[53]

Hannah and Mary could not have been entirely surprised to see the Abenaki forces descending on Haverhill in that spring of 1697. At the time, Hannah's husband was in the process of turning their home into a frontier garrison by order of the Committee of the Militia of Haverhill. During King William's War in particular, Haverhill was one of the exterior settlements that provided English settlements in the interior with a protective frontier. Surrounded by an immense and mostly unexplored forest, the town was constantly exposed to attack. From 1689 to 1697, Haverhill men went to work, and even to church, carrying loaded muskets. Like many in their community, both Hannah Dustin and Mary Neff had been living among the horrors and hardships of war for most of their adult lives.[54]

Hannah Dustin's fame has overshadowed the violent contributions of her fellow captive. Mary Neff, however, was actively engaged in the murders, swinging her hatchet alongside Dustin, whose desire for bloody vengeance against the Indians sprang from the personal tragedies she had experienced during the Indian Wars. In terms of the number of family members lost in the conflicts, and even perhaps the relative importance of those people in her life, Mary's losses were even greater than Hannah's. Indians had killed Mary's husband of twenty-three years, William Neff, at Pemaquid fort in 1688 while he was serving in the militia. Their son William Neff Jr. had been wounded in a surprise attack by Indians and French at Saco in 1691. Mary's aunt Jane Davis, as well as several of her cousins, were killed in the Indian massacre at Oyster River in 1694, and their family compound was destroyed. Two daughters of that family were also taken captive, including Mary's cousin. Indians irrevocably scarred the families of Mary's two sisters. Samuel Ladd, Mary's brother-in-law, was murdered during a raid on Andover in 1698, and his son was taken captive. Indians took John Robie, another brother-in-law, and Mary's nephew John Jr. captive near their home in Haverhill. John Sr. did not survive the ordeal.[55]

Such losses would have inspired a desire for revenge. Nevertheless, other considerations also appear to have played a role in the women's decision about when and how to kill their Abenaki captors. Their actions do not seem to have been those of two women filled with an uncontrollable rage for vengeance. Instead, the timing of the murders suggests that Hannah and Mary thoughtfully and deliberately took steps to protect themselves from further harm by their captors. At the time of their capture, the fate of their mutual relative Judith Emerson remained unknown, although Judith, taken captive by Indians in 1694, was presumed dead by the time Hannah and Mary were captured three years later. Both women also had other relatives who had been captured by Indians, many of whom did not survive. Hannah and Mary knew that their lives were in danger but chose to wait for the opportune moment to strike, traveling for several weeks with the Indians in peace. A few days before they launched their attack, news reached the women that when they arrived at Penacook village, they would be forced to "run the gauntlet through the whole army of Indians." Many English had "fainted and swoon'd away under the torments" of the gauntlet as an initiation rite for captives. After this unwelcome communication, Hannah and Mary set the time for the attack. Having lulled their captors into believing they were not a threat, Hannah and Mary waited until "the whole crew was in a dead sleep" before picking up their tomahawks and striking.[56]

Experience in slaughtering animals may have given Hannah and Mary the wherewithal to accomplish such a bloody task. As discussed previously in this book, women in seventeenth-century New England, including mistresses of households, commonly slaughtered pigs and other livestock when preparing food for their families. This would have involved a familiarity with wielding various domestic "weapons," such as knives and other implements for skinning hides. While killing an animal cannot be compared to killing a human being, Hannah and Mary may have been hardened to the act of taking life by fulfilling such duties. Hannah's will, recorded in Essex County probate records, lists a "flesh fork," a tool used for preparing meat, and her husband's will mentions that the family owned livestock in pigs and cattle. This implies that Hannah, at least, would have been familiar with caring for and probably butchering these animals. In addition, and as mentioned earlier, after the colonists had suffered through half a century of warfare against their native enemies, the sentiment had spread among them that the Indians were barely human, which could have made the women's actions somewhat easier to undertake.[57]

Hannah and Mary were also motivated to act by the promise of recouping some of their financial losses. Anger, of course, may have inspired the women to take trophies of their fallen enemies, but a tradition of scalp bounties in the Massachusetts Bay Colony also seems to have played a role. Both women had lost family property in the course of King William's War. After losing her husband to the conflict, Mary was left to fend largely for herself as a widow. In the estate inventory following her husband's death, the court noted that some of the family's goods "had been taken away by Indians" during his absence. Indians had also burned and ransacked the Dustins' home in the raid on Haverhill. Collecting scalp bounties could be a lucrative enterprise, and New England colonies had been offering bounties for heads and scalps of their enemies from the earliest years of settlement. Perhaps the women had this in mind as they carefully wrapped the scalps in a piece of linen and carried them back to their settlement. For her "just Slaughter of soo many of the Barbarians," and in consideration that "ye Petitionr havoing Lost his Estate in that Calamity wherein his wife was carryed into her captivity," the General Court awarded Hannah £50 as the leader of the attack. Mary Neff was given £10, twelve shillings, for her assistance.[58]

. . .

The settlers of New England paid a heavy price during King William's War. That "Lamentable Decade" had seen the progress of the English frontier "beaten back twenty years." The Treaty of Ryswick in 1697 brought a few years of peace, but war in Europe reignited hostilities in New England between Anglo-Americans and their Indian neighbors and French allies in Queen Anne's War.[59] With the outbreak of war, patterns of female violence from King Philip's and King William's Wars emerged again. Women on the frontier resorted to violence to protect their interests and those of their families. By this period, they had gained experience in defending against raids and even surviving in Indian captivity. It is little wonder that they would have used any and all weapons in their power to preserve their lives, as well as the lives of their children, and to avoid being torn away from everything they held dear.

During several raids on Haverhill, a Mrs. Bradley, who had been taken captive alongside Hannah Dustin and Mary Neff in 1697, took steps to try to ensure her family's safety and avoid being taken captive again. In 1704 she scalded two Indian attackers with boiling soap, killing one of them. This did not prevent her from being captured and dragged into the wilderness. Pregnant at the time, she gave birth to a child in captivity. The infant died of starvation and abuse by the Indians with whom she was living. Her husband was able to secure her release a year later, and she settled back into her life in Haverhill. One summer night in 1707, she, her husband, and their children watched a group of Indians approach their garrison home. Mrs. Bradley told her husband that she would rather die than be taken captive again. When the attackers rushed the garrison and had partially beaten down the door, Mrs. Bradley was the first to open fire. She shot and killed the first invader, and then the rest of the family fired into the group, causing them to retreat.[60]

During Queen Anne's War, as during the earlier Indian Wars, frontier towns bore the brunt of personal losses, while other communities were left to pay taxes, supply soldiers, and support refugees. In Salem and Marblehead, several women objected to the burdens placed on them during this period, and they responded with violence. Five Marblehead women were presented by the grand jury in 1706 for opposing "with force and arms" several colonial officials attempting to collect property in payment of debt. Lucy Codner, Mary Williams, Rebeckah Allen, Hannah Allen, and Miriam Allen were wives and daughters of poor fishermen in an area hurt by the disruptions of war. These women and their families lived a precarious existence even before the wars, and the Allens in particular found it difficult to support their family of fifteen children after rate increases. Thus, when collectors arrived to confiscate their property, these women banded together to defend their family interests against the constable and his men.[61]

A few years later, Mary Ordway of Salem took steps to avoid the increasing burden of financially supporting the conflict by "assaulting and hingering" a tax collector in the execution of his office in 1709. Mary apparently was far more aggressive than her husband during the incident; he was charged only with obstructing the office of the collector. The Ordway family had contributed soldiers to fight in the Indian Wars, and one of their daughters, Joanna, had been taken captive by Abenaki Indians five years earlier. Colonial officials had not been able to recover her. The Ordways also had relatives on the Massachusetts frontier, including in Haverhill. They were cousins to the Emersons and Hannah Dustin. Perhaps when the tax collector arrived looking for more money, Mary Ordway concluded that she and her family had given enough. Like other Anglo-American women before her, including her famous cousin, she used violence to try to preserve her life against the enemy at her door.[62]

These Anglo-American women's desire to defend themselves and their households led them to commit violent actions, and the hope of preserving their future influenced the measures they chose to take. It was as mistresses of households that most of these women entered into disputes with Indians or colonial authorities. In the context of women's everyday experiences with violence, household ideology and practical circumstance necessitated that wives conserve the integrity of their household, with or without their husband's participation. The uncertainties brought about by King Philip's War, King William's War, and Queen Anne's War, and the added demands placed upon colonial communities by their governments during these conflicts, encouraged women to take this a step further and use physical violence to defend their households. That women, the "hidden" foundations of colonial communities, would turn their aggression against colonial officials, those who should have been a protective and stabilizing force in their lives, illustrates the disruptive power of these conflicts. That women were forced to use violence to protect themselves and their families on the frontier demonstrates just how drastically colonial authorities failed to shield their own people from the hardships of war.

CHAPTER 4

☞ "The Devil will Bless himself, to find such a convenient Lodging"

Women and the Witchcraft Threat

In the spring of 1692, Dorcas Hoar, a poor resident of Beverly, was brought to court to answer charges for "High Suspicion of Sundry Acts of Witchcraft." Hoar had recently been widowed, some claimed under mysterious circumstances, and had a problematic relationship with her neighbors and local officials. She had previously been arrested, in the late 1670s, for the theft of household goods from her neighbor the Reverend John Hale and his family. With the help of Margaret Lord, the Hales' servant, Hoar had stolen food, including bushels of apples, beer, milk, and Indian corn, as well as jewelry and fabric.[1] After being fined for receiving stolen property, Hoar and her husband had retaliated against their accusers, thumping on the side of the Hales' house at all hours, and clubbing the Hales' cow to death. At the time, Goody Hoar was also accused of conspiring with the devil. The Hale children claimed that "she had a book in which shee Could read and call the diuell to kill." Hoar had a knack as well for predicting people's deaths and for fortune-telling. She had once gazed at a neighbor's healthy nine-year-old and remarked that he did not have long to live. He died within weeks.[2]

When, in 1692, Reverend Hale was called to Salem by the Reverend Samuel Parris to give his professional opinion about the "afflicted" girls of the Parris household, the stories of Hoar's problematic past with his family, and her association with dark forces, went with him. By now Hoar was a poor widow in her late fifties and thus easy prey for accusations of witchcraft. Soon her name was on the lips of eleven-year-old Abigail Williams, the Reverend Parris's niece, who lived in the Parris home and was one of the first accusers in the witch trials held in Salem. Hoar was arrested and locked in jail for months awaiting her trial. When brought before the court and her accusers, Hoar denied charges of witchcraft and defended herself against accusations that she had killed her husband. Her behavior in court did her few favors. She replied to the charges with "very greate pashtion," wringing her hands and stamping on the floor. You "wiked wretches," she cried at her accusers, who responded by claiming that she was "biting pinching and almost choaking them," revealing the "variety of tortors" she inflicted by showing the court marks on their bodies and "falling into fits." Whenever Hoar attempted to speak, her accusers only amplified the dramatic demonstrations of their afflictions, shouting, writhing, and pointing at Hoar as the source of their suffering.[3]

Hoar was indicted on the charge of witchcraft, but after confessing, she received a reprieve the day before she was to hang, as petitioned by John Hale and several others. By that time Hale had begun to lament his role in dragging Hoar's name into the Parris household drama, and into the hysteria overtaking Salem. It was too late for Hoar, however, whose property had been confiscated during her many months in prison. When she got home, she discovered that whatever meager property she had was gone—even her bed. Hoar was also probably not entitled to her widow's "third," being legally guilty of the crime of witchcraft. After her death, Hoar's family petitioned for restitution of her property on her behalf, as well as acknowledgment of her wrongful imprisonment and prosecution. They received some compensation and an official apology, but Hoar received nothing in the course of her lifetime.[4]

The trial of Dorcas Hoar illuminates several aspects of the witch trials that took place in Essex County, Massachusetts, at the end of the seventeenth century and their relationship with female violence. Like other witchcraft cases of its time, it also shines a light on the culture of violence in New England, licit and illicit, and the complex roles that women played in both diverging from and reinforcing cultural norms. As in the case of Dorcas Hoar, men and women had been accusing one another of practicing witchcraft from the earliest period of settlement in New England. In 1692, however, women's formal accusations of witchcraft became themselves a more overt form of violence, with devastating consequences.

The events of 1692 marked a shift in both the gender of the formal accusers and the consequences of a charge of witchcraft. It is important to distinguish between formal and informal accusations here. Clearly women had been involved in earlier witchcraft accusations prior to the events of Salem, but most complaints before this time were brought forward officially by men, with women providing testimony and "evidence." After the Indian Wars of the late seventeenth century, however, and in the midst of the political upheavals of the period, women took center stage in formal accusations, most drawn from existing interfamily disputes, with the support of colonial officials. The desire of some women to protect the interests of their families, households, and communities was twisted into a deadly colony-wide debacle by terrified believers, caught up in the fears of the moment, as well as by a few who saw the witch trials as a means of gaining personal and political advantage. As Cotton Mather stated in the aftermath of the trials, because of the "great wrath" of people toward one another during this time, the devil had been able to "Bless himself, to find such a convenient Lodging" among them. In the end, twenty-five people were dead, the lives of many others were destroyed, and all of New England was left reeling from the blow.[5]

As in Hoar's case, the Salem accusers picked up on earlier accusations of witchcraft and other inter-household disputes and added the names of those "disorderly persons" to their growing list of victims. Hoar had long been an unruly woman, who was known to use violent means to harass and bully her neighbors and damage property, clearly violating behavioral norms and the safety of the community as a whole. She represented both a practical and a spiritual threat, and her inappropriate use of violence made her a target for the sanctioned violence of accusation that would follow.

The idea of "violence of accusation" requires an explanation. In 1692, public accusations of witchcraft were accompanied by dramatic and violent representations of possession and the suffering imposed on the "afflicted." In this new era of witchcraft accusation, accusing someone of witchcraft became an effective way of getting rid of a threat to your person, your household, even your society, and one of the most effectual ways available to a woman. Either those accused would be imprisoned, their reputation in tatters, or they could be eliminated in the most final way possible, through execution.

As Hoar's case underlines, witchcraft accusation had been a common ingredient of disputes over property and reputation before 1692, it was not limited to Salem. Hoar was called to Salem for trial, but she was originally from Beverly, and it was there that the accusations of witchcraft against her originated. Other famous cases dating from before 1692 appeared all over

New England, and in Massachusetts as far away as Northampton in the Connecticut River Valley. Those are only the formal accusations of witchcraft that reached authorities' ears. Undoubtedly there were countless informal accusations that have been lost to history. Even in 1692, the witchcraft hysteria that gripped Salem was not limited to that town alone. The most infamous trials were conducted by the Court of Oyer and Terminer in Salem Town, but other trials also took place in Salem Village (now Danvers), Andover, and Ipswich. The accused came from twenty-two different places, fifteen of which were in Essex County. As Mary Beth Norton points out, a more accurate description for the hysteria of 1692, therefore, is the Essex County witchcraft crisis.[6]

We can trace how in 1692 the instinct to protect against disorderly or problematic forces was stretched and corrupted by a very real fear of the devil and his minions that existed in early New England, but also by other, non-spiritual influences. In the course of the trials in Salem, some women's willingness to protect their households and communities through violence took on a larger and darker scope after being embraced, even encouraged, by (male) leadership. Sometimes the connections between the accusers and these other conflicts were direct and clear. For instance, the Putnam clan's lengthy list of enemies corresponded in many respects with the list of people accused by the young members of the Putnam household. In other cases, as with Hoar, the connections between the accused and other conflicts can be discovered only by digging through court records and other sources. As Paul Boyer and Stephen Nissenbaum have illustrated, while the accusations being leveled against the accused witches were wild and otherworldly, the web of accusation that emerged through the trials seemed to be more of this earth.[7] This is not to discount the genuine belief in witchcraft and spiritual possession, and the real fear of the supernatural that permeated this society, nor is it intended to draw an anachronistic distinction between the natural and supernatural worlds that would not have existed in seventeenth-century New England.

THE VIOLENCE OF ACCUSATION

Most accusations of witchcraft before 1692 would not be considered "violent" in and of themselves, but because of the genuine belief in witchcraft, an accusation would still have been a terrifying experience. Those accused of being witches were understandably distressed. When Goodwife Seager of Hartford, Connecticut, was suspected of practicing witchcraft, she was "in great trouble, even in agony of spirit." In 1679 Goody Morse, of Newbury upon hearing that she had been associated with witchcraft, "fell on weeping," claiming she was as innocent as "the child unborn." She had reason to fear, and not just for the state of her soul. In addition to bearing the stain of accusation on her reputation, Morse was sentenced to death for her "crimes," although she was eventually reprieved. When friends Goody Jones and Alice Stratton of Charlestown learned that Jones had been formally indicted for witchcraft, they both burst into tears and looked to the Bible for comfort. It becomes clear from descriptions by victims and accusers alike that witchcraft cases produced significant emotional anguish.[8]

Eventually the performance of accusation became, in and of itself, a violent one. Physical torment and self-inflicted violence were hallmarks of "possession," whether the afflicted suffered in front of a few witnesses or in court before large, mesmerized crowds. As Mather noted in several narratives of possession he published during this period, which are discussed in greater detail in chapter 5, the afflicted would sometimes act out so aggressively they would injure bystanders and caregivers. These victims appeared to be abused and assaulted by a "Number of Spectres," to the horror of those who cared for them. Some were plagued by pins stuck in their skin and mouth, by scratches and pinches, or by unseen forces that prevented them from eating for days. When Hoar and others were called to answer charges of witchcraft in 1692, the afflicted showed their "sufferings" in court, often increasing in intensity in response to any denials or frustrations expressed by the accused.[9]

Against the advice of experienced jurors, witnesses were questioned in groups rather than individually. The accused were tried in the presence of not just the afflicted but the entire community. This allowed the afflicted to "demonstrate their torments" together, in front of an enthralled audience. According to observers, the racket in the meetinghouse, "thronged with spectators," was deafening. When one girl or woman would suffer from an affliction, the rest would soon join in, reacting to the responses and movements of the accused. When one accused witch on trial bit her lip, "severall of the afflicted were bitten," the Reverend Samuel Parris remarked. They would then produce the "Marks" for the "Magistrates, Ministers and others." During the examination in court of Parris's slave Tituba, the four victims appeared "greviously distressed" at the outset but were "immediately all quiet" when she made her confession. In the face of such violent behavior, many of the accused were intimidated into confessing and naming their "accomplices."[10]

In Puritan New England, it was otherwise unheard of for young women to command such sustained attention from grown men, let alone to wield such power. The accusations of women and girls were being taken very seriously, even those of lower rank, such as adolescent daughters and servants. As magistrates and ministers listened attentively to these young females and their denunciations of witches, societal roles in the early modern world was, for a moment, turned "topsy-turvy." Most authorities appeared to regard these afflictions as legitimate. For instance, during Hoar's testimony, the magistrates asked Hoar why she continued to "hurt" the girls who accused her during court proceedings.[11]

By demonstrating to colonial leaders the legitimacy, or at least the utility, of their witchcraft claims, the accusers shared with court officials and ministers the experience of holding power over life and death. As Rebecca Nurse stated in her testimony, "They accuse you of hurting them, and if you think it is not unwillingly but by designe, you must look upon them as murderers." It is possible that some of the accusers began to enjoy holding such power, even enhancing their stories of possession and affliction. It also seems clear, however, that when some of the accusers began to realize the violence they had inflicted, they wanted no more part in it. Some of the earliest accusers, perhaps shocked that their actions had helped send people to the gallows, stopped having fits and denouncing witches well before the trials came to an end.[12]

Female violence played a complex role on all sides of witchcraft accusations. Women who committed acts of overt violence, usually in addition to other inappropriate and offensive behaviors, were commonly the focus of accusation. A woman who abused her husband or children or raged against her neighbors might be accused of witchcraft. Poor, socially isolated, and vulnerable women may have resorted to "witch-like" behavior out of desperation. Poisoning, attempted assault through ritual magic, and displays of intense anger offered ways to engage in conflicts that played to their limited strengths. Such use of overt aggression went beyond the acceptable level of violence for women in Puritan communities, however, and sometimes was seen as crossing spiritual lines as well. For men, unnatural or supernatural violence was also the most frightening type of "aggression," because it could not easily be countered by men's superior strength. A thin line separated the violent nag from the woman who covenanted with the devil.[13]

Accusing another person of witchcraft was not necessarily disingenuous among the Puritans of New England, given the widespread belief in magic in the early modern world. The religion of the colonists was "infused with ancient attitudes and practices," some far older than Christianity. Belief in the idea that "murder will out"—that a dead body will bleed afresh when the murderer comes near—prophetic dreams and visions, superstitions for luck or the safety of loved ones, shape-shifting animals, and more remained commonplace. By the seventeenth century, much of this "old world" magic had fallen out of favor with the intellectual and religious elite but persisted among common folk. It is impossible to know the genuine feelings and motivations of those who accused others of being witches. Scholars have speculated endlessly about the female accusers of Salem in particular. There can be little doubt, however, that in the early weeks and months of the witch trials in Salem, most of the "witches" that these young women accused came from other families that appeared to pose a threat to the households of which they were a part. That the webs of accusation continued to spread, and produced such deadly consequences, is due to the way in which the male magistrates, judges, and religious leaders involved chose to handle the trials.[14]

WITCHCRAFT CASES BEFORE 1692

Prior to 1692, most New England courts reacted to witchcraft cases in line with how they were treated in most of western Europe. Magistrates were reluctant to credit accusations of maleficium, with proof often impossible to obtain, so convictions for this offense were rare. Imprisonment for charges of witchcraft was uncommon, execution for witchcraft almost unheard of. Of the 250 individuals formally accused of witchcraft in New England in the entire seventeenth century before 1692, some one hundred colonists were charged, twenty convicted, and sixteen executed.[15]

The number of women and men accused of witchcraft ebbed and flowed throughout the seventeenth century in New England, frequently in connection with local political upheavals, as well as with the standards of evidence that courts were willing to embrace. Between 1647 and 1663, about sixty people were accused in the region. Of the first twelve to be tried, eight were executed, most in Connecticut, which was the epicenter of New England witch trials into the 1660s. John Winthrop, one of the founders of the Connecticut Colony, had left for England to try to get a royal charter for the colony. He had long argued against witchcraft accusation, but without his calming influence, Connecticut became embroiled in a witch hunt. By 1663, however, the Connecticut leadership had joined Massachusetts in largely turning against accusations of maleficium as sufficient evidence for a conviction on charges of witchcraft.[16]

Four women were hanged for witchcraft in Massachusetts in the early years of settlement, including Margaret Jones and Elizabeth Kendall. Leaders of the colony began to have doubts about their trials, however, given that none of the accused had actually confessed to the crime. The conviction rate for witchcraft cases fell sharply again in the 1650s. Of the next forty-five trials, only seven people were executed, beginning with Mistress Anne Hibbens in 1655–56. Between Hibbens's trial, and the larger debacle that engulfed much of Essex County, only two people were convicted in Massachusetts, and one hanged, a community outsider and Irish Catholic named Mary Glover, who confessed to being a witch in 1688.[17]

These early cases commonly emerged out of inter-neighbor disputes over property or interpersonal relations, disputes that sometimes involved violence. New Englanders who were at odds with neighbors, or found a household in their community particularly problematic, sometimes resorted to accusations of witchcraft. These were hurled against neighbors, contractual parties, competitors—anyone who might be provocative, quarrelsome, or generally dissatisfied. Often, both the accused and accusers were involved in lawsuits over property, mistreatment, even divorce. Frequently the older women who became the focus of accusation were seen as obstacles to others' prosperity, as holders of property, tavern keepers, merchants, even healers or midwives—obstacles that could potentially be eliminated through accusations of witchcraft.[18]

The gender dynamics of early witchcraft cases also diverge from those of 1692. Early formal accusations emerged mostly from men, who claimed that a woman had used supernatural means to harm them, their property, or members of their household. Women participated in these trials, though usually as witnesses, giving testimony to back up the claims of the primary male accusers, creating a web of accusation that would grow to involve many members of the households in question. Unlike in 1692, however, women as accusers remained largely in the background in these early cases. And because of their secondary role, it is difficult, if not impossible, to reconstruct the involvement of every single deponent or witness in each case before the court.[19]

Jane and Erasmus James of Marblehead seem to have had a contentious relationship with several neighboring families, resulting in charges of witchcraft being leveled against Jane in particular. Both Jane and her husband were charged with the theft of items from a neighbor and bound on "good behavior" by the court, but it was Jane who bore the brunt of accusations of witchcraft. In 1646 Peter Pitford, who lived near the Jameses, claimed that Jane was a witch and that he had seen her "in a boat at sea in the likeness of a cat." At the time, it was commonly believed that witches could turn themselves into animals in order to commit their evil deeds without being recognized. Pitford also claimed that the proximity of his farm to the James residence was a cause of his misfortune. His "garden frughtes" would not prosper as long as he lived near "that woman," whom he repeatedly referred to as a "Jesable." Another neighbor, Richard Rowland, who was, like Erasmus, a shipbuilder and had a difficult working relationship with him, claimed that Jane came in through the window in his home one night and choked him in his bed. Jane was never found guilty of witchcraft, and Erasmus and Jane repeatedly sued the Pitfords and Rowlands for slander for calling Jane a witch. Rumors surrounding Jane continued to swirl, however.[20]

In 1648 Margaret Jones of Charlestown became the first person in Massachusetts to be executed for witchcraft. Jones was known as a "cunning woman," someone who performed a variety of healing services, including midwifery. As one who existed on the margins of Puritan society, Margaret was carefully watched by local authorities. According to the Puritan leader John Winthrop, as he noted in his journal, she seemed to have the ability to foretell the future and had a "malignant touch." Suspicions about Jones came to a head after some angry words passed between her and her neighbors. In the wake of their public quarrel, some "mischief befell such neighbors and their creatures." These neighbors were "supposed to be bewitched, or have a charm upon them." They also appear to have suffered a house fire, which they subsequently blamed on Jones and her supernatural powers. Margaret's husband, Thomas Jones, was suspected of committing witchcraft too but was never prosecuted. Margaret denied that she was witch until her dying day. A minister and several of her neighbors went to the jail to visit her on the day of her execution, urging her to confess her sins. Jones admitted to the crime of theft, but "as for witchcraft she was wholly free from it, and so she said unto her death."[21]

Heated disagreement over ownership of a "dwelling house" in Salem led to accusations of arson and witchcraft against Edith Craford in 1666 and 1667. Mordicha and Edith Craford had formerly been in possession of a local inn. Although the circumstances through which they lost the property are not clear, it can be assumed that financial difficulties led to two men, a Captain Savage and Anthony Asbie, taking control of the property. Edith had "given out threatening speeches concerning the house," according to court records. When the building later caught fire, Savage and Asbie accused Edith of starting the blaze. In addition to being committed to prison in Boston to await her trial, Edith was also accused of witchcraft during the proceedings. Asbie announced that "hee would have [Edith] Hanged If ther were no more wimen In the world for shee was A witch & If shee were nott a witch allreaddy shee woudl bee won & therefore It was as good to Hang her att first as Last." Asbie did not get his wish. Edith was exonerated.[22]

The infamous case of John Godfrey follows previous patterns of witchcraft accusation in that the allegations emerged in the context of other disputes with neighbors, but his case stands out, given the sex of the accused and the sheer number of accusations laid against him. John was male and not connected to a woman accused of witchcraft. Like the women usually accused, he was vulnerable, however, because of his poverty and his status as a troublemaker and social outsider. No fewer than twenty-four witnesses from six different towns came forward to testify against him. Between 1658 and his death in 1675, Godfrey appeared in court at least once a year on account of various legal actions, most involving property in land, money, bonds, crops, livestock, and so on. As John Demos notes, "Taken as a whole, the records depict a man continually at odds with his peers, over a host of quite specific, personal, and mundane affairs." Godfrey's disagreements with his Andover neighbors also spilled over into the supernatural. At least eleven people came forward in a petition to the court in 1658, claiming that because of him, they had "sufered loses in ther estates and some aflickshen on ther bodyes also: which as they supose doth not arise from any natural cause." They cited the mysterious death of oxen, the loss of a child; one woman noted "hearing voyce and being aflicted in her body." In another case, two men brought forward eighteen witnesses to accuse Godfrey of having "consulted with a familiar spirit" and "done much hurt and mischief by several acts of witchcraft to the bodies and goods of several persons." Unsurprisingly, the names of many of those involved in these cases also appear in opposition to Godfrey in lawsuits over property or debt. He was narrowly acquitted on charges of witchcraft.[23]

The widow Ann Burt of Lynn was accused of witchcraft on several occasions, largely as a result of her status as a healer, which left her open to accusations from disappointed patients, distrustful neighbors, and her competitors. While not personally "afflicted," the main witness against Burt in these cases before the court was Dr. Phillip Read, a self-professed physician who visited those who claimed to have been struck down by Burt's curses and torments after going to her for treatment of various ailments. Read testified that he had visited Sarah Townsend, who told him that "Burt had afflicted her and told her if ever she did relate it to anyone she would afflict her worse." An hour later, Sarah "had a sadder fit than any ever she had afore," Read claimed, stating that he "did plainly perceive there was no natural cause for such unnatural fits." Thomas Farrar blamed sickness and "extreme misery" in his family on Goody Burt, as reported by Read, who claimed that Farrar's son was now "bewitched to his understanding." In the context of other court cases, Read appears to have been threatened by the presence of women healers and had sued others for slander when his professional reputation or competence was questioned by them. Accusing Burt of witchcraft was perhaps one way of getting rid of the competition.[24]

Jealousy, and one family's failures and grief, led to accusations of witchcraft against Mary Bliss Parsons over several decades. The Parsons family moved to Northampton in 1654 and soon became one of the wealthiest families in town. Mary and Joseph Parsons had eleven children, most of whom lived to adulthood. In an ironic twist, it seems that the Parsonses' successes are what drew the ire of their neighbors. Joseph Parsons was frequently involved in lawsuits, usually as a plaintiff, related to his ventures as a merchant. Rumors began to circulate that the family's prosperity came at the expense of other families, and through the work of witchcraft. Sarah and James Bridgman were the source of most of the accusations. The

Bridgmans arrived in Northampton soon after the Parsonses, but where the Parsonses enjoyed success, the Bridgmans did not. They experienced financial difficulties, and Sarah kept losing children in infancy, plagued with a variety of ailments. After the death of their infant in 1656, members of the Bridgman household began to speak ill of Mary Parsons, claiming that she was connected, through witchcraft, to the death of the child. Other neighbors piled on, blaming Mary for various childhood illnesses and loss of livestock. Joseph Parsons brought a lawsuit against Sarah Bridgman for slander. The magistrates issued their decision in favor of the Parsonses and ordered Sarah to make a public apology for her slander or else pay a fine. It appears that despite the financial hardship, Sarah chose to pay the fine rather than submit to the public humiliation.[25]

The decision in the slander case did not stop the feud between the Bridgman and Parsons clans nor end community speculation that Mary was a witch. She was officially brought to trial for witchcraft in 1674 after the death of another Bridgman child, this time a grown married woman, Mary Bridgman Bartlett, at age twenty-two. The widower, Samuel Bartlett, filed a complaint against Mary Parsons, claiming in his grief that his wife had died "by some unusuall meanes . . . of some evell Instruemt." According to court records, he presented "diverse evedences to shew the grounds of his feares & suspicioun." The following January, county magistrates conducted a hearing. Mary spoke for herself, proclaiming her innocence, yet the court ordered that her body be searched by a "jury of . . . chast woman" for any "markes of witchcraft" that might appear. Afterward, magistrates decided that the matter was beyond their jurisdiction, so they sent the case to the Court of Assistants in Boston. Mary was held in prison in Boston for several months awaiting trial. Her family wealth may have allowed her to pay for a larger cell and purchase decent food and water—prisoners at the time were responsible for their own food and lodging while in prison—but it would not have been a pleasant experience. Eventually Goody Parsons was acquitted by the court of the charges of witchcraft, but the family does not seem to have been eager to return to Northampton. They stayed in Boston for a time, and eventually moved to Springfield. When the Parsonses' son Ebenezer was killed in September 1675 battling Indians at Northfield, some in the community must have considered it punishment for Mary's communing with the devil.[26]

A SHIFT IN ACCUSATION

Ebenezer Parsons was killed fighting in King Philip's War (1675–1678), a conflict that marked the end of an era of peace, commercial expansion, and prosperity in the region and wiped out almost 30 percent of the Anglo-American population of New England. Fighting continued to bring devastation to the region a decade later, especially in northern New England, during King William's War (1688–1697). It is difficult to quantify the impact of these conflicts on the Puritan settlers. They regarded their losses in the wars, and the resulting loss of prosperity, as God's punishment for their sins. With increasing desperation, people looked for someone, or something, to blame. Perhaps, some surmised, it was the work of the devil himself. New England was under attack by outside forces—physical as well as spiritual—that had intruded upon them and threatened their very survival.[27]

The dramatic increase in accusations of witchcraft in the late seventeenth century cannot be examined outside the context of these wars. For Essex County towns in general, the proximity to New Hampshire and Maine meant that their residents were involved in both wars with the natives. Essex County militiamen served on the Maine frontier. Many had relatives and friends who had suffered from the aftermath of Indian raids. As several scholars have shown, a number of people involved in the witchcraft crisis in Salem and its surrounding towns had intimate experience with the Indian Wars. At least in part, it was the impact of those wars that made the Essex County witch trials different from those that had preceded them. Several of the accused, and their accusers, were refugees from Maine and had experienced the conflicts firsthand. These accusers, many of whom were young women who had lost their families in the wars, began residing in Salem and other towns nearby in Essex County. They brought their fears and memories of the horrors of war with them, and as these anxieties spread, they helped fuel the witch trials of 1692.[28]

After King Philip's War there was a marked shift in the sex of most formal witchcraft accusers. Increasingly, and culminating in the Essex County witchcraft crisis, women and girls took the lead in openly accusing others of consorting with the devil and bringing malevolent forces into their communities. This shift must be seen within the context of how women in Puritan New England tended to use violence more generally. In the midst of the trauma of the conflicts with the Indians, and the collective sense of panic that resulted from that threat, women began to level accusations against those they perceived to be sources of disruption and deprivation in their lives and the lives of their families, households, and communities. Many of the accused had threatened their neighbors and communities with disorderly physical or spiritual violence emerging from previous inter-household and community disagreements. These accusations began to evolve into a form of colony-wide violence, given the outcome of the trials of 1692. Most of the convicted witches lost their lives, and many of them their property. Families also felt the consequences of conviction, both emotional and financial. Even those who were acquitted lived on in the shadow of accusation.

The violence of the 1692 witch trials can be read as an extension of colonial women's use of violence as a means of preserving family interests, or the interests of kin groups, in the midst of turmoil and loss. Women's willingness to resort to overt, sometimes deadly violence under extreme circumstances was exploited by leaders in Salem and Andover, in particular, in the name of protecting the colony as a whole, and sometimes to serve their own purposes. The trials offered an opportunity to "release pent-up fears and to root out persons who seemed threatening to the community," as Richard Godbeer argues.[29] In turn, the accusers themselves may have enjoyed wielding power that would ordinarily remain well out of their grasp. The fact that the "witches" the women and girls were accusing in 1692 were not actually a supernatural threat to themselves, their households, or the safety of the colony is irrelevant in this context. The perception of threat, and the amplification of those fears through the course of the trials themselves, mattered far more than any actual physical danger.

One issue that has perplexed scholars who have studied the witch trials is the question why these women and girls targeted other women. In the context of this inquiry it is important to consider why women would have been considered more of a threat to their households and communities than men. In seventeenth-century New England, women were seen as more of a threat socially as well as spiritually. As Carol Karlsen has shown, those accused of witchcraft in early New England tended in general to be disorderly women who either failed or refused to follow the behavioral norms of their society. As I have discussed in this book, women operated within a more limited scope of appropriate behavior than men, including when acting in violent ways. Many of the women accused of witchcraft demonstrated uses of violence that threatened the male-dominated social order and drew the ire of men and, in turn, their female dependents. With no real sense of gender solidarity in this society, women's primary loyalty remained to their kin group, their household, and, secondarily, their community. As Ann Kibbey has argued, women's identity during this period was an extension of the men in their lives, and thus conflicts between women could "easily be exploited to express conflicts between the men with/by women they were identified." Divided from one another by a patriarchal social structure and dependent on the goodwill of men, women attacked other women. On a larger scale, women also focused on those who, by their disorderly behavior, seemed to threaten the stability of the community as a whole. This was particularly relevant during the chaos and disruption of war.[30]

In a spiritual sense as well, women could be more "dangerous" than men. If, as Cotton Mather and other Puritan divines explained, the Indian Wars were indeed a scourge sent by God for the people's sinfulness, one obvious solution for ending the terror, loss, and hardship of war was to root out the primary sins in their society. Women were seen as more susceptible to sin and wickedness, more likely to commune with the devil, and therefore more likely to be caught in his snare.[31] Practicing witchcraft was an obvious sign of sinfulness and rebellion against God, and a threat to the community at large. Puritan New Englanders believed themselves to be a people chosen by God, meant to bring his word to a previously heathen land, and were thus particularly inclined to see themselves as antagonists of the devil. Identifying witches, and ridding themselves of the threats they posed, was an aspect of that fight in which women and girls could participate, even excel, if encouraged by members of the clergy and community leaders.

THE ESSEX COUNTY WITCHCRAFT CRISIS

One of the most fervent supporters of the hunt to identify disorderly forces in their midst turned out to be the embattled minister Reverend Parris. Taking the reins of the new Salem Village church a few years before the witchcraft crisis, Parris seemed determined to use his position to achieve the respect and status he had long sought. A history of professional failures, his personal insecurities, and the precarious position of the village in relationship to Salem Town more generally were all obstacles in his way. Parris was thirty-six years old in 1689 and had failed as a merchant in both Barbados and Boston before accepting the post in Salem Village. After his ordination, Parris had subjected the village to a year of divisive negotiations before he agreed to take up the position. By most accounts, Parris was a sensitive individual, easily miffed at perceived slights and "scoffing" or "rough" behavior toward him. Compared to its prosperous neighbor Salem Town, Salem Village was only just able to support an organized church. The small village was not yet a fully established community.[32]

Parris's arrival, rather than uniting Salem Village, deepened the divisions between church members and nonmembers, between those who supported Parris's ministry versus those who sought to remove him. Parris repeatedly stressed the difference between full church members and everyone else. He had nonmembers dismissed from the meetinghouse after the sermon on sacrament days before the members took communion. He also supported the church's position of allowing the sacrament of infant baptism only for children who had at least one church-member parent. Opposition to his ministry grew, especially among the nearly three quarters of adult villagers who had not officially joined the church. They repeatedly refused to contribute to his salary or deposit firewood at his door, an expression of deference which Parris had demanded. Parris responded by attacking his opponents and portraying opposition to his ministry as a struggle between good and evil.[33]

Parris often took the fears, anxieties, and concerns of his listeners and turned them into a conflict between good and evil, Christ and Satan, heaven and hell, "us" versus "them." As other scholars have noted, the prevailing motif of Parris's sermons from 1689 to 1692 "is one of encircling menace: a menace which thrusts closer and closer to the heart of the Village." Church members branded outsiders as "other," even at times as evil. In employing such imagery from a position of influence, and among a people still reeling from the horrors of war, Parris's rhetoric helped set the stage for the larger witchcraft crisis of 1692. As Benjamin Ray has calculated, "65 percent of the Village accusers (41 out of 65) belonged to the households of church members or supporters of Parris," while 71 percent of the accused did not belong to the church. In general, supporters of the trials and those who opposed them were divided along the lines of pro- and anti-Parris factions. Those who supported the trials were generally pro-Parris partisans, and opponents of the trials were overwhelmingly anti-Parris.[34]

Most of the accusers during the Essex County witchcraft crisis were the women of pro-Parris households. Before Parris's own nine-year-old daughter Betty and his slightly older niece (or female relative) Abigail Williams began to behave in strange and mysterious ways, they would have been treated to Reverend Parris's sermons railing against those who opposed him, threatening to make "thine enemies thy footstool," and presenting Salem Village as in the midst of a spiritual war against the devil. Forces of evil sought to destroy the church entirely, Parris claimed, and they would be aided by "Assistants of Satan" who were "Wicked." It was up to "the Saints on Earth . . . to intercede for one [an]other," he preached. It is logical to conclude that such rhetoric continued within the Parris household after church services had concluded. To those who spent any time listening to Parris, the question of who were among the wicked would have been clear. By mid-January 1692, Abigail and Betty were showing signs of engaging in this spiritual war themselves.[35]

By February, Ann Putnam Jr. and her friend Elizabeth (Betty) Hubbard had also started to suffer from similar fits. As Reverend Hale reported, like Betty Parris and Abigail Williams, they were being abused and afflicted by "invisible agents" who bit and pinched them, twisted their bodies back and forth, and caused them to fall dumb, their "throats choaked . . . limbs tormented."[36] Ann, the twelve-year-old daughter of Thomas Putnam Jr., was the most active of the "afflicted" girls. By March, her mother, Ann Putnam Sr., had joined her, suffering from violent fits and claiming to be haunted by specters. The extensive Putnam clan were supporters of Reverend Parris and dedicated members of his church, accounting for almost one-fourth of the total church membership in these years. As others turned against Parris and sought his removal, the majority of the Putnam family remained loyal, even after the witch trials were concluded.[37]

The Putnams were instrumental in expanding the witch trials. At least eight members of the family, drawn from all three of its branches, were involved in the prosecution of no fewer than forty-six accused witches. Many of the people they accused had had previous disagreements with members of the Putnam family, whether over land claims, their loyalty to Samuel Parris, or some personal slight or insult. The Putnam family remained wealthy, but recent generations had seen their worth and influence begin to lessen, and some members of the Putnam clan were determined to regain their previous footing. One of them was Thomas Putnam, who was heavily involved in Salem Town politics, and who wrote more than 120 depositions and testimonials against accused witches during the trials. His success rate for getting grand juries to act against the accused, frequently on the testimony of his own family members, was remarkably high. Putnam was known for adjusting court documents to fit legal needs, for example, signing someone else's name to a document, or adding language to strengthen a case. When Putnam filed his last formal complaint, on July 1, 1692, his name had appeared on more than half of all felony complaints of witchcraft that had appeared before that time in the trials. Questions remain about whether Putnam was simply a conscientious citizen, or if he was acting in service of other motives, or some combination of both. Similar questions also arise about the role of Ann Putnam Jr. and Sr., as well as other women of the household, in destroying several enemies of the Putnam clan through accusations of witchcraft.[38]

One of the first three people accused of witchcraft in Salem was Sarah Warren Prince Osborne, a woman with an unconventional personal life as well as a contentious history with the Putnam family. She was named by Ann Putnam Jr., Betty Parris, Abigail Williams, and Elizabeth Hubbard as one of the witches who had been "afflicting" them. Thomas Putnam and his son Edward filed official charges against her. Sarah was the widow of Robert Prince, whose sister had married into the Putnam family. Robert had purchased an extensive piece of land next to the Putnams' property, which was entailed to his and Sarah's two young sons (who were also Ann Jr.'s second cousins). After Robert's death, Sarah scandalized her neighbors by marrying her former servant, an Irish immigrant named Alexander Osborne. The two attempted to take possession of the property, which brought them into conflict with the father and uncle of Thomas Putnam, who had been named executors of Prince's estate and who defended the claims of Sarah's sons. It appears that by upsetting social norms and attempting to claim land outside of proper inheritance practices, Sarah had made herself a target.[39]

Sarah was called to appear in the Salem meetinghouse on March 1, 1692. Her examination and testimony reveal the influence of the Indian threat that continued to lurk on the edges of Essex County communities at the time. Sarah's accusers confronted her, having been instructed to "stand up and looke upon her" in order for them to identify her as "the woman that did afflict" them. After being questioned for hours, Sarah continued to deny having any part in harming the children. She did admit, however, to being "frightened one time in her sleep" by dark visions. She "either saw or dreamed that shee saw a thing like an indian all black," she recalled, "which did pinch her in her neck and pulled her by the back part of her head . . . to the dore of the house." As Cotton Mather noted, reports of dark figures, or specters that resembled native peoples, were common in cases of possession and were often stand-ins for Satan. That images reflecting the horrors of Indian raids had crept into Sarah's dreams is not surprising in the context of late seventeenth-century New England.[40]

Another of Sarah's accusers was Tituba, Reverend Parris's slave. She had come with him to New England from Barbados and was often described as being an "Indian" herself. Tituba was accused of being a witch by her young mistress Betty Parris. The reverend then demanded that she name other witches, and some accounts claim he beat his slave until she was willing to confess and name names. Sarah Osborne was one of those she mentioned, having seen her name signed in the devil's book, written in blood, Tituba claimed. In her testimony, Sarah revealed that the dark figure who had appeared to her had also encouraged her to separate herself from Parris's church. A "voice" had told her that she should "go no more to meeting." Although Sarah claimed she had resisted the command, her husband revealed that Goody Osborne had not attended church for a year and two months. Sarah then pleaded that illness had kept her away, but the magistrates disagreed, accusing her of "yielding to the devil" to "never goe to meeting." Whatever Sarah's reasons for avoiding going to the Reverend Parris's church, in a community as small as Salem Village her absence could not have been overlooked. In the end, it was the testimony of women from both the Parris and Putnam households that sealed Sarah's fate. She died in prison on May 10, 1692.[41]

Ann Putnam Jr. was the first to name Rebecca Towne Nurse, of nearby Topsfield, as a witch, but it was largely the testimony of Ann Putnam Sr. that led to her conviction. When Nurse was accused, it sent shock waves through both Salem and Topsfield. Despite the fact that her mother had been accused of witchcraft years earlier, though never arrested and brought to trial, Nurse did not fit the standard profile of an accused witch. She was a respectable matron and church member, and her family was of good personal and financial standing, except with the Putnam and Parris families. Thus, her fellow churchgoers were very surprised when Ann named Goody Nurse as one of her spectral attackers during the second week of March. It appears that previous disputes between the Nurses, Putnams, and Parrises, as well as the taint of accusation inherited from her mother, were enough to drag Rebecca into the Salem debacle.[42]

The Nurses had managed to get on the wrong side of both the Putnam and Parris families, threatening the economic interests of one and the livelihood of the other. The Putnams had a long-standing dispute with the town of Topsfield, into which town officials claimed some of their land extended. A central piece of this dispute involved the question of who had legitimate access to the trees on that property. Several members of the Nurse family lived in Topsfield and became involved in these boundary disputes. Rebecca and her husband, Francis, lived on a rich three-hundred-acre farm near the Ipswich road. In the 1670s, Francis had been involved in a legal dispute with the Putnams over some mutually bounded acreage. Again, in the 1680s, the Nurses and Putnams were back in court, this time over rights to timber on land that both families claimed. The Putnam women would have been familiar with these disputes prior to lodging accusations of witchcraft against Rebecca Nurse. The Nurses also opposed Reverend Parris. Francis was a member of the anti-Parris village committee, and in 1689 Rebecca had decided not to transfer her church membership from Salem Town to Parris's church in Salem Village. As a member of Parris's household, Abigail Williams probably witnessed her uncle's frustration over the Nurses' opposition to his ministry.[43]

The disputes between the Nurses, Parrises, and Putnams were eventually played out in court, recast around charges of witchcraft leveled against Rebecca by the women of these households. The case would, of course, have deadly results. Rebecca was convicted largely on the basis of spectral afflictions that befell Ann Putnam Sr. in late March 1692. As the word of an adult, Ann Sr.'s testimony carried more weight in court than that of the younger witnesses, although their dramatic testimony would also have moved those who came to watch the proceedings. The violent nature of the afflictions described attests to the level of threat Rebecca appeared to represent. Ann accused Goody Nurse of appearing before her "only in hir shift" and tormenting her with "hellish temtations" in order to get Ann to add her name to the devil's "little Red book." When Ann refused, Rebecca threatened to tear her soul from her body. During Nurse's examination before the court, Ann Sr. was apparently so "dreadfully tortured" by Nurse that her husband had to carry her out of the meetinghouse. Ann Jr. confirmed her mother's story that Nurse, or her "apparition," was attacking her. Abigail Williams shared a similar tale, claiming she "hath been pulled violently [and] often pinched & almost choked" by Goody Nurse. She was also "tempted sometimes to leap into the [fire and] sometimes to subscribe a book the said apparition brought." Court magistrates convicted Rebecca Nurse of witchcraft on the basis of such testimony. She was hanged on July 19, 1692.

That disputes over territory were coming to light during the late seventeenth century is not surprising. That they could result in such deadly consequences deserves exploration. According to the historian David Konig, the people of Massachusetts were "particularly sensitive to the violation of boundaries during the years leading up to the witch hunt." Wandering or destructive animals, the crossing of boundaries, and general intrusions onto private property appear frequently in depositions from the 1692 witch trials. Konig argues that this sensitivity to intrusion was linked to the general insecurity of the moment in the midst of the Indian Wars and the political crises that accompanied them. With colonial authority and power in question, local fences and boundaries became a stand-in for control and safety. When viewed in the context of women's willingness to use violence to preserve household security, the Putnam women's bringing land disputes into the witch trials, and focusing on those who would threaten to intrude on their own family's claims, becomes more explicable.[44]

Several other women with connections to the Topsfield land disputes found themselves at the mercy of the Putnam women in court, accused of witchcraft. Testimony from Ann Putnam Jr. and Sr. was central in bringing down Rebecca's sister Mary Towne Easty, whose husband had also been involved in the Topsfield incidents. She was executed in September 1692. Rebecca's sister-in-law Elizabeth Howe was also dragged into the debacle. Her family's involvement in the disputes, and her relationship with the Nurse clan, helped condemn her, aided by earlier accusations of witchcraft and strange behavior.[45]

In 1682, when ten-year-old Hannah Perley began falling into fits and feeling as if she were being pricked by pins, her parents sought an explanation. They visited several doctors, who eventually diagnosed Hannah as being "under an evil hand." Her condition persisted for two or three more years until "she pined away to skin and bones and ended her sorrowful life." Before she died, Hannah had claimed that the Perleys' neighbor Goody Howe was responsible for her suffering. "I could never afflict a dog as Good Howe afflicts me," she cried. Apparently, even before she was accused of being a witch, Howe was judged in Topsfield to have an unsavory character. In 1654, Goodwife Batchiler was hesitant to go over to Goody Howe's home and borrow some draft cattle "because she feared there was some evil practice in it." How's reputation made Hannah's claims seem all the more plausible.[46]

In retribution for what they believed Elizabeth Howe had done to their daughter, the Perleys sought to prevent her from joining their church in Ipswich. They began a campaign against her membership in the church, reminding their fellow parishioners of Elizabeth's misdeeds, including the "grete scandal" involving their daughter. Howe must have realized that her exclusion from the church would only ostracize her further, so she reached out to other neighbors for help. She pleaded with the wife of Joseph Safford to represent her in the congregation, and even persuaded Goody Safford to approach the church elders. When Safford was unsuccessful in influencing church leaders to accept Howe, things seemed to take a dark turn. Soon afterward, Safford and her daughter both fell ill, and she began to suspect that Howe had some hand in her misfortune. Recanting her statement in the church meeting supporting the Howes' petition, she stated, "I was mistaken . . . for I thought goode how had bene a precious saint of god but now I see she is a witch for shee hath bewitched mee and my child and we shall never be well till ther is testemoney for her that she may be taken into the church."[47]

The Perley family suspected that Elizabeth had taken her revenge against them as well. Samuel Perley testified during Howe's trial that after his family had prevented Elizabeth from "coming into the Church," their cow fell ill; the cow suddenly went "mad" and ran into a pond, drowning herself, he claimed. Another neighbor, sixty-year-old Nehamiah Abot, also blamed Elizabeth for his loss of livestock after a disagreement with James Howe. "After any difrencis with James Hows wif elizabeth," he reported to the court, "how ofen Evill a curents did falow som straing loses I met withall amongst our Catill."[48] Several other neighbors and rivals showed up to give testimony against her. Isaac Cummings Sr. regaled the court with a strange tale. Eight years earlier, Cummings had refused to allow James Howe to borrow his horse. The next day, the horse refused to eat and had several mysterious bruises and injuries. After concluding that the horse must have a stomachache, he tried a folk remedy which involved lighting a pipe of tobacco to "put it in to the fundement of the mare." A blue flame shot out of the pipe, lit the horse's hair on fire, and almost burned down the barn. He attributed this remarkable occurrence to the work of Goody Howe. Even Elizabeth brother-in-law John testified against her. He stated that he had told her if she would confess to being a witch, he would go with her to Salem, but she had become angry and refused. The next day, his sow jumped high in the air, gave a squeal, and fell dead as if it "was bewitched." To test whether the sow was truly dead, he cut off its ear. The hand he used became "numb and full of paine." He thus concluded that Elizabeth Howe was to blame. It is perhaps not a coincidence that John would have been in line to inherit his brother's estate, given that James and Elizabeth had no sons. With Goody Howe out of the way, he would have one fewer obstacle to claiming the property.[49]

As with most of the accused from Topsfield, the Howes had had the misfortune to run afoul of the Putnam family. In the early 1680s, Elizabeth's husband, James, had been one of the men who met with Thomas Putnam and informed him that they had liberty from the town of Topsfield to clear trees from lands the Putnams claimed on the Topsfield side of the town line. The men then cut down a tree in front of him. Outnumbered at the time, Putnam could do nothing to respond to the insult. Later, however, he and several other family members returned to cut down and claim the trees themselves. Mercy Lewis, a nineteen-year-old servant in the Putnam household, acted as a key player in dragging Elizabeth Howe into the Salem debacle. During Howe's trial, Lewis threw herself on the floor as soon as Howe entered the meetinghouse. Court records report that "Mercy Lewis at length spake & charged this woman with hurting & pinching her." Her fits increased in intensity as Howe claimed her innocence. Elizabeth Howe was convicted of witchcraft and hanged on July 19, 1692, the same day as Rebecca Nurse.[50]

Sarah Avery Wilds's nonconformity, tendency toward disruptive behavior, and prior offenses made her a disorderly figure, and thus a target for accusations of witchcraft in the 1680s and again in 1692. Ending up on the wrong side of a member of the extended Putnam clan did not help her situation either. In particular, the matriarch of the Reddington family, Mary Gould Reddington, considered Sarah an undesirable, even dangerous addition to her extended family and made her views well known. (Sarah married John Wilds very soon after the death of his first wife, who was from the Gould family.) Prior to her marriage, Sarah had been sentenced to be whipped for fornication in 1649. Later, she would be brought to court for violating Puritan sumptuary laws by wearing a scarf. The now Goodwife Wilds and Mary Reddington got into a fight in which Mary claimed that Sarah had pulled her backwards off her horse into a brook and "held her doune so as she Could not helpe her selfe." Clearly Sarah was a threat, and it was after this altercation in the 1680s that Mary Reddington began claiming that Sarah Wilds was a witch. The story grew and spread until it finally reached such proportions that John Wilds threatened to prosecute John Reddington for his wife's actions. Mary retracted her claims, but the groundwork had been laid for future accusations of witchcraft.[51]

Since the Goulds were related to the Putnam family, it comes as little surprise that Sarah Wilds's name was soon being spoken by Ann Putnam in association with acts of maleficium. Ann informed the wife of Thomas Dorman that Sarah was responsible for the death of the Dormans' livestock, telling her that "good wif wils had whoried away my Cattell," Thomas reported. Dorman was amazed that Ann would be familiar with such a detail, which seemed to verify the claim. "I wondred an putman should know I lost my Cattle so long agoe," he testified. During Goody Wilds's 1692 trial for witchcraft, Ann also claimed that "a woman that tould me hir name was willds did greviously torment" her, as well as several other accusers. It was also revealed that before the trial, Mary Reddington had asked her brother to record her testimony in writing, lest Wilds use her magic against her and strike her down before she could speak to the court. Before he had the chance to record her statement, however, she fell ill, so "as she Could not declare any thing," her brother testified. "The Last words I herd sister Redington say was that it was GoodWife Wilds that brought her into that Condition." It seems that Mary used her dying breath to ensure Sarah's downfall. She was assisted by several others who told stories of Sarah's malevolent deeds, including Elizabeth Symonds, who claimed that she had been "afflicted" by Wilds after a disagreement over moving some hay. After they argued, Elizabeth said she saw figures in her room at night, and experienced strange sensations and pains. The court agreed that Sarah was a danger to society, and she too was hanged on July 19, 1692.[52]

AN INDIAN-DEVIL CONSPIRACY

It was women from the Putnam household whose testimony would help alter the course of the Essex County witch hunts in its later stages, confirming fears of the "war the devil has raised . . . by wizards and witches" of Reverend Parris's description. Ann Jr., along with the Putnams' servant Mercy Lewis, provided accounts of an Indian-devil conspiracy lurking at the edges of their settlements, spreading the web of accusation farther from Salem. Mercy Lewis was an orphan of the Indian Wars, her parents and grandparents having been killed by Wabanaki Indians before she came to live and work in the Putnam household. Mercy, who was nineteen years old during the witch trials in Salem, had probably been tasked with caring for the young afflicted girls of the Putnam household, until she began to demonstrate symptoms of affliction herself. Lewis brought what she had heard and witnessed as a young girl on the Maine frontier with her to Salem, and it seems to have informed not only her testimony but also the testimony of others around her. Together, she and Ann reported doing battle with the spectral scene of tortures committed by a witch who had "a speet at the fire with a man upon it." Mercy took a stick to strike the vision, so reminiscent of reported Wabanaki torture techniques, only to become wracked with pain in the attempt. Many of the spectral apparitions reported by the girls began to take on the brutal imagery of Indian warfare.[53]

The young women were also instrumental in accusing several persons who were already of interest in the witch hunt, if not yet formally named. Mercy would have known both Abigail Hobbs and the Reverend George Burroughs from her time in Maine. Abigail and Mercy would likely have known each other while both were settled at Falmouth in Casco Bay, and may even have been distant relatives. In addition to her previous acquaintance with

Lewis, fourteen-year-old Abigail's behavior helped ensure she would be a target of accusation. She openly spoke of having "sold her selfe boddy & Soull" to the devil and claimed she had made a bargain with him. She was soon accused of afflicting Mercy Lewis and Ann Putnam Jr., among others. Like only Tituba before her, Abigail was coerced to confess by the chief examiner of the trials, and her statement confirmed what many had feared: that she had met Satan among the Indians "at the eastward at Casco Bay." Her confession would set the stage for the arrest of Reverend Burroughs, a former minister of Salem Village as well as Falmouth, and a man of dubious reputation. Soon after Abigail's confession, Ann Putnam Jr. testified that Burroughs's apparition had tormented her, trying to force her to sign the devil's book.[54]

Mercy must have provided much of the information about Burroughs's time in Maine as suspicions against him continued to mount, but the reverend had other enemies in Salem. Lewis had been sent to live as his servant in Maine before later being placed in the Putnam household. Lewis's family had been tragically killed by the Wabanaki, but Burroughs had managed to survive several attacks on Falmouth and had conveniently vacated Casco Bay before a fatal attack in the spring of 1690. The reason for Burroughs's mysterious good fortune soon became clear: he was a witch working with diabolical Indian forces against his own people. Ann Putnam Jr. revealed that Burroughs "had bewicthed a grate many souldiers to death at the eastword" to ensure an Indian victory and his own survival. He was clearly a danger not just to those closest to him but to the colony as a whole. Previously, in Salem, Burroughs had also managed to offend the Putnam family, among others, during his brief stay as the minister of Salem Village between 1680 and 1683. Several disapproving residents of the village had refused to pay Burroughs's salary. Burroughs refused to preach unless he was paid, and openly spoke of leaving. He borrowed money from the Putnams and left before it was repaid. Thomas Putnam issued a warrant for his arrest, but upon Burroughs's returning to Salem, the debt was canceled by town authorities. It seems the Putnams had not forgotten the slight in the decade that followed.[55]

Mercy Lewis and the other afflicted girls, along with male leaders in the region, thus began to transform the accusations of a small number of women and girls into a regional crisis and conspiracy by the summer of

1692, one that would soon envelop Andover and spill over into Billerica, Reading, Haverhill, Boxford, and Rowley. In mid-July the focus of accusations moved to these communities to the northwest of Salem, after two of Salem's afflicted girls—Mercy Lewis and Betty Hubbard—were brought to Andover as "witch hunters" to identify potential witches in their midst.[56] Soon, seventy-two-year-old Ann Foster, her daughter Mary Lacy Sr., and her granddaughter Mary Lacey Jr. all stood accused. All three Andover women quickly confessed to the crime. Guided by the magistrates' questions, they relayed specific details of their Satanic meetings, which grew in size upon every report, and listed the names of neighbors who were fellow witches; they even turned on one another. Many of those accused followed suit in confessing and naming others. By the end of the trials, Andover had seen more than forty-five of its residents accused of witchcraft—more than Salem Village and Salem Town combined. Three of those were convicted and hanged, with one dying in prison while awaiting execution.[57]

It was during the "Andover phase" of the trials that the idea of witchcraft as a region-wide conspiracy—rather than acts of "maleficium" by individual witches—gained prominence. In her confession on July 15, Ann Foster named several people who were involved in attempting to recruit her into their "witch meeting" after the devil initially failed to do so. One called "Goody Carier" appears most conspicuously, the unruly Martha Carrier of Andover. According to Ann's remarkably detailed testimony, "it was Goody Carier yt made her a witch" after coming to her in person promising "prosperity" if she would agree and threatening that the "diuill should tare her in pieces" if she did not. Ann agreed to serve the devil and use her powers to bewitch certain people in the community. She also accompanied Goody Carrier to a large meeting of witches in Salem Village, to which "she & Martha Carier did both ride on a stick or pole" as "they ware caried in the aire aboue the tops of the trees." The meeting was well attended—by George Burroughs, among others—and Ann heard at the meeting that there "was three hundred & fiue [witches] in the whole Country" and "that they would ruin that place ye Vilige" of Salem. This testimony corresponded with other stories that emerged during this period about large groupings of witches. Deliverance Hobbs testified that Burroughs had administered a sacrament with "Red Bread, and Red Wine Like Blood" to a gathering of witches. Sarah Cloyse spoke of a meeting of forty witches who took a similar sacrament at the Parris house. William Barker, also of Andover, reported meeting with over three hundred witches in Salem Village. Burroughs appeared in several accounts as a leader of these groupings of witches, summoning them to Satan.[58]

Martha Carrier was also named as a ringleader of these groups, a "Rampant Hag" and "Queen of Hell," as Cotton Mather described her. It came as little surprise when Goody Carrier was named as a witch by the afflicted girls in Salem, who would have been familiar with her reputation. She was notorious in the region for her outspokenness and her aggressive hostility against anyone who encroached on her family's land, what little they had. She was not deferential to her more prosperous neighbors, and she and her five children were considered a burden on the community. When Martha and her children caught smallpox in 1690, Andover's town fathers tried to force the Carriers to leave. Martha refused and remained quarantined within their house. Still, at least six other Andover residents outside of Martha's family died of the disease. The community, of course, blamed Martha, as if she had deliberately brought the epidemic to town. Rumors that Martha was a witch continued to swirl and emerged again in 1692. She was accused of witchcraft months before anyone else in Andover. Her "leadership position" among the witches only increased interest in Andover as the trials continued.[59]

As word spread that Martha was a witch, old grudges and interfamily disputes again saw the light of day. The Carriers and the Abbots had a difficult relationship as neighbors. Martha was angry because the town had granted the Abbots some land next to the Carriers' property, and she did not hold back in expressing her frustrations. Benjamin Abbot claimed that a year before her trial for witchcraft, Goody Carrier had accosted him and made the ominous threat that he "should Repent of it afore seauen years Came to an end" and that no doctor would be able to cure him. He later developed swelling in his foot, pains in his side, and sores in his groin. The local doctor attempted to lance and drain several of these sores, but it did not provide him any relief. He only began to improve when Carrier was taken away by the constable, and he reported having felt well ever since. Sarah Abbot testified about her husband's strange affliction, and also about the sudden death of their cow under strange circumstances. Other cattle, she reported, began acting strangely, and "would come out of the woods wth their tounges hanging out of their mouths in a strange & affrigtening manner." Her only explanation for their behavior was "Martha Carriers threatnings."[60]

Other Andover neighbors added their stories of run-ins with Martha, some more fanciful than others. Samuel Preston reported that after having a "difference" with Goody Carrier two years before, his cow, who had been "Lusty" in June, was dead two months later. Martha had predicted the animal's death, Preston claimed, and later the cow "pined & quickly lay downe as if she was asleep & dyed." Through the course of her trial, it became clear that Martha had taken on the status of a local legend, which helps explain why her name was on the lips of the afflicted girls early on during the trials. Twelve-year-old Phoebe Chandler was approached by Carrier in the meetinghouse one day, and Martha asked her where she lived. Phoebe was immediately suspicious and afraid. Later, while walking down the street, Chandler heard a voice which she thought was Martha Carrier's. The voice told her that she would be poisoned within two or three days, and afterward there was swelling in her face and hand, a "strange burning" in her stomach, and intense pain. She saw Martha's son Richard during meeting looking "uery earnestly" at her, after which she was momentarily struck deaf.[61]

Goody Carrier remained outspoken during her trial as well, challenging the magistrates and inquiring why they "should mind these folks that are out of their wits," as her afflicted victims writhed and screamed, demonstrating her "Tortures." At Carrier's trial, in particular, the courtroom was in chaos. The afflictions of her accusers grew so violent that Martha had to be escorted out, "bound hand & foot," for fear she had "almost killed" them. Magistrates and community members seemed determined to use whatever means necessary to prove her guilt. Martha's own children were coerced into testifying against her. Two of her teenage sons, as their fellow prisoner John Proctor recalled, were tortured into confessing, "tied neck and heels till the blood was ready to come out of their noses." They confessed and named others, including members of their extended family among the Toothakers and Emersons. Such forms of judicial torture were allowed in England but had been outlawed by the Massachusetts General Court in 1641. Not so in 1692. The new governor, William Phips, had set up the Court of Oyer and Terminer on an emergency basis to handle the witchcraft issue during a period in which all laws and courts in the colony had been invalidated under a new charter and had yet to be reestablished.[62]

Political and religious leaders in Andover were also willing to embrace radical methods to uncover the witches in their town. In September 1692, assistant minister Reverend Thomas Barnard arranged for all those accused of witchcraft to come together at the Andover meetinghouse for a "touch test." Some believed that if a witch touched the body of the person he or she had afflicted, that person would become well and could identify the witch. Reverend Barnard prayed, and then, as the accused recalled, "we were blindfolded, and our hands were laid upon the afflicted persons." Immediately, all of the girls "were well" and claimed "we were guilty of afflicting them." All eighteen accused persons were seized and imprisoned to be taken to Salem for trial. They were advised by "gentlemen" present to confess their sins. When the women later recanted their confessions, they recalled the "hard measures" the men had used, which "rendered us incapable of making our own defense." It can be assumed from this testimony that Reverend Barnard was involved in these incidents and in "encouraging" the confessions.[63]

Some in the community may have been suspicious when several female family members of the Reverend Francis Dane were swept up among the accused, given Barnard's role in the identification ritual. Tensions between the senior clergyman, Dane, and his assistant (and eventual replacement), Barnard, had run high since Barnard had been hired to replace the sixty-five-year-old minister. In March 1681, Dane, who had served as minister and schoolmaster for more than two decades, informed the town that he could no longer perform all his duties unassisted. This was clear to the town, whose members had already sent a complaint to the General Court that Dane had been failing to hold regular worship services. The town wasted no time in hiring his replacement, a Harvard graduate in his twenties, and promptly placed Dane in retirement and canceled his salary. Dane refused to accept his full retirement, given that he had continued to deliver public prayers and an occasional sermon. A committee of legislators and local ministers met in Andover and decided that the two men would have to divide the minister's salary, as long as Dane could "carry on part of the work."[64] Neither man was pleased with the arrangement, nor were several in the community.

Perhaps, as for Reverend Parris and Thomas Putnam in Salem Village, the witch scare in Andover now presented Reverend Barnard and his supporters with an opportunity. Reverend Dane himself was too well respected to be accused directly, at least at first. By using the afflicted girls of Salem as his "witch finders," Barnard could target Dane's daughters, daughter-in-law, and five grandchildren, discrediting the old clergyman and, he no doubt hoped, ridding himself of his older rival permanently. Dane's unwillingness to be involved in the witch hunts, and his refusal to administer the "touch test" himself, would have added to the suspicions. As many as twenty-six of those accused in Andover were related to the Danes, including the Carrier family. Most were coerced into confessing in the hope of sparing their own lives, spreading the web of accusation throughout the region. If destroying the extended Dane family had been part of Barnard's plan, he did not succeed. Instead, Dane was instrumental in bringing an end to the turmoil in Andover and Salem, continually pushing back against the trials and petitioning the governor and General Court on behalf of the accused. In the end, Andover's forty-five confessions became an embarrassment for those involved in the witch hunt and helped inspire questions that would eventually bring an end to the trials. By January 1693, even Barnard had grown concerned that "persons of known integrity and piety were accused."[65]

FATEFUL DECISIONS

That the trials reached the size and scope they did at the end of the seventeenth century in Essex County was largely due to several unusual decisions made by male leaders at the time—decisions on how to deploy the "afflicted" and display the violence of female accusation—which turned the trials into a colony-wide spectacle. In the end, the trials were a "collaborative creation" between the female accusers and the men who influenced, encouraged, and guided them. It is impossible to determine how much genuine fear was felt by all of those involved, and the extent to which other considerations played into their decisions about how to proceed. In the aftermath of the Indian Wars, the leaders of Massachusetts Bay—several of whom presided over the trials—were desperate for someone to blame for their military failures and losses. Perhaps, in this moment, the devil was both a real source of fear and a convenient scapegoat. Local leaders as well, as we have seen, seem to have incorporated their own priorities into the trials. For the female accusers, being taken so seriously and wielding power over the lives of others would have been an overwhelming and perhaps intoxicating experience.[66]

One of the most consequential decisions made early on in the trials was to conduct public examinations of both the afflicted and the accused. Customary procedure in cases of affliction was to hold preliminary examinations in private and focus on stopping the afflictions and limiting the numbers of those exposed. In earlier instances, as Cotton Mather and other ministers had done, religious leaders would meet with those suffering at the hands of unseen forces and, through prayer and reflection, relieve their suffering and rid them of the dark forces possessing them. The accused would be interviewed, at least initially, in private. In Salem, those in power chose to deviate from these practices designed to avoid encouraging the spread of affliction and accusation. Samuel Parris failed to defuse the situation in his own home, and encouraged, even demanded, that the women in his household name their tormentors. At the beginning of the trials, Salem magistrates John Hathorne and Jonathan Corwin decided to interrogate the first three women accused of witchcraft in public, fueling interest in the trials and leading many witnesses to decide to come forward. In early spring, with the ground still frozen, local farmers and their families would have had little to do in their fields and had time to devote to the trials. Public interest in the trials was so intense that the proceedings were moved from Nathaniel Ingersoll's tavern to the meetinghouse, the largest building in town.[67] Thus the trials became public spectacle, spreading the network of accusation, and eventually leading to imprisonments and executions.

By the end of the Essex County witchcraft crisis, the phenomenon of witchcraft accusation had evolved from a formerly male-dominated practice that rarely ended in the execution of the accused to a female-led process that contained within it a very tangible risk to life and limb. Fears among the settlers of the looming Indian threat in the aftermath of years of horrific warfare help explain why accusations of witchcraft increased in number and intensity in the last few decades of the seventeenth century. Such destruction had to be the work of the devil and his minions and could only have been inflicted on New England Puritans because of the sinfulness in their midst. Perhaps, initially, women and girls in Essex County began to accuse witches out of a desire to root out such a threat and prevent the intrusion of physically and spiritually destructive forces. In so doing, they focused largely on those who challenged cultural norms and standards of behavior and, in an ironic twist, helped reinforce existing power structures as they themselves appeared to operate outside of them.

The webs of accusation that began to emerge in 1692 and spread throughout the region strongly suggest, however, that while women and girls were the face of the "afflicted," they were not solely responsible for the destruction that followed, nor did the threats remain limited to the spiritual. It is too much of a coincidence that so many women and girls accused primarily those in other families that they perceived to be a threat to the prosperity and well-being of their own households. The active involvement of male leaders in validating the trials, examining the accused, and coercing testimony also suggests that they were willing to take advantage of the female accusers in the midst of the witchcraft scare to bolster their own positions and try to rid themselves of enemies and rivals. Whether these male leaders regarded those enemies and rivals as genuine threats to their communities is impossible to determine.

Unfortunately, we have few statements from the women involved to explain their actions. Later in her life, when Ann Putnam Jr. wished to join the church in Salem Village, she was required to submit a public statement describing her conversion experience and confessing past sins. In her statement she refers to the trials in Salem as "that sad and humbling providence that befell my father's family in the year about '92," and claims that in her childhood, she was party to the "accusing of several persons of a grievous crime." She acknowledges that she was involved in bringing upon herself and this land "the guilt of innocent blood" of those she no longer believed were guilty. Ann does not, however, claim ultimate responsibility for the violence her accusations wrought. She was "deluded," she claims, "by Satan." Evidence suggests, however, that the Salem Village church was perhaps too hasty in accepting Ann's deflection of guilt. Tracing the web of accusation also indicates that Satan was not alone in turning Ann, and the other female accusers in and around Salem, into violent "instruments" of accusation.

CHAPTER 5

☞ Female Violence

From Potential Threat to Cultural Weapon

> The Walls of the whole World are broken down! The usual Walls of defence about mankind have such a Gap made in them that the very Devils are broken in upon us.
>
> —*Cotton Mather,* Wonders of the Invisible World, *1693*

> She is a monument of divine severity; and the Lord grant that all that see or hear may fear and tremble.
>
> —*Samuel Willard, "A Brief account of a strange and unusual providence of God befallen to—Elizabeth Knapp of Groton by me, Samuel Willard," 1671*

At the end of the seventeenth century, political upheaval joined the disruption of war in exacerbating a feeling of disorder and vulnerability in New England, and Massachusetts Bay in particular. King Philip's War, then the revocation of the original Massachusetts charter in 1685, followed by renewed fighting during King William's and Queen Anne's Wars, political restructuring under the new charter in the 1690s, and the witchcraft threat all combined to make the colonists feel as if they were under constant attack. In addition, as population growth continued in the eighteenth century, religious observance among third- and fourth-generation Puritans began to wane. A growing divide in religiosity between the clergy and the laity emerged around the turn of the century. New England appeared to be under threat, and its leaders worried about a loss of control over their "experiment in the wilderness."[1]

Cotton Mather voiced the loudest warnings during this time. He often framed his concerns in the imagery of invasion, both literal and metaphorical. In the face of these invading forces, he felt that worldly issues had begun to divert attention from the Puritans' divine mission and feared that New England was backsliding in its commitment to religious devotion. Mather was not alone in his concern about the Puritans' future and the leadership's role within it. The Puritan leadership was generally united in expressing this sentiment. As Perry Miller explains, in the 1640s, a lament had commenced in the sermons of New England over "the waning of primitive zeal and the consequent atrophy of public morals." This lament would become an "incessant chant" within forty years. Michael Wigglesworth in *God's Controversy with New-England,* a poetic jeremiad from 1662, bewailed the languishing state of faith in New England and cited a recent drought as God's punishment. Joshua Moody, Increase Mather, and Eleazer Mather all expressed concerns that "profanation" had spread beyond the unregenerate and had begun to infect the "saints" themselves.[2]

By the late 1670s, the subject dominated sermons and jeremiads increasingly and at length. Clerics in Massachusetts responded to these concerns with a call for moral and social reform which took shape in the Reforming Synod of 1679. The meeting of church representatives was called to answer crucial questions about New England's future, including "What are the evils that have provoked the Lord to bring his judgement on New England?" And "What is to be done so that those evils may be reformed?" Puritan belief dictated that God had a rational plan, and that according to that plan, there should be at least one person able to read the patterns in His works of creation and providence; to reconstruct at least part of God's infinite wisdom through the study of objects and events. The ministers saw it as part of God's plan that they had been blessed with the ability to read the signs and interpret His warnings, among them divine judgments in the guise of Indian wars, natural disasters, disease, and political unrest. These signs convinced the clergy that America was facing God's judgment. The synod was, at least in part, an attempt to support the authority of both the ministers and magistrates in bringing New England back in line. An unlikely group of people also assisted in this endeavor, however unintentionally. Stories of violent, problematic women of the age offered a means through which the Puritan leadership could spread this message.[3]

Under normal circumstances, colonial authorities tolerated women's violence only when it was contained within acceptable boundaries, most notably the household. Such behavior actually served to reinforce household, and therefore social, order and tended to receive the tacit approval of the authorities as long as it did not become disruptive to the community at large. Prosecutions for "household violence" disappear almost completely from the records at the end of the seventeenth century. The cessation of prosecutions for violence against servants, children, and spouses, and neighborly routs, does not indicate a change in people's behavior. With the upheaval at the end of the century—and the Anglicanization of the court system following the new charter—policing these types of violence became less of a priority for those in charge.

Other types of violence in which women engaged, however, remained a genuine and growing concern for colonial authorities. These authorities focused on violence perpetrated by accused "witches" and the threat they posed to society as a whole. Violence against colonial authorities during the Indian Wars had drawn the court's attention and became particularly problematic during a period in which the leadership of the colony was under threat from without. Women were also necessarily drawn into violent confrontations during the Indian Wars as a matter of survival. Although most women would have preferred to avoid such actions, some were forced to use violence to protect themselves and their families from the constant threat of attack from their Indian neighbors on the frontier. The attention some of these women received, and the necessity of women's violence for protection on the frontier, highlighted the failings of the colony to protect its settlers.

Also, at a time when the population of English colonists had received several severe blows as a result of the Indian Wars, the practice of infanticide became a focus of increased concern. Women gained the attention of their communities when they allowed themselves to be led astray and then committed murder to conceal their missteps. Not only was infanticide at odds with efforts to repopulate New England, but also it signaled a woman's willingness to defy the dictates of her community and government, something that could not be tolerated during this turbulent period. The change in the law governing prosecutions for infanticide signaled heightened concerns about the secrecy and subversive nature of the act.

While addressing these types of unacceptable or revealing acts of violence, as well as their concerns about declension and their own leadership during this period, colonial authorities produced contrasting stories of female victimization and heroism in many of the sermons, narratives, and narrative histories they created. Cotton Mather led the charge in reframing women's violence through the written and spoken word. Authorities repackaged women's expressions of violence and, in doing so, reasserted the authority of male colonial leadership, while providing powerful examples for society of the consequences of both positive and negative behavior. In this chapter I explore some of the most famous examples—narratives of demonic possession, execution sermons for women convicted of infanticide (beginning with Elizabeth Emerson), the captivity narrative of Hannah Dustin, and, finally, narrative histories of the Indian Wars—to discern how and why some forms of women's violence were transformed from socially disruptive to practically and symbolically useful. These women's actions, and the publicity that they inspired, became one means of preserving the Puritans' way of life in their struggling New Jerusalem.

It was almost a foregone conclusion that the leadership of New England would embrace the power of literacy and the spoken word in their struggle. The godly valued direct access to the word of God as one of their most precious privileges, and this ensured that the region had nearly universal literacy. As David Hall has shown, most people had access to a Bible and learned to read as children. Literacy figured "at the heart of cultural politics." Spiritual education was augmented by books and pamphlets exhorting people to faith, as well as spoken sermons, which most regarded as just as sacred as the printed page and were often written down for more extensive distribution. A "shifting coalition of ministers, printers, booksellers" in New England made these godly works available to a desiring public. According to patterns of production and consumption, laymen and women preferred religious books, pamphlets, and sermons to other kinds of written or spoken works. An "ideology of print," and a general respect for what the clergy said and wrote, "strengthened the role of the clergy as 'ambassadors' of Christ." The Puritan leadership was not afraid to take advantage of both newsworthy events and the cultural resources of the literary marketplace in order to reinforce their orthodoxy in the minds of the general public. Narratives that "mated terror and evangelical inquiry" were by far the most popular.[4]

NARRATIVES OF POSSESSION

Few types of literature during this period had the capacity to inspire as much fear and curiosity as the possession narrative. Possession narratives were designed to tell stories of those afflicted and invaded by otherworldly spirits, the suffering the possessed endured, and the heroic process of their salvation through the power of God, guided by the clergy. The narratives were usually written about a single person or group of persons, frequently women, and told from the point of view of a third party. The personal elements of the tale would have allowed individual colonists to relate to the struggles of the afflicted, while the third-person narration added the sheen of objectivity to the story. These stories were simultaneously entertaining and educational, proving the power of the invisible world and the dark forces that lurked within it, as well as the power of belief to overcome them. As the historian Erika Gasser has argued, Mather used such works to stoke a "profitable fear" in his audience, a fear that could be used to bolster his own position in defiance of his "detractors."[5]

In the wilderness of the New World, these tales held a particular fascination and power. Possession narratives offered a "psychological rescue from the devil," as Richard Slotkin argues, in which ministers could emerge triumphant. In so doing, Mather and other Puritan leaders hoped to restrain the "atomism and individualism" encroaching on New England in the late seventeenth century. Not everyone involved in the possession narratives was necessarily self-consciously using them for a purpose, however. Janice Knight reads many of the "victims" of possession as "confused, fractured," and unconsciously overlaying personal traumas onto the possession narrative, such as those resulting from Indian captivity or other hardships. The young women who are the subjects of the narratives were certainly confused and probably not involved in plans surrounding their creation.[6] For Mather and other men of his standing, however, instances of possession—like captivity stories, tales of violent crime, and accounts of the events of war—provided not only a vehicle to address the latest news in the region but also a means of spinning that news to spread their message.

Cotton Mather's treatment of Elizabeth Knapp, Mercy Short, and Margaret Rule, victims of demonic possession during the 1670s and 1690s, came at an important moment. A genuine believer in the ever-presence of both God and the devil, as well as the power of providence, Mather attempted to save these female sufferers of unholy, unseen torments and to document and distribute his accounts thereof. In publicizing his recollections of the young women's battles against their "Devilish Masters," Mather identified a source for New England's troubles: the dark forces of the devil testing the Puritans' resolve in their spiritual mission. Through his narratives, the instances of women's violent "possession" Mather described, he displaced rumblings of popular discontent, either due to the societal changes that were overtaking New England or surrounding the losses that the Indian Wars had brought to the people of that region. The narratives also showed that Mather was a leader capable of helping the colony spiritually survive those crises.

In centering on a young female servant employed in the household of a respected Puritan minister, Elizabeth Knapp's case in 1671 anticipated possession tales that would emerge during the panic in and around Salem in the 1690s. Although her possession did not involve an explicit connection to the trauma of the Indian Wars—as did Short's and Rule's—strange and violent behavior similar to what Knapp exhibited would appear among the young women afflicted decades later. And like other young women so afflicted, Knapp also demonstrated a personal discontent with her position and a violently aggressive attitude toward the figures of authority in her life, in her case her family and the Reverend Samuel Willard of Groton. When Knapp began to exhibit her "very strange manner" and "violent agitations," the Reverend Willard reached out to Cotton Mather for help. Mather documented her afflictions, as Willard described them, and published her story many years later along with his other possession narratives.[7]

The daughter of English immigrants, James and Elizabeth Warren Knapp, Elizabeth was employed as a servant in the Willard household at the age of sixteen. The Willards' was a more respected and prosperous household than her own. Scandal and suspicion seem to have haunted the Knapp family. Prior to their move to Groton, her father, James, was charged with adultery (though not convicted) and was suspected of being the father of an illegitimate child. He had also confessed to drunkenness. Elizabeth's uncle John had been convicted as a thief. Although she was an only child, something relatively rare in this period of large families with many children, Elizabeth was "bound out" to the Willards soon after the Knapps' arrival in Groton. This suggests, perhaps, that the domestic upheaval that had plagued the family before their move may have followed them to their new establishment, and perhaps her family thought Elizabeth would be better off under another roof.[8]

Elizabeth Knapp may have come under the protection of a more respectable role model, but this does not appear to have made her content with her life. Being exposed to the luxuries that accompanied a larger income and a stable home life seems to have caused her to resent her lesser circumstances. As she later explained, it was her discontent with her "condition" as a servant, the "burdensome" nature of her labor, and her desire for worldly extravagance that left her open to the influence of the devil in her life. Reverend Willard noted that in the midst of her possession, Knapp confessed that "she was neither content to be at home nor abroad; and [that she] had oftentimes strong persuasions to practice in witchcraft, had often wished the Devil would come to her at such and such times, and [had] resolved that if he would she would give herself up to him soul and body." The devil preyed upon her weaknesses, "presenting the treaty of a covenant . . . [with] such things as suited her youthful fancy, money[,] silks, fine clothes, ease from labor, to show her the whole world." In the midst of her agitations, she was known to call out "money! money!" while sometimes "weeping" or "roaring."[9]

Both Mather's and Willard's accounts of her possession suggest that it was Knapp's discontent that was the cause of her affliction, a detail that both men felt was important to communicate with their New England audiences: Knapp's dissatisfaction itself had inspired the devil to attack her, and had she been satisfied with her position, with her limited opportunities and resources, she would have avoided the traumatic experience. Her sin was to question her place in the "divinely planned social order." It was a tendency that was symptomatic of larger societal changes and had the potential to leave the colony itself open to attack from its spiritual foes.[10] Knapp's story became a cautionary tale about the dangers of striving for greater individuality or prosperity beyond one's station or place.

Knapp's possession involved a great deal of physical violence. Willard recounted, "She was violent in bodily motions, leapings, strainings and strange agitations, scarce to be held in bounds by the strength of 3 or 4." In his version of events, Mather increased the number of men necessary to restrain her, writing, "Six men were scarce able to hold her in some of her fits." Knapp would lash out at those who held her, spit in their faces, and "if any time she had done any harm or frightened them she would laugh." The afflicted young woman seems to have reserved her most disturbing outbursts and violent threats for those in positions of authority in her life. Perhaps this stemmed from their inability to fully care for her. The devil "urged upon her constant temptations to murder her parents, her neighbors," Knapp claimed. "Once he put a bill hook into her hand" and instructed her to murder the Reverend Willard himself. As Mather noted, "The chief things that the daemon [within Knapp] spoke were horrid railings against the godly minister of the town." Sometimes the demon took this a step further and "belch'd out most nefandous blasphemies against the God of heaven."[11]

The solution for Knapp's possession was not a change of circumstance but a wiliness to accept her position in the community and relieve her personal sense of discontent. Willard urged Elizabeth as a "subject of hope" for all to acknowledge her sin and repent, thereby cleansing herself. Mather offered a similar solution to her affliction: prayer, reflection, acceptance of her place in the divine order. Once Knapp "confess'd, that she had been deluded by satan, and compell'd by him unreasonably," she began to improve. As she prayed alongside those in the community she had targeted and accused as her possessors, and agreed not to "speak evil . . . without a cause," her cruel torment seemed to subside. Through the guidance of these Puritan divines, Knapp was able to recover fully, and even successfully marry and start a family three years after her possession. She became a good Puritan wife and mother, almost completely disappearing from the public record after 1673.[12]

Two decades later, Mercy Short was one of several persons afflicted during the course of the Salem witchcraft crisis who had intimate experience with the Indian Wars. Though residing in Boston, like many of the Salem accusers Short was young and female. She had been held captive and left orphaned as a result of the war on the Maine frontier. As Mather recounted, Short was captured by "cruel and Bloody Indians in the East" who "horribly

Butchered her Father, her Mother, her Brother and her Sister, and others of her Kindred, and then carried her, three surviving Brothers with two Sisters . . . unto Canada." The manner of her return to civilization is unclear. Like other afflicted girls in Salem, Short was left without any emotional or financial support in the wake of the Indian Wars.[13] She had since found work as a servant to support herself.

According to Mather's narrative of her possession and redemption, *A Brand Pluck'd Out of the Burning* (1693), Short met several persons who had been imprisoned on "suspicion of having an Hand in that most Horrid and Hellish Witchcraft" after being sent by her mistress on an errand to the "gaol" in Boston. One of the suspected witches, Sarah Good, asked Short for some tobacco. In response "she affronted the Hag . . . (since executed at Salem) by throwing a Handful of Shavings at her and saying, That's Tobacco good enough for you." Good "bestowed some ill words upon her," Mather commented, and Short was taken ill soon after.[14]

Short's possession thus began with an act of physical aggression—throwing the shavings—and her expressions of violence and anger only increased as it continued. When Short fell ill in the meetinghouse, under the influence of her "Invisible Troublers," her physical reaction was so disruptive that she had to be restrained and carried from the building by "many strong men with an united Force." Even these men, however, "could not well carry her any Further than the House of a kind Neighbor." Short was "Insolent and Abusive to such as were about her," and "it was no Rare Thing for the Standers-by to have their Arms cruelly scratch'd, and Pins thrust into their Flesh." Short was also abused and assaulted by a "Number of Spectres," to the horror of those who were caring for her. She was plagued by pins stuck in her skin and in her mouth, by scratches and pinches, and by unseen forces that prevented her from eating for days on end. These attacks, Short reported, were committed by spirits "resembling the persons of several people in the countrey" who "obeyed their Devilish Master."[15] It is impossible, however, not to surmise that at least some of these injuries were the result of self-inflicted violence.

Physical torment, and self-inflicted violence, were also hallmarks of Margaret Rule's spiritual affliction a few months later, as chronicled by Mather in *Another Brand Pluck'd Out of the Burning* (1693). Indeed the "Afflictions" of the girls were so alike that Mather commented, "The relations I have given of the one, would almost serve as the full History of the other." The evening before "Margaret fell into her Calamities" in September 1693, she had been "bitterly treated" and "threatn'd" by a "Miserable Woman, who had been formerly Imprisoned on suspicion of Witchcraft." The following day Rule caused a considerable "disturbance" in the meetinghouse and had to be carried home. From then on, she would fall into "odd Fits" and began to see specters. Tormented by spirits "in a manner too Hellish to be sufficiently described," she was confined to bed. "In obedience to [the devil] they addressed themselves into various ways of Torturing her," Mather wrote. Accordingly, she was "cruelly pinch't with Invisible hands very often in a Day, and the black and blew marks of the pinches came immediately visible unto the standers by." Her attendants found pins "stuck into her Neck, Back and Arms" and noted "she would also be strangely distorted in her Joynts, and thrown into . . . Convulsions."[16]

It was in these fits of violence that the different impact of the Indian Wars on the two women became most apparent. As both Short and Rule reported it, the "Divel" who taunted and controlled them was clearly an Indian. "Having the Figure of A Short . . . Black man," the specter who possessed Short "was of a Tawney, or an Indian colour." Though Rule, by contrast, had not lost family members to the Indian Wars, her fears of the conflicts also caused her tormentor to manifest as the same Indian figure, a "Short . . . Black man" whom the other spirits "call'd their Master." By physically acting out against this Indian, Knight explains, the women could express their anxiety and anger in a socially acceptable way, without fear of reprisal. For Short in particular, some of that anger sprang from the "impotence of pastoral surrogates" and the failures of other colonial leaders to protect her. Short's violence and frustration were directed more outwardly as a result. When Mather came to pray over her, she "flew upon him," seized the Bible from his hands, and tore it. This was not a random act of violence but was representative of Short's suffering during captivity and her frustrated hopes after her return to civilization. Short was also seen and heard to argue with the specters, shouting at them and rejecting their false promises of a husband, fine clothes, and a place in heaven.[17] In so doing, Short was calling attention to her personal losses in the wars. Like so many women, she was missing loved ones, had been alienated from the promise of prosperity, and denied the comfort of security because of the conflict.

According to Mather, Short's and Rule's illnesses were the same as that "which held the Bewitched people then Tormented by Invisible Furies in the County of Essex." In relating the women's possession to the events in Salem, Mather portrayed them as part of a larger demonic attack on the colony. The spectral "Black Man" who possessed them had "exactly the same Dimensions and Complexion and voice, with the Divel that has exhibited himself unto other infested People . . . in other parts of this Country." In Mather's narratives, the devil and the Indian were one and the same, imbuing the Indian enemy with unforeseen powers and giving the Puritans' struggles against them a spiritual basis and urgency. As others afflicted by spirits had testified before her, Short saw meetings take place among witches in which "there had been present some French Canadians, and some Indian Sagamores, to concert the methods of ruining New England." The conspirators took "Directions for their Devotions" at these meetings from a book of Catholic devotions they had stolen from Mather's own study. As a united effort, Mather shows, the witches and the Indians, with their French Catholic allies, planned to destroy the Puritan colonies. Against such an organized invasion, colonial authorities could do only so much.[18]

Witchcraft "had brought in the Divels upon several parts of the Country," but Mather and other Puritan leaders were willing to do spiritual battle against these aggressors. In his narrative of Short's possession, and his account of the similar afflictions that plagued Margaret Rule, Mather demonstrated that he held the answer to the upheavals that threatened their society, and their very souls. Short would frequently quote Mather "in her Arguments against the Divel," he recounted. These quotations and arguments held a great weight and served as powerful weapons against these unseen forces because "the Divel had a very particular Provocation and Malignity" against Mather himself. Mather also reported that both Short and Rule were visited by a "white spirit" during the worst of their possession who encouraged them to maintain their faith in God. For Rule, this spirit also explicitly called on her to consider Mather her "Father." According to Mather's recollections, the white spirit said to her, "Margaret, you are now to take notice that (such a Man) is your Father, follow his counsels and you shall do well." As Gasser notes, the entirety of Mather's narrative can be regarded as "propaganda on behalf of patriarchal authority."[19]

Evidence that Mather was chosen by providence to lead the colony out of its spiritual suffering was in the results he achieved for both women: each was "delivered" from harm by his holy efforts.[20] Mather and the people of the neighborhood were ceaseless in their prayerful devotion to Short "for the Deliverance of the Afflicted Maid." He wrote, "There was, I think, scarce a Night for near a Month together, which was not All spent in the Exercise of Devotion, by those that Watched." Eventually their prayers were answered when one evening an "unseen Defence" protected Short from the specters' attacks: "The Spectres Try'd all the Evening long to inflict their Tortures on her, but . . . they were unable to Touch her." Shortly thereafter, "God was pleased at length to hear the multiply'd prayers of His people for her Deliverance." Similar efforts, accompanied by a three-day fast, were enough to protect Rule from spirit attacks. Unable to prick her with pins, her "Tormentors . . . flew out of the Room," never to return, and she gave thanks for her deliverance. By their "unwearied Cares and Pains," the faithful had rescued these girls from their suffering and banished the dark forces that threatened them.[21]

In order to use stories of demonic possession in this way, Mather presented the female sufferers of possession as innocent victims in the ordeal. These were not flawed women capable of violence against themselves and others, but instead young, vulnerable victims of circumstance and Satan's meddling. While Mather was able to depict Mercy Short as a poor orphan of the Indian Wars reliving the conflicts in spectral form, he had a more difficult time fitting Margaret Rule—born of "sober and honest Parents, yet Living"—into the mold of innocent victim. Mather could not comment on Rule's "Character" with "exactness," he claimed. Instead, he emphasized her youth, mentioning it on almost every page of his narrative of her possession, giving vague hints about rumors that surrounded her previous life. Mather argued that "wherever the Devils have been let loose to worry any Poor Creature amongst us," people would always "inquire and relate all the little Vanities of their Childhood, with such unequal exaggerations, as to make them appear greater Sinners than any whome the Pilate of Hell has not yet Prayed upon." He assured the reader, however, that whatever misdeeds had marked Rule's past had been behind her "for about half a year before her Visitation" and that "she was observably improved in the hopeful symptoms of a new Creature" by then. She had become "seriously concern'd for the everlasting Salvation of her Soul and careful to avoid the snares of Evil Company" at the time she was taken ill.[22]

Mather's efforts to use these women's expressions of violence for the good of the colony during the trials did not turn out as he intended. He and other colonial leaders could not make up the authoritative ground they had lost during the Indian Wars and were continuing to lose during the upheavals of the 1690s. Ultimately, Mather's involvement with the afflicted during the witch trials backfired, as did his unwillingness to renounce the trials strongly in their aftermath. Although Mather kept his physical distance from the Salem debacle—he did not attend the trials or even come to Salem except to witness the execution of Reverend George Burroughs in August 1692—his early support of spectral evidence had kindled the flames of the Salem witch hunt. Mather was also tainted by the trials after writing letters and narratives vindicating them and their work. At the end of his narrative of Margaret Rule's possession and deliverance, Mather responded to his detractors with dismay. After all his efforts "to rescue the Miserable from the Lions and Bears of Hell, which had seized them," and after all his "Studies to disappoint the Devils in their designs," he found it unfathomable that he would be "driven to the necessity of an Apologie."[23] The dominance of Cotton Mather and other men of his ilk was showing signs of strain.

EXECUTION SERMONS

Even as men in positions of power tried to solidify their authority, the post-Salem renunciation of spectral evidence and a new skepticism about interpreting the workings of providence all contributed to the marginalization of men like Mather, or those who had been the loudest proponents of belief in witchcraft. Mather, however, continued to present women's violence in narrative and sermon form to offer examples to the community and demonstrate his leadership. In the aftermath of the trials, he shifted his focus to a topic that would cause little controversy: women's violence that sprang from sexual sin and filth. One of the major avenues he and other Puritan ministers utilized was the execution sermon.

During much of New England's early history, the public execution process often included a sermon given by a member of the clergy. These sermons were addressed to the condemned but also contained messages for the local population, who came to partake in the spectacle. Execution sermons were not unique to Puritan New England, but the sermons, in both spoken and written form, appear to have had unprecedented popularity there compared to the rest of the Western world in the seventeenth and eighteenth centuries. In addition to being accounts of the crimes committed by the condemned, or recordings of their final words—although those elements were incorporated into them—execution sermons were opportunities for Puritan divines to impose their vision of moral order on their flocks. Most were structured around particular passages from the Bible, examined as doctrine, and then drawn out as exhortations to improvement: to the accused and the audience in general.[24]

Focusing on cases of infanticide, and the sinfulness and uncleanness of a society that could foster women who would commit such a deed, offered a way for Mather and other ministers in New England to demonstrate their moral authority. Mather referred to executions as "opportunities" to spread his message of salvation. The timing for Mather to diagnose the ills of Puritan society could not have been better; Elizabeth Emerson's execution for that crime came just a month after the last of the Salem imprisoned were reprieved and released by Governor Phips.[25] Mather wrote in his diary about Emerson, "I had often wished for an Opportunity; to hear my Testimonies, against the Sins of Uncleanness [when] A young Woman of Haverhill (and a Negro Woman also of this Town) were under sentence of Death, for the Murdering of their Bastard-children." He spoke of the time he spent trying to save their miserable souls and held them up as examples to "vast Multitudes of others." He attributed it to providence that their execution should fall on his lecture day: "Their Execution, was ordered to have been, upon the Lecture of another, but by a very strange Providence . . . the order for their Execution was altered and it fell on my Lecture Day. I did then with the special Assistance of Heaven, make and preach, a Sermon."[26]

Female violence could be used in this guise as a very public instrument to reaffirm Puritan leadership in the colony. Execution sermons for women being put to death for infanticide offered a powerful platform, and authorities soon realized that these women's executions were a perfect combination of public spectacle and spiritual theater. Huge crowds would gather to witness a public hanging and jostle for a glimpse of the accused as she listened to her final sermon. Describing the scene at Emerson's execution, Mather claimed, "Whereat one of the greatest Assemblies, ever known in these parts of the World, was come together."[27] The execution of Sarah Threeneedles for infanticide in 1698 also offered an opportunity to spread the word to a massive and enthralled audience. As Samuel Sewall noted in his diary on the occasion of Mather's execution sermon for Threeneedles, the meetinghouse was filled with a "very vast Assembly, and the street full of such as could not get in." Mather himself commented that "four or five thousand Souls" had come to hear him speak and to watch Threeneedles die. There were so many people crammed into the meetinghouse that he "could not get unto the Pulpit, but by climbing over Pues and Heads." Cotton Mather was not the only spiritual leader to take advantage of such an enormous and attentive crowd. Samuel Willard and Increase Mather also treated the gathering to their exhortations on the nature of sin and its consequences for New England.[28]

The large crowds were not merely incidental to the spectacle; they were a necessity. Execution sermons and the executions that immediately followed were frequently scheduled on lecture days to ensure maximum attendance. Threeneedles's execution sermon was given at noon on a lecture day, a time when it could hardly be missed by the community at large. She was not an exception. In Puritan New England "the condemned met their fate in the middle of the day or early afternoon, after the dire public sermons of the ministers." Mather noted feeling elated by the large numbers who had come to hear him speak. When he later described the spectacle of Threeneedles's lecture, he admitted that on the day he'd felt "weak," faint, and spent. After seeing the crowds that had come, however, he was reinvigorated by the "Spirit of the Lord." Presented before as many people as possible, execution was a drama meant for public consumption, as it reinforced the social order by reaffirming the values that had been threatened by the crime and the legitimacy of those who had condemned the accused.[29]

Ministers were aware of this and adjusted their execution sermons to address the public at large. Mather's sermon given prior to Emerson's execution is an example of this. The minister himself called the event a "dismal Spectacle" and urged his listeners to take her example to heart: "You have before your Eyes, a Couple of Malefactors, whose Murderous Uncleanness ha's now in ther Youth brought upon them a most miserable Death. May your Hearts now give a profitable Attention unto the Use that should be made of such." The majority of Mather's sermon was in this same tone, and though ostensibly for the benefit of the condemned, was not actually directed at Elizabeth herself. Mather used the pronouns "him" and "he" throughout and referred to Emerson only in vague terms until the very end of his sermon, when he offered her "confession," called *Warnings from the Dead.* He used her name just once, and never referred to the other woman being executed that same day by name, calling her only "thy Black Fellows-Sufferer there." When Mather did address Emerson directly, it was just for a few minutes before leading her to the gallows. The rest of the sermon Mather devoted to the generalized "You" in the audience. "I demand this from all the rest of You," he called out, "that the Circumstances of These, do quicken your all to mind . . . the Lamentble Desolations, which an Unclean Life do's bring upon the Children of men."[30]

While execution sermons were directed to the audience as a whole, when women were the condemned it bolstered the power of public punishment as both deterrence and an example of redemption. Mather acknowledged that the sight of the weaker sex about to be executed—those "unhappy and condemned Malefactors, who make a Sight in this house at this Time"—was "very moving unto all Spectators." Women, as physically and legally more vulnerable than the men who might be punished, were a pitiable object to those who came to witness their suffering. In her shame and pain, even the most hardened of female criminals could usually elicit a sympathetic chord, and in turn, her punishment proved particularly moving and cathartic to the multitude. N. E. H. Hull observes, "In her punishment [the audience] could feel the lash or the noose and be purified of sin—at least for a moment." At the same time, ministers' narratives of women's sins offered vivid lessons for others about the road to ruin.[31]

Publication amplified the effects of confessions and execution sermons beyond the meetinghouse and the gallows. A larger audience than those who attended the event could partake of a dramatic execution experience through a literary re-creation of the ritual. Sermons and confessions were printed and distributed soon after the execution to take advantage of the public's curiosity and to meet demand at its peak. These works were also sold cheaply and were thus available to people from a wide range of social ranks and classes. Cotton Mather was known to pass out copies of his work to people he met on the street. He appreciated the lingering impact published sermons could have. "Sermons Preached, are like Showres of Rain, that Water for an Instant," he wrote. "But Sermons Printed, are like Snow that lies longer on the Earth." The effect of an execution sermon and confession together was made particularly "profitable" via publication. When discussing his use of Emerson's execution, Mather wrote: "Take these Affectionate Warnings . . . Give Ear unto the Dying Speeches of the Young Woman, whose Execution you are to see this Afternoon. She has put into my Hand . . . these Dying Expressions of her Distressed Soul; which it will not be unprofitable for me to publish this Day among you."[32]

In their execution sermons, and the women's "confessions" that were attached to them, ministers in the 1690s returned again and again to the argument that a failure to listen to those in positions of social and spiritual authority led inevitably to ruin. Drawing parallels to the situation plaguing the colony—the threat of declension and destruction inherent in the wars—ministers hoped to reassert their political and theological upper hand through these interpretations. In her confession, published as part of Mather's *Warnings from the Dead* sermon in 1693, Elizabeth Emerson cited "disobedience" to her parents as "the chief thing that hath, brought me, into my present Condition." Elizabeth was quoted as saying: "I despised all their Godly Counsils and Reproofs; and I was always an Haughty and Stubborn Spirit. So that now I am become a dreadful Instance of the Curse of God."[33]

Similarly, for Sarah Smith and Sarah Threeneedles—both executed for infanticide in 1698—ignoring Godly counsel and "undutiful carriage" toward authority led them to their unfortunate position as sinners condemned before God. Smith, since disdaining the advice of her pious father-in-law to rectify her sinful ways, was bound for the gallows. "Her Despising the continual Counsils and Warnings of her Godly Father-in-law laid the Foundation of her Destruction," Mather wrote. The chief sin for Sarah Threeneedles was also her failure to listen to authority and tailor her behavior accordingly: "But the chief Sin, of which this Chief of Sinners, now cries out, is, Her undutiful Carriage towards to her parents . . . [T]hey often told her, It would come to this." Mather placed Threeneedles's morality tale at the beginning of his compilation of sermons and confessions, appropriately titled *Pillars of Salt* (1699). Like Lot's wife, the women condemned for infanticide had failed to heed the warnings and advice of their righteous counselors and had paid the ultimate price.[34]

Disobedience had doomed these women to a life of sin and to their own destruction. In describing the events that led them to commit their heinous deeds, ministers painted the lives of the condemned in vibrant sinful shades. In his sermon *Warning to the Unclean,* given at the execution of Sarah Smith for infanticide in 1698, John Williams set the murder within a pattern of sinful behavior. After her husband had been taken captive in an Indian raid on Deerfield, Smith had a sexual relationship with a neighbor. She became pregnant, and according to the court, after giving birth she smothered the infant to conceal her "Sins of unchastity." In his sermon on her execution, Mather noted Smith's "Hardness of Heart" and continual uttering of "New Lyes" while in prison following the murder of her child. She even fell asleep in church during an exhortation for her benefit. She "seem'd the most unconcern'd of any in the Assembly," Mather observed.[35]

Female perpetrators of infanticide were easy targets for the tarnishing brush of colonial authorities' written expressions. Most of these women were single or widowed and had a history of previous sinful behavior. Many were reluctant to reform and become ministers' muses for lessons on the consequences of sin and uncleanness. Although he brought Elizabeth Emerson to the point where she was willing to confess her sins and allow that confession to be published for the good of others, Mather doubted that Emerson's initial confessions were sincere. He claimed that she "has more to confess, I fear" and held little hope for her salvation. According to Mather, "there never was a Prisoner more Hard-Hearted, and more Unfruitful" than Emerson. Her history of sexual impropriety made this easy to believe for Mather. In *Warnings from the Dead* he referred to her previous "Uncleanness," which had resulted in the birth of her first illegitimate child, a girl. Had she seriously repented her transgression the "First Time [she] fell into it," Mather wrote, she would not have been led into the more serious sin of murder that followed.[36]

If these particularly sinful and unrepentant women could be brought to see the error of their ways, however, there was still hope for all. Their redemption, of course, could come only through the efforts of Puritan ministers. Even as hardened a sinner as Smith could be brought to heel. During her visits with Williams, as he fought to redeem her soul, "sometimes violent pangs of Horror would come upon her, wherein she detected her own Lying and seemed greatly to Bewail it." Before being hanged, she was moved to acknowledge some of her sins and to warn other women not to emulate her behavior. In the end, she "desured to Give Glory unto God, and to take shame unto her self," Mather wrote. "She would warn all others, to beware of Sins, that had brought her unto this miserable End."[37]

Some women refused to be brought to heel. Sarah Threeneedles's darker tendencies lurked not far beneath the surface and did not lessen as she awaited her execution and the "gallows theater of repentance." Far from reforming her sinful behavior, Threeneedles had sexual relations with another prisoner while awaiting her execution. She also failed to either repent or accept blame for her actions. According to Samuel Sewall, who witnessed her presentation in court on the day of her trial, Threeneedles bitterly described herself as "ruin'd" by the father of her child, "Thomas Savage, junr, shopkeeper." It was his fault, not hers, that matters had taken such a disastrous turn. "She said . . . if he would have promis'd her any thing, it had not come to this," Sewall recorded in his diary. Highlighting these sins, Increase Mather, Cotton Mather, Samuel Willard, and Sewall used Threeneedles as a cautionary figure for others with regard to the disaster that accompanied sinfulness. All four used the "horrible Sight" of her execution to transfix their spiritual and reading publics in New England. In order to depict Threeneedles as a villain, all but Samuel Willard failed to address her status as a covenanted church member before her fall from grace. Willard alone seemed bothered that one of the "Flock" who "had received the Seal of the Covenant" could commit such an act.[38]

Just as these women's sinful ways and hardened hearts had led them to be "Extinguished by the Justice of God," sinful corruption within Puritan New England had brought down the scourge of God upon the community in the Indian Wars. In the turbulent 1690s, Mather and others like him seized the substantial weapons they possessed to craft their own versions of events and deflect blame for the devastation the colony had suffered. Linking sin to the losses of war, Mather made it clear that the sinful corruption of women like Emerson, Threeneedles, and Smith was a specimen of the larger corruption that would continue to destroy them all if not purged. The young were the most prominent victims. "This Land is making the Lamentation that was made by the Church of old, The Lord ha's called an Assembly against me, to Crush my young men," he wrote. "How many Scores of Young men have . . . been lost . . . by the Disastrous Plagues and Wars that have been upon us! Unto us may our God say, He said unto Isreal of old, Your Young men have I Slain." The reasons for the decimation were clear: "Wickness & Especially the Uncleanness . . . should be acknowledged, among the Causes of these Calamities." New England was weak with sin and ripe for the taking: "So little Joy indeed ha's our God in our Young people, that He is evey day saying over them, Indians, Do you come: Frenchmen do you come . . . cut off as many of those young People, as come in your way!"[39]

THE CAPTIVITY NARRATIVE OF HANNAH DUSTIN

In the midst of this destruction and loss, another literary creation emerged in the late seventeenth century to serve as a rallying point for the colonial experiment in distress: the captivity narrative. Written and distributed by Puritan divines and historians, these narratives of Indian capture, English suffering, and eventual redemption frequently highlighted female captives as sympathetic heroines and described them suffering from, and sometimes engaging in, physical violence. The narratives traced an individual's "progress through the temptations of sin and disbelief," enhancing the "terrors which surrounded the soul" for dramatic and moving effect. The women in these narratives served as symbols of the larger suffering of New England as a whole, as well as its potential for restoration.[40]

The suffering of female captives rallied political and spiritual unity, demonstrating in dramatic fashion the literal and metaphorical "invasions" of Puritan society about which Cotton Mather and others had warned. The captives' actions, however violent, also demonstrated what was possible with the assistance of the divine and when directed for the good of the colony. Mather used Hannah Dustin's narrative to just such effect in the late seventeenth and early eighteenth century. In so doing, he harnessed a dramatic act of female violence to accomplish three aims: to negate Dustin's troubling actions by illustrating their divine origin, to bolster his own position and relevance as the interpreter of God's message, and to rally the public to unite politically and spiritually against their common enemies.

Dustin was not the only woman to use violence, and even deadly violence, in late seventeenth-century Massachusetts. The scale of her violence, however, and the destruction she left in her wake, placed her beyond other colonial women of her time. While her story is exceptional, she was still a part of what appeared to be an increasingly visible trend among women toward more open expressions of anger and aggression, particularly in response to threats to household safety, security, and property. By the summer of 1697, Dustin's actions were known around the colony. Thomas Dustin claimed that his wife's story had already become public knowledge when he petitioned the General Court for scalp bounty that June. Hannah's "Slaughter of soo many of the Barbarians" was an extraordinary act worthy of "Considerable Recompense from the Publick," he argued before the court. Furthermore, regardless of the fact that the policy rewarding bounties for Indian kills had been revoked a few years before, it was still a "matter of universal desire thro the whole Province" that her heroism "Should not pass unrecompensed."[41]

Mather addressed his concerns about colonial men's inefficacy and inaction—weaknesses that had pushed Dustin and other women to take violent action—and their role in the current calamities troubling New England in his publication of Dustin's narrative. In that story, as elsewhere in his *Decennium Luctuosum,* it was colonial men's procrastination and cowardice that had forced colonial women to defend themselves bodily. The very name that Mather gave to Dustin's narrative in *Decennium Luctuosum* and *Magnalia Christi Americana,* "Dux Femina Facti," which translates as "a woman the leader in the achievement," revealed his frustration, and perhaps amazement, that a woman would lead the way in battling these heathen elements. While using her tale of female heroism to shame men into action, Mather also recognized the dangers inherent in allowing a woman to become such an active, and violent, public figure. Dustin's aggressive individual action—her ability to escape capture through her own strength and cunning—might suggest that anyone, even a woman, could rely on himself or herself for survival and salvation. To undermine this idea, Dustin's narrative required Mather's careful explanations to make it acceptable for public consumption. In order to avoid perpetuating, or even exacerbating, trends toward female action, Mather had to remove the agency for Dustin's actions from her hands and place it elsewhere.

From the beginning, Mather used Dustin's position as mistress of a household, and the fact that Dustin had just given birth to her eighth child the week before her capture, to justify her behavior as the natural response of a wife and grieving mother. In the beginning of the narrative, still recovering from the ordeal of childbirth, Dustin was forced to helplessly witness the destruction of her home and her children. Mather recounted how the "furious tawnies" came into their home, the center of Puritan society, to ransack it and "set the house on fire." They had easily bypassed the "usual Walls of defence" protecting colonial societies—both literal and metaphorical—as Mather had warned in his earlier work *Wonders of the Invisible World* (1693). The "raging dragons" then seized Dustin and her newborn child: "But e're they had gone many Steps, they dash'd out the Brains of the Infant, against a Tree." Neither did the "Salvages" provide the child, or any others they had killed, with a proper burial, but instead left "their Carcases on the ground, for Birds & Beasts to feed upon." Witnessing this destruction, Mather claimed, made Dustin a law unto herself: "Being where she had not her own Life secured by an Law unto her, she thought she was not Forbidden by any law to take away the Life of the Murderers, by whom her Child had been butchered."[42] In emphasizing her suffering as a goodwife and mother, and enlisting sympathy for her actions as a result, Mather hoped to divert attention from the more problematic aspects of Dustin's narrative while reminding readers of his earlier warnings about the threat posed by invading forces to Puritan life itself.

In all his versions of Dustin's narrative, Mather also emphasized the hand of God in her act of retribution. From the beginning, it is clear that Dustin and the other captives passively "received" their "Deliverance" from captivity by humbling themselves before the Lord. Dustin and Mary Neff, her midwife and fellow captive, were passionate in their religious observance, defying their Indian captors to sneak off and pray. Like another Hannah, Samuel's mother from the Hebrew Bible, Dustin and Neff were persistent in "pouring out their Souls before the Lord." As a result of their devotions, God heard their supplications and enabled their escape. But their means of attack were not their own but were instead part of God's "Favour." In slaying their Indian "Oppressors," the women were merely imitating "the Action of Jael upon Sisera."[43]

In his *Humiliations Follow'd with Deliverances* (1697), Mather attributed Dustin's agency to the prayerful public of New England as a whole. The "Praying Friends" of Dustin and Neff did not "forbear to pour out Supplications for them." It was by their friends' fervent belief and their willingness to humble themselves as Christians before God, as opposed to any action by the two women themselves, that this praying public successfully "besought

His Mercy for our poor Captives that were become the Prey of the Terrible." The women, as passive, seemingly helpless victims, had others to thank for their return to civilization. Mather wrote, "Yea we have done it."[44] In so doing, he carefully contained Dustin's captivity experience and expressions of violence within his own interpretations. He was also able to illustrate the divine sanction of Puritan violence against the Indians more generally.

Through a careful re-framing of Dustin's story, Mather simultaneously neutralized a particularly visible act of female violence while crafting a powerful narrative weapon. By presenting his own interpretations of religious doctrine as read through those dramatic events, Mather also asserted his relevance as a religious leader of the colony. Time and again through Dustin's narrative, Mather defined both sin and the road to redemption. He warned the Puritans that the only means of saving them all from destruction was by following his instructions for salvation. He used the women in Dustin's narrative as a primary example. At the end of the narrative, he pointed out that the former captives themselves were actually in the church at that moment, to hear his sermon and "to give Thanks unto God their Saviour." While offering praise for their brave deed, he took the opportunity to present them with a warning as well: they would need to become the "sincere Servants of the Lord," who "by his Blood has brought [them] out of their Dungeon," or else become "the Slaves of Devils," which was "worse than to be in the Hands of the Indians."[45]

Mather's meaning in making this statement was clear. If these women who had felt God's presence so powerfully in their lives were still in danger from the dark forces of Satan, no one in Puritan New England was safe. Mather spoke of the sinfulness that had opened the "Flood gates for Innumerable . . . Woes." If such sinfulness persisted—in the form of sexual "uncleanness," the "Decay of good Family Discipline," and other "wicked sorceries"—no one would be spared. "Have Bloody, Popish, and Pagan Enemies, made very dreadful Impressions upon us, and Captived and Butchered multitudes of our Beloved Neighbours?" Mather wrote. If so, he continued, "Let us Humbly Confess, our Sins have [been] Deserved." The "Scourges of Heaven" in the form of such "Pagan Enemies" would continue to be employed against the community for "Crimes against the Holy and Just . . . Laws of the Lord."[46]

While Mather was defining the nature of the sin that had brought God's wrath upon them, he also pointed out that all was not yet lost, and that the Puritan leadership, as appropriate interpreters of God's word, knew the path to redemption. Humility before the Lord, first and foremost, and trust in those chosen to present His message were the answer. And as his narrative plainly demonstrated, if a weak woman like Dustin could prostrate herself before God and achieve her redemption, surely others could as well, for "when a Sinful People Humble themselves before the Almighty God, it is an Hopeful and Happy Symptom, that He will not utterly Destroy [them]." While the people of New England had felt the "Anger of God" most acutely, the Lord had not completely "Turned away" from them. Through confession of sin, reformation of behavior, and a demonstration of complete humiliation by fasting, they could once again feel God's saving Grace.[47] Although Dustin was not necessarily of the "chosen people," not being a church member at the time of her capture, her actions, as inspired by God, turned her into one of the elect.

Perhaps more than any other violent woman used by colonial propagandists, Hannah Dustin failed to fit neatly into the mold of a colonial heroine. While the narrative depicted her as a devout woman of faith, unlike Sarah Threeneedles, Dustin would not become a member of the church until the end of her life. Mather was preaching a form of religious practice that featured, as Teresa A. Toulouse states, a "performed passivity that grants all to Christ's humiliation," and one that ostensibly brought about a desire for both the public as well as personal benefits of church membership. The unconverted Dustin's individual aggressive female action failed to fit this model. In addition, Dustin's family history was less than ideal. Her father was violent, prone to abuse his children and quarrel with neighbors. Her sister Elizabeth Emerson, of course, had been fined for fornication and executed for infanticide.[48]

Without the softening lens of Mather's interpretation, Dustin's own deeds also made her an unlikely woman to shoulder the burden of sainthood. Dustin was far from the passive victim of circumstance of Mather's imaginings. Stealthily waiting for the cover of darkness, Dustin planned the attack in advance with her fellow captives. She also embraced two prominent symbols of Indian barbarity for her own purposes: using the very tomahawks the Indians had used to slay her brethren to commit the murders and collecting the scalps of the fallen as trophies. Six of the ten Indians slain and scalped by Dustin were children. Mather does not include these aspects of the story in his version of Dustin's tale and glosses over the most brutal details. He is not afraid to embrace her violent methods more generally, however.

The violent language that Mather employed in presenting his road to salvation mirrored the violent methods Dustin herself used in making her escape. "A fasting Day must be a . . . Sin killing Day, or 'tis nothing," he wrote. "Our Fasts are to Slay our Lusts; those are the Beasts, which are then to be slaughtered." In using this language alongside Dustin's story, Mather repackaged her violence in order to place his listeners and readers on the front lines of the war with the Indians and present his message of solidarity under Puritan leadership. Changes and catastrophes, most prominently Indian war and political upheaval, were interpreted as signs that New England was backsliding. Sermons and narratives served as a means of drawing Puritan audiences into a greater war against this evil, the greatest of all battles, as opposed to a war against the authorities. Through "imaginative involvement they demonstrated that every individual was part of this eternal and spiritual war and that every soul was at stake."[49]

Using the narrative in this way, Mather sought to unite Massachusetts residents against their common foes—most prominently the Indians and their French allies—to rally the colony and promote internal stability. The intense anti-Indian feeling that had emerged during King Philip's War was reawakened during King William's War. Adapting captivity narratives, Mather and others embraced this antipathy, and bent it toward eventually creating a unified citizenry in the colonies following these conflicts. Mather described the Indians as "Barbarous" wolves and as "Angels of Death shooting the Arrows of Death," while recounting in detail the raid on Haverhill, the slaughter of civilians, and Dustin's capture.[50]

Not until later in the narrative does the reader discover that the Indians themselves were Christians, converts to Catholicism and under the sway of the French. The Indian family that had carried out the raid and taken Dustin and Neff into captivity were fervent Catholics who prayed "no less than Thrice every Day" in "Obedience to the last injunction the French had given them." In making this a prominent element of the tale and linking the Indian "Idolaters" to their French "whiter Brethren," Mather also took advantage of anti-French and anti-Catholic sentiment among New Englanders. Certainly fears of French encroachment had a basis in reality. The French had been fighting alongside their Indian allies in northern New

England to try to retake territory from the English, and many colonists believed that the French and Indians were conspiring with the devil to destroy them. In Dustin's narrative, Mather simply encouraged their hatred of both "savagery" and "popery" by depicting the French and their Indians allies as part of a "Spiritual Plague" that had attacked New England and threatened to overwhelm them all.[51] In doing so, he could confirm and rally their spiritual and political loyalties as Puritan New Englanders.

NARRATIVE HISTORIES

As the seventeenth century drew to a close, and the more immediate state of emergency associated with the Indian Wars began to lessen in all but the northernmost areas of New England, the concerns of colonial authorities turned more explicitly toward shoring up political stability and reestablishing secure domestic relations within both the colony and the household. The narrative histories that colonial historians produced in the eighteenth century thus focused less on the spiritual dangers that lurked in the shadows and more on the necessity of effective male leadership for the challenges still to come. These narratives embraced more transparent political and social agendas and represented a discursive shift in the way they approached female violence. They framed women's past acts of anti-Indian violence during the Indian Wars less as instances of practical and spiritual heroism to be emulated than as deeds born out of only the greatest necessity. By showing women forced into performing distinctly "unwomanly" acts, colonial historians sought to encourage male New Englanders to rise to the occasion and reaffirm their position at the top of the social hierarchy. They also urged the public to rally behind men in positions of political authority, thus negating the need for such behavior by women in the future.

Cotton Mather's history of the Indian Wars, *Decennium Luctuosum*, was one of his more political works published in the late seventeenth and early eighteenth centuries. The dedicatory and concluding comments to the Earl of Bellomont, who in 1697 was designated the royal governor of Massachusetts, made it clear that the work was an expression of solidarity with the new leadership, as well as with King William, during a period of yet another political transition. At the end of the work, Mather praised the king and called Bellomont the "Illustrious Image of His own Royal Virtues."[52] Mather had high hopes that Bellomont's tenure would end the political upheavals that had plagued the colony throughout the 1680s and 1690s. He also hoped that by tying his fate to the new leader he could distance himself from earlier political missteps. Mather had strongly backed the temporary government of Simon Bradstreet, including his ill-fated expeditions against the "Armies of Indians and Gallic Blood Hounds" in Canada.[53] Mather had also been pleased to support his father's choice for royal governor, Sir William Phips, prior to Phips's political disgrace. In addition, the Mather family had a personal stake in the establishment of political stability under the latest, and unpopular, Massachusetts charter. Increase Mather had negotiated the charter in London, and both Mathers had been defending it since the early 1690s.

In his narrative history, Mather used instances of female violence to demonstrate the need for both political and domestic stability as well as effective male leadership in these realms. Mather discussed the actions of colonial Englishwomen, including the women of Wells, Maine, and their defense of a garrison against Indian attack in the midst of King William's War. He recounted that Englishwomen in the garrison "took up the Amazonian stroke, and not only brought ammunition to the men, but also with a Manly resolution fired several times upon the enemy." While appearing to applaud their actions, Mather's description of the women as "Amazonian" and "Manly" also painted them as uncivilized, un-Christian, and unfeminine. The presentation of women acting like men revealed Mather's awareness that such female action had the capacity to fundamentally disrupt the English patriarchal domestic order, even as the women themselves fought to defend it. It was the ineffectiveness of men, however, that forced the women to act in this way. Mather emphasized that the attacking Indians badly outnumbered the Englishmen willing to take up arms against their foes: some fifteen men to the Indians' several hundred. Of these few brave Englishmen, at least one had spoken of surrendering.[54]

Such chaotic results of ineffective male leadership—examples of the "Feebleness discovered by my Countrey-men, in some of their Actions, during this War"—littered the pages of Mather's *Decennium Luctuosum.* At the same time, however, he held up Bellomont, with the support of the king and united colonies behind him, as the hope for the future of New

England. "But that which yet more assures a Break of Day after a long and sad Night unto us, is, That . . . the Greatest Monarch, that ever Sway'd the Sceptre of Great Britain, hath Commissioned a Noble Person . . . to take the Government of these Provinces," Mather wrote. He credited Bellomont, the "Greatest person ever to set Foot on the English Continent of America," for installing William in power during the Glorious Revolution, and remarked that the "Continent of America must now Share in the Influence of that Noble Person." Undoubtedly Bellomont's "Great and Good Influences" as Governour—his "Virtus et Summa potestas" (virtue and highest power)—would help reinstall manly leadership in the colony.[55] His nobility would thus end the need for women to step out of their appropriate gender roles.

Samuel Penhallow also used stories of gender dynamics in chaos—and the female violence that resulted from it—to encourage male leadership and political stability in New England in the uneasy 1710s and 1720s. New England had yet to achieve political homeostasis under secure leadership during the first quarter of the eighteenth century. Poorly conducted diplomacy with respect to the Native American Wabanaki Confederacy of northern New England had even led to yet another war with the Indians, Dummer's War, from 1722 to 1725. Originally settling in Massachusetts, Penhallow found his political calling in the upper echelons of New Hampshire politics. Near the end of his life, while still the chief justice of the Superior Court of Judicature, Penhallow published his *History of the Wars of New-England with the Eastern Indians, or a Narrative of their Continued Perfidy and Cruelty* (1726). Penhallow's scathing portrayal of the Indians is clear from the title of his work; to other narrative histories, Penhallow added accounts of colonists being burned alive and even cannibalized by their Indian captors.[56] These barbaric forces routinely invaded women's sphere in Penhallow's work, forcing Englishwomen to use manly, violent action to defend themselves and their families.

Penhallow's treatment of an unnamed "oxford woman" and her response to an Indian attack on her home is a prime example of this. According to Penhallow, in the midst of Queen Anne's War, the woman shot and killed an Indian who was attempting to break in through her roof. According to local legend, she had two muskets and two pistols charged and ready for his three companions. The woman had apparently been left unprotected by the men of the house. More disturbing, however, was that her preparedness indicated that she did not expect assistance from masculine rescuers. Having several different kinds of guns for her own use went against New English social custom with regard to firearms. Men in New England "seem to have held their guns in special regard," Ann Little argues, as symbols of their masculine dominance as householders. Owning and knowing how to operate a gun was a privilege of their sex. Women did not usually own or keep guns. When they were widowed, New England women did not keep their husband's gun or other weaponry in their homes. Thus, the Oxford woman's familiarity with firearms, and her willingness to use not just one but four, would have been seen as an undeniable disruption of the gender order. Her actions as Penhallow described them were to be lauded but also needed to be rectified.[57]

The trope of women stepping out of their prescribed gender roles in the context of war was well known in England at the time. Popular literary tales suggested that simply by adopting men's clothing and armor, Englishwomen might successfully impersonate English manhood. "Images of cross-dressing women, and of women masquerading as soldiers in particular, were familiar figures in English pamphlet literature and popular ballads," Little notes. Stories of these "warrior women" circulated quite broadly, and on the surface seemed to praise those women who were willing to put on men's clothing and fight alongside men. They even, at times, showed that women might fight as equals to men, displaying a form of "manly virtue" in the process. In reality, however, these women were not taken seriously as enlistees fighting for the honor and glory of the English nation. Instead, these stories functioned as both popular entertainment and moral lessons. They were "meant to humiliate cowardly or defeated men by implying that even women could be better soldiers than the present lot."[58]

This theme appeared in many of the historical narratives of the Indian Wars of early eighteenth-century New England. For a people recovering from those wars while struggling with the social disruptions of a growing and expanding population, messages regarding paternal, masculine dominance and appropriate gender roles were both relevant and timely. As the population of New England continued to rise in this period through both natural increase in the region and immigration, land in the older agricultural communities was becoming scarce by the third and fourth generations. Young people coming into maturity found that they either had to go into non-farming occupations or move. As a result, outmigration from old communities and the founding of new towns proliferated after 1715. As New Englanders became increasingly mobile and young adults more willing to migrate away from the traditional farming household establishment, male-dominated parental authority seemed in jeopardy, and with it a clear understanding of gendered household roles. "The imperatives of autonomy and independence that had been so powerfully manifest everywhere else in the English American world throughout the seventeenth century" had finally arrived in New England.[59]

The story of the courageous—and cross-dressing—women of Oyster River reflects the discomfort that accompanied many of these changes in the early eighteenth century. Local minister Jabez Fitch of Portsmouth, New Hampshire, relayed the tale in his *Brief Narrative of Several Things Respecting the Province of New Hampshire in New-England,* published in 1728–29. Fitch's appointment to North Church in Portsmouth in 1724 from a church in long-settled Ipswich, Massachusetts, paralleled population expansion away from the oldest New England communities to more outlying areas. As a result, this graduate of Harvard College witnessed the troubling social shifts and "unhappy consequences" for Portsmouth as it emerged as a commercial port in the early eighteenth century. In recounting in his narrative an Indian assault on a garrison in Oyster River in April 1706, Fitch emphasized the fact that Englishmen were not at the helm during the crisis. The garrison under attack "had not a man in it at the time," he wrote, which forced the women to assume "an Amazonian courage and put on the Habit of men" in order to defend the garrison. By donning men's attire, they acted their part so well that they frightened away the enemy.[60]

When Fitch's narrative of the event is compared to another account of the Oyster River incident, it appears that Fitch exaggerated the absence of men, as well as the women's counterattack. In his journal, the Reverend John Pike of Dover and Portsmouth made note of the assault on the garrison, writing, "The Indians came in upon the south part of Oyster river, by the little bay, and killed ten persons." Among those killed in the exchange were "brother John Wheeler, and his wife, John Drew, &c." Thus, according to Pike's recollections, not only were men present during the attack but also several were killed defending the settlement. The Indians did not run and hide in the face of female force but stayed long enough to dispense with ten English settlers. Pike was widely regarded, even by Jabez Fitch, as a "person of great humility, meekness and patience . . . without gall or guile." It is unlikely that Pike's version of the events, which included the actual names of those killed in action, varied significantly from reality. Fitch, therefore, must have amplified the women's role in the incident, as well as their gender-bending attire and behavior, in order to play on existing social anxieties for dramatic effect. In so doing, he emphasized the moral that the absence of effective male leadership, and the resulting female violence, threatened to undermine whatever patriarchal order still remained.[61]

A gendered hierarchy was central to the structure and functioning of colonial and provincial society. The destruction of the well-ordered and secure domestic realm appears throughout many of the narrative histories of the wars from this period. The importance of the household in early New England meant that attacks on English homes were seen as attacks on Englishness itself. The narrative histories pointed out that no staple of New English family life was safe; even the Sabbath "became a Day of Danger," Penhallow remarked, "in which [the Indians] often did Mischief, as at Dover, Oyster-River and Berwick." Mather's *Decennium Luctuosum* catalogued numerous frontier atrocities in King William's War, reading, in Little's words, "like a rusticated Book of martyrs."[62] Families and young English children were the frequent targets of destruction in these accounts. While these works excuse women's behavior as recounted in the narratives as understandable reactions to Indian encroachment on the sanctity of the community and household and the loss of loved ones, they also demonstrate the chaos that ensued as a result. In publishing these narratives, authors expressed their implied hope that the eighteenth century would bring a return to traditional structures of domesticity. Once men took their rightful place atop the political and social hierarchies, women could return to their normal duties, as well as a less visible, less violent place in society.

The failure of men to protect her forced Hannah Bradley to step out of the orderly picture of household domesticity into a world of violence and horror in Penhallow's *History*. When the Bradleys' garrison in Haverhill was "unhappily surpriz'd" by a small band of Indians, they found that the Englishmen were not at their posts. "Seeing the Gates open and none on the Sentry," Penhallow writes, the Indians were able to enter the garrison without meeting any manly resistance. As a result, the savages "became

Masters thereof." The only person who fought back against the incursion was the pregnant "Housewife" working in her kitchen. "Perceiving the Misery that was attending her," Hannah Bradley attempted to defend herself using a primary tool of domesticity itself, a kettle of boiling soap. Throwing it on one Indian attacker, she scalded him to death before being dragged into the wilderness to endure continual horrors at the hands of the Indians. Despite "being with Child," Bradley was "yet oblig'd to travel in a deep snow, under a heavy burden, and many Days together without Subsistance." After Hannah gave birth while in captivity, her baby died from want of food, as well as the "Cruelty of the Indians, who as it cry'd threw hot Embers in its Mouth."[63]

In Penhallow's hands, however, Bradley's narrative ends on a hopeful note. While men's leadership failures had led to her capture and suffering, her eventual redemption was the result of masculine effort. After a year in captivity, Bradley was finally rescued through the valiant exertions of her husband. "After a Years Bondage she was sold to the French for eighty Livers," Penhallow recorded. Upon hearing of her sale, Bradley's husband, Joseph, traveled to Montreal to "redeem" her. Penhallow's history does not record that Bradley attempted to escape on her own or negotiate her own release during this period. According to local history, Joseph was so determined to rescue his wife, he traveled on foot and dogsled into Canada to find her and purchase her freedom. The couple then took a boat to Boston, and then on to their home in Haverhill. In a dramatic demonstration of the possibilities for male action and leadership, Joseph Bradley had successfully "redeemed" his wife from the wilderness and brought her back into the peaceful domestic fold.[64]

Historians of colonial New England tried to avoid the moral ambiguity that plagued "real" women of the period in their narrative histories. Some attempted to downplay the barbaric influences of life on the frontiers of New England and their English heroines' interactions with Indians. In his depiction of Hannah Bradley's attack on an Indian invader, Penhallow mentions briefly that her resulting capture was "the second time of her captivity." Unlike later authors who would use Bradley's story, Penhallow offers no details about Bradley's earlier experience with the Indians, which lasted almost a year. Later historians would refer to the impact of her first captivity, and her earlier loss of a child to the Indians' barbarity at that time, as an explanation for her behavior during the second invasion. These later authors would also, however, include other, more disturbing details about Bradley's attack on the Indian in her home. Benjamin Mirick, in his *History of Haverhill*, recorded that "having been brought home by her husband," Bradley was taken a second time, "but not before she had finished and wounded an Indian by pouring boiling soap into his mouth." In this account, instead of simply throwing the soap on an attacker, Bradley used it as a targeted weapon. The intimate violence of holding down an Indian intruder and actually forcing him to ingest the boiling liquid changes the nature of Bradley's act almost entirely.[65] In avoiding such detail, as well as any mention of her earlier experience among the Indians, Penhallow also carefully avoided the taint of uncivilized behavior in his tale. Bradley's effectiveness as a symbol, therefore, remained intact.

In order to use the violent women in their stories as symbols of the need for male social and political leadership, other colonial historians presented their female characters as anonymous figures compelled by the circumstances of war. In his own narrative of the Oyster River heroines, Jabez Fitch never names any of the specific women involved in the incident, although as later accounts illustrated, the names of those involved in the attack were well known. Instead, in his *Brief Narrative* and other works that would follow, the cross-dressing women who displayed such "Amazonian courage" remained unidentified. None of them could rise to the level of "heroine" for their violent deeds, as Hannah Dustin had done decades earlier.[66] Historians also did not spend any time describing their appearance, aside from their male attire and behavior. They focused much more effort and page space on recounting the looming Indian threat, and Englishmen's failures, which had forced the women to step outside of gender norms.

Despite the appearance of female characters in narratives of possession, execution sermons, captivity narratives, and narrative histories as either morally corrupt villains or self-sacrificing heroines, the actual differences between these women were much less significant than their literary depictions claimed. All of the women discussed in this chapter, on either end of this artificial dichotomy, employed violence in brutal ways and for their own ends. The violent tenor of colonial New England society—combined with the burdens imposed on many women in the context of the Indian Wars and other struggles of the period—meant that most women were unlikely to be ideal inspirational symbols. Therefore, while it was easy to villainize the "bad" women as using violence as a last desperate act in a life filled with sin—at least prior to their last-minute redemptions—shaping the "good" ones into heroines appropriate for public consumption was more difficult.

The decision of colonial authorities to use these women as inspirational symbols becomes easier to comprehend when we examine the everyday realities of life for women in colonial Massachusetts and the violence they experienced and employed. Although these women were thrown into remarkable circumstances, the moral ambiguity of their actual lives was not unusual. Like other colonial women, they were exposed to violence in war and between family members, against servants, and among neighbors. Also like other women in seventeenth-century New England, they employed violence for their own ends. As part of a colony and a people reeling from the destruction of war and internal upheaval, they were among those women willing to use violence to protect themselves and their interests when the authorities either could not or would not. As far too visible representations of this troubling tendency, their stories had to be negated, appropriated, and repackaged for the spiritual, political, or social good of the colonies.

At the end of the seventeenth century and through the turn of the eighteenth, the political, social, and religious changes that were occurring in New England through war—against real and spiritual enemies—as well as the inevitable changes that accompanied an expanding society—combined to cause the Puritan leadership to worry that their experiment in the wilderness was under threat from without and within. In response, Puritan leaders took some of the most problematic narratives of their time—stories of women violently possessed by demonic spirits, the tales of those who had committed the unforgiveable by killing their children, the narratives of those who had fought to escape the barbaric wilderness, and the histories of those who had done battle against the encroaching Indian threat—and used them in remarkably creative ways to unite the colonial population and solidify their positions.

Mather led the push to rescue the colonies from both internal discontent and demonic invaders as he helped free Elizabeth Knapp, Mercy Short, and Margaret Rule from possession. When the witch trails in Salem failed, ultimately, to bolster the cultural authority of the Puritan leadership, Mather and other religious leaders shifted their focus to women more clearly guilty of evil deeds. Their execution sermons for women convicted of infanticide outlined the path for New England's redemption and the ministers' role in that endeavor. When warfare again threw the colonies into hardship, narratives like Hannah Dustin's rallied colonists against both the Indians and their French allies. Finally, when the ministers sought to reestablish their society in the new century, secure domestic relations, and inspire men to take on effective leadership roles, they turned to narrative histories of women forced to commit unwomanly acts in defense of themselves and their communities. Through all of these efforts, the Puritan leadership transformed these women and their actions from potential threats into weapons for the societal and cultural survival of colonial New England.

NOTES

Introduction

1. Massachusetts Archive, Felt Collection, vol. 40, 279, 625; Massachusetts Archive Court Records, *Records of the Superior Court of Judicature,* vol. 1, 1692–1695, Commonwealth Museum and State Archives, Boston, Massachusetts; *The Diary of Cotton Mather,* vol. 1, ed. Worthington Chauncey Ford (Boston: Massachusetts Historical Society, 1911–12), 164–65; Cotton Mather, *Warnings from the Dead* (Boston, 1693), 70, 71.
2. *Samuel Sewall's Diary,* ed. Mark Van Doren (New York: Russell & Russell, 1963), 142; Cotton Mather, *Humiliations Follow'd with Deliverances* (Boston, 1697), 40, 47.
3. Mather, *Warnings;* Cotton Mather, *Pillars of Salt: An History of Some Criminals Executed in This Land for Capital Crimes* (Boston, 1699); Mather, *Humiliations*; Cotton Mather, *Decennium Luctuosum: An History of Remarkable Occurrences in the Long War which New England hath had with the Indian Salvages* (Boston, 1699); Cotton Mather, *Magnalia Christi Americana or The Ecclesiastical History of New-England* (London, 1702).
4. John Winthrop, "A Model of Christian Charity," in *A Library of American Literature: Early Colonial Literature, 1607–1675,* ed. Edmund Clarence Stedman and Ellen Mackay Hutchinson (New York, 1892), 304–7.
5. This is not to argue that women did not commit acts of sexual violence against others, more particularly their subordinates. As Thomas Foster has shown, white women committed acts of sexual violence against enslaved men in southern societies much more frequently than historians have recognized. We cannot assume that women in colonial New England would not also have been capable of similar behavior just because it was not addressed by colonial courts. Thomas Foster, *Rethinking Rufus: Sexual Violations of Enslaved Men* (Athens: University of Georgia Press, 2019).
6. As Marylynn Salmon explains, in early New England "the inability of wives to act as individuals at law arose as a corollary to their inability to own property. After marriage, all the personal property owned by a wife came under the exclusive control of her husband." Marylynn Salmon, *Women and the Law of Property in Early America* (Chapel Hill: University of North Carolina Press, 1986), 15. I borrow the idea of the "dignity of anonymity" for colonial good wives from Laurel Thatcher Ulrich, *Good Wives: Image and Reality in the Lives of Women in Northern New England, 1650–1750* (New York: Vintage Books, 1991), 3, 37.
7. Proverbs 31:10–31. Seventeenth-century Puritan advice literature frequently included references to the proverb of Bathsheba; e.g. John Dod and William

Hinde, *Bathshebaes Instructions to Her Son Lemuel* (London, 1614); and Cotton Mather, *Ornaments of the Daughters of Zion* (Cambridge, MA, 1692). See Ulrich, *Good Wives,* 3, 11, 246.

8. Mather, *Ornaments,* 5–6; Proverbs 31:10–31.
9. John Demos, *A Little Commonwealth: Family Life in Plymouth Colony* (1970; New York: Oxford University Press, 2000), 134–37; Philip Greven, *The Protestant Temperament: Patterns in Child-Rearing, Religious Experience, and the Self in Early America* (Chicago: University of Chicago Press, 1988), 35–37.
10. *OED Online* (Oxford: Oxford University Press, March 2016), s.v. "violence," http://www.oed.com.proxy.uchicago.edu/view/Entry/223638?rskey=ajSLR6&result=1 (accessed May 6, 2016); Susan Dwyer Amussen, "Punishment, Discipline and Power: The Social Meanings of Violence in Early Modern England," *Journal of British Studies* 34, no. 1 (January 1995): 2–3.
11. David D. Hall, *Worlds of Wonder, Days of Judgment: Popular Religious Belief in Early New England* (New York: Alfred A. Knopf, 1989), 15; Elizabeth Reis, *Damned Women: Sinners and Witches in Puritan New England* (Ithaca: Cornell University Press, 1997), xvii; Perry Miller, *The New England Mind: The Seventeenth Century* (1939; Boston: Beacon Press, 1961), vii; Richard Archer, *Fissures in the Rock: New England in the Seventeenth Century* (Hanover: University of New Hampshire Press, 2001).
12. Amy J. Fitzgerald, "A Social History of the Slaughterhouse: From Inception to Contemporary Implications," *Human Ecology Review* 17, no. 1 (2010): 59. Ulrich, *Good Wives,* 22–23, makes the connection between Hannah Dustin's experience with slaughtering pigs and her ability to scalp her Indian victims. See also Jay Allen Anderson, "A Sold Sufficiency: An Ethnography of Yeoman Foodways in Stuart England" (PhD diss., University of Pennsylvania, 1971), 101.
13. Helena Wall, *Fierce Communion: Family and Community in Early America* (State College: Pennsylvania State University Press, 1990); Richard J. Ross, "Puritan Godly Discipline in Comparative Perspective: Legal Pluralism and the Sources of 'Intensity,'" *American Historical Review* 113, no. 4 (2008): 977. See also Laurence Friedman, *Crime and Punishment in American History* (New York: BasicBooks, 1993), 37.
14. Natalie Zemon Davis, "Women on Top," in *Society and Culture in Early Modern France* (Stanford: Stanford University Press, 1975), 146. See also E. P. Thompson, "The Moral Economy of the English Crowd in the Eighteenth Century," *Past and Present* 50 (February 1971): 115–18; Olwen Hufton, "Women in the Revolution, 1789–96," *Past and Present* 73 (November 1971): 90–108; Patricia Higgins, "The Reactions of Women," in *Politics, Religion, and the English Civil War,* ed. Brian Manning (London: Edward Arnold, 1973), 179–222; Robert Southey, *Letters from England,* vol. 2 (London: Longman, Hurst, Rees, Orme and Brown, 1814), 47.
15. Demos, *A Little Commonwealth,* 40, 131–32; Gloria Main, *Peoples of a Spacious Land: Families and Cultures in Colonial New England* (Cambridge: Harvard University Press, 2001); Wall, *Fierce Communion.*

16. Ulrich, *Good Wives*, 186–87.
17. There has been a great deal of scholarship on New England women's experience as captives in war. Ulrich's *Good Wives* dedicates much of the closing third section of the book to female captivity; Ann M. Little's rich study *Abraham in Arms* (Philadelphia: University of Pennsylvania Press, 2007) covers gender and female captivity with a nuanced approach. See also Douglass Leach, *Flintlock and Tomahawk: New England in King Philip's War* (New York: Macmillan, 1966); James K. Folsom and Richard Slotkin, *So Dreadfull a Judgment: Puritan Responses to King Philip's War, 1676–1677* (Middletown, CT: Wesleyan University Press, 1978); Annette Kolodny, *The Land Before Her: Fantasy and Experience of the American Frontiers, 1630–1860* (Chapel Hill: University of North Carolina Press, 1984); Russell Bourne, *The Red King's Rebellion: Racial Politics in New England, 1675–1678* (New York: Oxford University Press, 1990); Patrick Malone, *The Skulking Way of War: Technology and Tactics among the New England Indians* (Lanham, MD: Madison Books, 1991); Teresa Toulouse, "'My Own Credit': Strategies of (E)Valuation in Mary Rowlandson's Captivity Narrative," *American Literature* 64, no. 4 (December 1992): 655–76; Lorrayne Carroll, *Rhetorical Drag: Gender, Impersonation, Captivity, and the Writing of History* (Kent: Kent State University Press, 2007); David Stephen and Jeanne T. Heidler, *Daily Lives of Civilians in Wartime Early America: From the Colonial Era to the Civil War* (Westport, CT: Greenwood Publishing Group, 2007); Alden T. Vaughan and Edward W. Clark, *Puritans among the Indians: Accounts of Captivity and Redemption, 1676–1724* (Cambridge: Harvard University Press, 2009).
18. Historians who have explored the impact of the Indian Wars on New England as a whole include Mary Beth Norton in *In the Devil's Snare: The Salem Witchcraft Crisis of 1692* (New York: Knopf, 2002); and Janice Knight in "Telling It Slant: The Testimony of Mercy Short," *Early American Literature* 37, no. 1, "Interiority in Early American Literature" (2002): 36–69; David Corlett in "Forced to Flee for Our Lives: New England Refugees In King Philip's War," paper presented at the Society for Military History annual meeting, February 26, 2005; Leach in *Flintlock and Tomahawk*; and Kyle F. Zelner, *A Rabble in Arms: Massachusetts Towns and Militiamen during King Philip's War* (New York: New York University Press, 2009).
19. Thavolia Glymph, *Out of the House of Bondage: The Transformation of the Plantation Household* (New York: Cambridge University Press, 2008), 28–29.
20. Lois Green Carr and Lorena S. Walsh, "The Planter's Wife: The Experience of White Women in Seventeenth-Century Maryland," *William and Mary Quarterly* 34, 3rd ser. (October 1977): 542, 546, 547–49; Cynthia A. Kiernan, "Women, Gender, Families, and Households in the Southern Colonies," *Journal of Southern History* 73, no. 3 (2007): 644–45.
21. Glymph, *Out of the House of Bondage*, 19, 23–25, 28–31, 33, 36 42, 45.
22. Jane Kamensky, *Governing the Tongue: The Politics of Speech in Early New England* (New York: Oxford University Press, 1999), 6, 10.

23. Davis, "Women on Top," 124–25, 146–49. See also Thompson, "The Moral Economy of the English Crowd," 115–18; Hufton, "Women in the Revolution"; Higgins, "The Reactions of Women," 179–222.
24. Davis, "Women on Top," 130. See Marilyn J. Westerkamp, "Puritan Women, Spiritual Power, and the Question of Sexuality," in *The Religious History of American Women: Reimagining the Past,* ed. Catherine A. Brekus (Chapel Hill: University of North Carolina Press, 2007), 52–54.
25. Norton, *Devil's Snare;* Paul Boyer and Stephen Nissenbaum, *Salem Possessed: The Social Origins of Witchcraft* (Cambridge: Harvard University Press, 1974). The historiography of the Salem witch trials is extensive. For my purposes, some of the most pertinent other works include Carol Karlsen, *The Devil in the Shape of a Woman: Witchcraft in Colonial New England* (New York: Norton, 1987); Reis, *Damned Women*; John Demos, *Entertaining Satan: Witchcraft and the Culture of Early New England* (New York: Oxford University Press, 1982); Richard Godbeer, *The Devil's Dominion: Magic and Religion in Early New England* (New York: Cambridge University Press, 1992); Knight, "Telling It Slant; Peter Charles Hoffer, *The Salem Witchcraft Trials: A Legal History* (Lawrence: University Press of Kansas, 1997); Diane E. Foulds, *Death in Salem: The Private Lives behind the 1692 Witch Hunt* (Guilford, CT: Globe Pequot Press, 2010); Bernard Rosenthal et al., eds., *Records of the Salem Witch-Hunt* (New York: Cambridge University Press, 2009); Marilynne K. Roach, *The Salem Witch Trials: A Day-by-Day Chronicle of a Community under Siege* (Lanham, MD: Taylor Trade Publications, 2004); Margo Burns and Bernard Rosenthal, "Examination of the Records of the Salem Witch Trials," *William and Mary Quarterly* 65, no. 3 (2008): 401–22.
26. Cornelia Hughes Dayton, *Women before the Bar: Gender, Law, and Society in Connecticut, 1639–1789* (Chapel Hill: University of North Carolina Press, 1995), 4–5, 8–9, 10, 12; David Konig, *Law and Society in Puritan Massachusetts: Essex County, 1629–1692* (Chapel Hill: University of North Carolina Press, 1979), chap. 7; G. S. Rowe and Jack D. Marietta, "Personal Violence in a 'Peaceable Kingdom': Pennsylvania, 1682–1801," in *Over the Threshold: Intimate Violence in Early America,* ed. Christine Daniels and Michael Kennedy (New York: Routledge, 1999), 29–30.
27. Kidada Williams, *They Left Great Marks on Me: African American Testimonies of Racial Violence from Emancipation to World War I* (New York: New York University Press, 2012).

Chapter 1: The Limits of Household Violence

1. George Francis Dow, ed., *Records and Files of the Quarterly Courts of Essex Co., Massachusetts,* vols. 1–9 (Salem, 1911–1921), 2:50; "Relation of Elizabeth

Woodbery," Essex County Court File Papers, April 1657, Massachusetts Judicial Archives, vol. 3, 127–1.

2. Dow, *Quarterly Courts of Essex Co.,* vols. 1–9; Records of the Essex County Court, Massachusetts Archives, microfilm reel 0877433, item 1; Records of the General Sessions of the Peace, Massachusetts Archives, microfilm reel 877466; Records of the Massachusetts Court of Assistants, Superior Court of Judicature (after 1686), and the Massachusetts General Court; Christine Daniels and Michael Kennedy, eds., *Over the Threshold: Intimate Violence in Early America* (New York: Routledge, 1999), 4–5; G. S. Rowe and Jack D. Marietta, "Personal Violence in a 'Peaceable Kingdom': Pennsylvania, 1682–1801," in Daniels and Kennedy, *Over the Threshold*, 30.
3. Barry Levy, *Town Born: The Political Economy of New England from Its Founding to the Revolution* (Philadelphia: University of Pennsylvania Press, 2009), 51–52; Peter Charles Hoffer and N. E. H. Hull, *Murdering Mothers: Infanticide in England and New England, 1558–1803* (New York: New York University Press, 1981), 35.
4. Laurel Thatcher Ulrich, *Good Wives: Image and Reality in the Lives of Women in Northern New England, 1650–1750* (New York: Vintage Books, 1991), 3; Elizabeth Pleck, *Domestic Tyranny: The Making of American Social Policy against Family Violence from Colonial Times to the Present* (New York: Oxford University Press, 1987), 18.
5. W. Henry Whitmore, ed., *The Colonial Laws of Massachusetts . . . Together with the Body of Liberties of 1641* (Boston: Rockwell and Churchill, City Printers, 1890), 31; David H. Flaherty, ed., *Essays in the History of Early American Law* (Chapel Hill: University of North Carolina Press, 1969); C. Dallett Hemphill, "Women in Court: Sex-Role Differentiation in Salem, Massachusetts, 1636 to 1683," *William and Mary Quarterly*, 3rd ser., 39 (1982): 164–75.
6. Dow, *Quarterly Courts of Essex Co.,* vols. 1–9; Records of the Essex County Court, Massachusetts Archives; Records of the Massachusetts Court of Assistants; Superior Court of Judicature (after 1686); Records of the Massachusetts General Court.
7. Daniels and Kennedy, *Over the Threshold,* 9; John Demos, *A Little Commonwealth: Family Life in Plymouth Colony* (1970; New York: Oxford University Press, 2000), 184; Gloria Main, *Peoples of a Spacious Land: Families and Cultures in Colonial New England* (Cambridge: Harvard University Press, 2001), 165; Garthine Walker, *Crime, Gender and Social Order in Early Modern England* (Cambridge: Cambridge University Press, 2003), 77; Ulrich, *Good Wives,* 36, 38.
8. Dow, *Quarterly Courts of Essex Co.,* vols. 1–9; Records of the Essex County Court, Massachusetts Archives, microfilm reel 0877433, item 1; Records of the General Sessions of the Peace, Massachusetts Archives, microfilm reel 877466.
9. Susan D. Amussen, "Punishment, Discipline and Power: The Social Meanings of Violence in Early Modern England," *Journal of British Studies* 34, no. 1 (January 1995): 13–14; See Rowe and Marietta, "Personal Violence," 29–30; Jon Pahl, *Empire of Sacrifice: The Religious Origins of American Violence* (New York:

New York University Press, 2010), 18; Konig, *Law and Society in Puritan Massachusetts*; Peter Charles Hoffer, *Law and People in Colonial America* (Baltimore: Johns Hopkins University Press, 1992).

10. Demos, *Little Commonwealth;* Main, *Peoples of a Spacious Land*; Ulrich, *Good Wives*; Mary Beth Norton, *Founding Mothers & Fathers: Gendered Power and the Forming of American Society* (New York: Alfred A. Knopf, 1996), 73–74; Helena Wall, *Fierce Communion: Family and Community in Early America* (State College: Pennsylvania State University Press, 1990); Ann Marie Plane, *Colonial Intimacies: Indian Marriage in Early New England* (Ithaca: Cornell University Press, 2000); Whitmore, *The Colonial Laws of Massachusetts*, 31; David H. Flaherty, ed., *Essays in the History of Early American Law* (Chapel Hill: University of North Carolina Press, 1969); Hemphill, "Women in Court," 164–75; Amussen, "Punishment, Discipline and Power," 18; Dow, *Quarterly Courts of Essex Co.*, 2:344, 431, 4:108, 280–82, 8:101–2.
11. Randolph A. Roth, "Spousal Murder in Northern New England, 1776–1865," in Daniels and Kennedy, *Over the Threshold,* 75; Pleck, *Domestic Tyranny*, 23, 24.
12. See Wall, *Fierce Communion,* 8, 81; Pleck, *Domestic Tyranny,* 31, 8.
13. Dow, *Quarterly Courts of Essex Co.*, 8:272–73.
14. Dow, *Quarterly Courts of Essex Co.*, 8:104–5.
15. William Perkins, "*Christian Oeconomie. Or a short survey on the right manner of ordering a familie, according to the Scriptures*," in *The Works of William Perkins*, ed. Ian Breward (Appleford, England: Sutton Courtenay Press, 1970), 429; Ulrich, *Good Wives*, 36–38; John Winthrop, "History of New England, 1630–1649," ed. James Kendall Hosmer (New York: C. Scribner Sons, 1908), 239; Benjamin Wadsworth, *The Well-Ordered Family* (Boston: B. Green, 1712), 25, 36.
16. William Secker, *A wedding ring for the finger; the salve of divinity, on the sore of humanity* (1690), 67–72.
17. Dow, *Quarterly Courts of Essex Co.*, 1:136; Essex County Court Papers, WPA transcription, "Deposition of Jabish Hackett, November 1647," 1–97–1; Dow, *Quarterly Courts of Essex Co.*, 1:184.
18. Essex County Quarterly Court File Papers, June 1674, Massachusetts Judicial Archives, vol. 22, 31–1; Dow, *Quarterly Courts of Essex Co.*, 6:193; Essex County Court Papers, WPA transcription, "Depositions of John & Jone Baker, June 1676," 25:89–2; Dow, *Quarterly Courts of Essex Co.*, 8:59–60; "Pudeator, Ann," in *The Salem Witchcraft Papers*, vol. 3, ed. Paul Boyer and Stephen Nissenbaum (New York: Da Capo Press, 1977), 701; Carol Karlsen, *The Devil in the Shape of a Woman: Witchcraft in Colonial New England* (New York: Norton, 1987), 129, 130, 142.
19. "A Coppie of the Liberties of Massachusets Colonie in New England," in *Collections of Massachusetts Historical Society,* ser. 3, 8 (1843): 299; Nathaniel B. Shurtleff, ed., *Records of the Governor and Company of the Massachusetts Bay*, vol. 3 (Boston: W. White, 1853–54), 212; Lyle Koehler, *A Search for Power: The "Weaker Sex" in Seventeenth-Century New England* (Urbana: University of Illinois Press, 1980), 49.

20. Thomas Platter, *Travels in England, 1599,* trans. Clare Williams (London: Jonathan Cape, 1937), 182; Susan Dwyer Amussen, *An Ordered Society: Gender and Class in Early Modern England* (Oxford: B. Blackwell, 1988), 50, 103; Amussen, "Punishment, Discipline and Power," 9; Natalie Zemon Davis, *Society and Culture in Early Modern France* (Stanford: Stanford University Press, 1975), 136, 140.
21. Hemphill, "Women in Court," 173; Norton, *Founding Mothers & Fathers,* 78.
22. Dow, *Quarterly Courts of Essex Co.,* 1:25; W. B. Trask, ed., *The New England Historical and Genealogical Register,* vol. 21 (Boston: Samuel G. Drake, 1867), 256; Dow, *Quarterly Courts of Essex Co.,* 1:25.
23. Pleck, *Domestic Tyranny,* 26; David Hackett Fischer, *Albion's Seed: Four British Folkways in America* (New York: Oxford University Press, 1989), xxiii; Hoffer, *Law and People,* 52; "Massachusetts Laws and Liberties of 1648," in Whitmore, *The Colonial Laws of Massachusetts,* 6.
24. Demos, *Little Commonwealth,* 97; Karlsen, *Devil in the Shape of a Woman,* 168–69.
25. Norton, *Founding Mothers & Fathers,* 27; Dow, *Quarterly Courts of Essex Co.,* 1:133, 135, 136, 138, 156, 173, 174, 194, 198, 254, 271, 298, 304, 305, 414, 424, 425; John Bezis-Selfa, *Forging America: Ironworkers, Adventurers, and the Industrious Revolution* (Ithaca: Cornell University Press, 2004), 56; Alanzo Lewis, *History of Lynn, Essex County, Massachusetts,* vol. 1 (Boston: Shorey, 1865), 225.
26. Fischer, *Albion's Seed,* xxiii.
27. Dow, *Quarterly Courts of Essex Co.,* 5:146; Fischer, *Albion's Seed,* xxiii; Essex County Court Records, March 25, 1673, entry 67, Massachusetts Archives, microfilm reel 877462.
28. Dow, *Quarterly Courts of Essex Co.,* 8:101–2.
29. Hoffer, *Law and People,* 46; Lawrence Stone, *The Family, Sex and Marriage in England, 1500–1800* (London: Weidenfeld & Nicolson, 1977), 284; Philip Greven, *The Protestant Temperament: Patterns in Child-Rearing, Religious Experience, and the Self in Early America* (Chicago: University of Chicago Press, 1988), 35–37; Main, *Peoples of a Spacious Land*; Wall, *Fierce Communion;* Cotton Mather, *Help for Distressed Parents* (Boston: John Allen, 1695), 28; Demos, *A Little Commonwealth,* 134–37; Koehler, *A Search for Power,* 13; Norton, *Founding Mothers & Fathers,* 119.
30. Demos, *A Little Commonwealth,* 134–37; Greven, *The Protestant Temperament,* 35–37; *The Works of Anne Bradstreet,* ed. Jeannine Hensley (Cambridge, MA: The Belknap Press of Harvard University Press, 1967), 285.
31. Norton, *Founding Mothers & Fathers,* 119.
32. Pleck, *Domestic Tyranny,* 27; Dow, *Quarterly Courts of Essex Co.,* 6:141; Kenneth Davis, *America's Hidden History: Untold Tales of the First Pilgrims, Fighting Women, and Forgotten Founders Who Shaped a Nation* (New York: HarperCollins, 2008), 50; Charles Henry Pope, *The Haverhill Emersons* (Boston: Murray and Emery Company, 1913), 15.
33. *The Journal of John Winthrop,* ed. Richard S. Dunn, James Savage, and Laetitia Yeandle (Cambridge: Belknap Press, 1996), 229–30, August 5, 1637, 391–92, and

May 1642; John Noble and John Cronin, *Records of the Court of Assistants of the Colony of the Massachusetts Bay, 1630–1692*, 3 vols. (Boston: County of Suffolk, 1901–1928), 2:126; Hoffer, *Law and People*, 41; Dow, *Quarterly Courts of Essex Co.*, 1:130.

34. Dow, *Quarterly Courts of Essex Co.*, 1:174, 147.
35. Dow, *Quarterly Courts of Essex Co.*, 1:257; Norton, *Founding Mothers & Fathers*, 48; Dow, *Quarterly Courts of Essex Co.*, 2:39; Franklin B. Dexter, ed., *Ancient Town Records: New Haven Town Records, 1649–1684*, 2 vols. (New Haven: New Haven Colony Historical Society, 1917, 1919), 2:222–23.
36. Dow, *Quarterly Courts of Essex Co.*, 5:306; Samuel Eliot Morison, ed., *Records of the Suffolk County Court, 1671–1680* (Boston: Colonial Society of Massachusetts, 1933), 478–79.
37. Wall, *Fierce Communion*, 2, 8, 11, 12.
38. "Deposition of Mary Sollas," March 1674, Essex County Court Papers, WPA transcription, vol. 31, 35–1; "Deposition of Hana Gray," March 1674, vol. 31, 35–2; "Deposition of Freeborne Black," March 1674, vol. 21, 36–1; Dow, *Quarterly Courts of Essex Co.*, 5:291, 7:46–55.
39. Dow, *Quarterly Courts of Essex Co.*, 3:143, 4:179.
40. Wall, *Fierce Communion*, 8, 9, 94–96; Dexter, *New Haven Town Records*, vol. 2; Shurtleff, *Records of Massachusetts*, vol. 4.
41. Dow, *Quarterly Courts of Essex Co.*, 1:123.
42. "Statement of Thomas Jones against Elner Jackson," September 1660, Massachusetts Judicial Archives, Essex County Court File Papers, vol. 6, 69–1, 2; Dow, *Quarterly Courts of Essex Co.*, 2:249; "Deposition by William Vinsoon," 1680, Essex County Court Papers, WPA transcription, vol. 6, 68–2; Dow, *Quarterly Courts of Essex Co.*, 3:273–74; "The Deposition of Martha Coye," September 1665, Essex County Court Papers, WPA transcription, vol. 11, 12–3, 4; "Depositions of Martha Coye and Richard Coye," Essex County Court Papers, WPA transcription, September 1665, vol. 11, 13–1.
43. Rowe and Marietta, "Personal Violence," 30–31; Roger Thompson, *Sex in Middlesex: Popular Mores in a Massachusetts County, 1649–1699* (Amherst: University of Massachusetts Press, 1986), 170, 186.
44. John Demos, "Developmental Perspectives on the History of Childhood," *Journal of Interdisciplinary History* 2, no. 2, "The History of the Family" (Autumn 1971): 322.
45. Mary Beth Norton, "The Evolution of White Women's Experience in Early America," *American Historical Review* 89, no. 3 (1984): 593–619; Walker, *Crime, Gender and Social Order*, 77.
46. Dow, *Quarterly Courts of Essex Co.*, 2:100–101, 10; Essex County Court Records, September 1656, Massachusetts Judicial Archives, vol. 38, entry 38.
47. Dow, *Quarterly Courts of Essex Co.*, 3:414; "Testimony of Richard and Mary Downing," June 7, 1667, Essex County Court Papers, WPA transcription, vol. 12, 88–1; "Arrest Order against [Mi]gilligan and Wife," June 7, 1667, vol. 12, 87–2;

Dow, *Quarterly Courts of Essex Co.*, 3:420; "Testimony of Frances Gilliginn," June 1667, Essex County Court Papers, WPA transcription, vol. 12, 89–4; Dow, *Quarterly Courts of Essex Co.*, 3:443.

48. Dow, *Quarterly Courts of Essex Co.*, 5:215–16.
49. Dow, *Quarterly Courts of Essex Co.*, 5:306–7; Essex County Court File Papers, Massachusetts Judicial Archive, vol. 21, 41–44; "Deposition of Thomas Waite," May 1674, vol. 21, 43–1; vol. 21, 53.
50. Jane Kamensky, *Governing the Tongue: The Politics of Speech in Early New England* (New York: Oxford University Press, 1999), 4, 6–7, 15; William Hubbard, *Benefit of a Well-Ordered Conversation* (Boston, 1684), 45; Whitmore, *The Colonial Laws of Massachusetts*, 49, 35; Cotton Mather, *Ornaments of the Daughters of Zion* (Boston, 1692), 49.
51. Essex County Court Record Books, September 1656, Massachusetts Judicial Archives, vol. 4, entry 30; Dow, *Quarterly Courts of Essex Co.*, 2:10, 6:54, 8:14.
52. "Testimony of Hanah Merrek, wife of James, and Hanah Merek, his sister," March 1682, Essex County Court File Papers, Massachusetts Judicial Archives, vol. 37, 47–1; Dow, *Quarterly Courts of Essex Co.*, 8:260, 262; "Petition of John Atkinson," September 26, 1682, Essex County Court File Papers, Massachusetts Judicial Archives, vol. 38, 86–1; "Petition of Sarah Atkinson," April 10, 1683, vol. 39, 65–1.
53. Daniels and Kennedy, *Over the Threshold*, 9, 30; Pleck, *Domestic Tyranny*, 8–9; Norton, *Founding Mothers & Fathers*, 100–101, 116; Dow, *Quarterly Courts of Essex Co.*, 3:224; Pleck, *Domestic Tyranny*, 28; Cotton Mather, *A Good Master well Served* (Boston, 1696).
54. Pleck, *Domestic Tyranny*, 8–9, 22; Whitmore, *The Colonial Laws of Massachusetts*, 30, 105. Hoffer, *Law and People*, 46; Amussen, *An Ordered Society*, 90, 96.
55. Ulrich, *Good Wives*, 35–50; Main, *Peoples of a Spacious Land*, 69; Linda Kerber, "Separate Spheres, Female Worlds, Woman's Place: The Rhetoric of Women's History," *Journal of American History* 75, no. 1 (1988): 9–39.
56. Dow, *Quarterly Courts of Essex Co.*, 1:133, 2:62, 63, 104, 134, 356, 3:376, 143, 4:200, 5:291, 7:46–55, 334, 8:347–48, 9:145.
57. Daniels and Kennedy, *Over the Threshold*, 25; Pahl, *Empire of Sacrifice*, 18.
58. Dow, *Quarterly Courts of Essex Co.*, 8:223–26.
59. Dow, *Quarterly Courts of Essex Co.*, 6:340.
60. Dow, *Quarterly Courts of Essex Co.*, 8:91–92.
61. Dow, *Quarterly Courts of Essex Co.*, 7:421–22; Henry Fritz-Gilbert, *The New England Historical Genealogical Register*, vol. 42 (1888; New England Historic Genealogical Register, Heritage Books, 1996), 363.
62. Dow, *Quarterly Courts of Essex Co.*, 8:295, 5:293.
63. Dow, *Quarterly Courts of Essex Co.*, 7:147–49; Marilynne K. Roach, *The Salem Witch Trials: A Day-by-Day Chronicle of a Community under Siege* (New York: Taylor Trade Publications, 2004), 296.
64. Pleck, *Domestic Tyranny*, 28; Dow, *Quarterly Courts of Essex Co.*, 8:302–3.

65. "Deposition of Esther Bishop," March 1682, Essex County Court File Papers, Massachusetts Judicial Archives, vol. 37, 113–1; Dow, *Quarterly Courts of Essex Co.,* 8:315–16.
66. "Deposition of Anthony Day," September 1660, Essex County Court Papers, WPA transcription, vol. 6, 61–1; "Testimony of Zacheus Curtis," September 1660, vol. 6, 17–1; Dow, *Quarterly Courts of Essex Co.,* 2:238; Rebecca Tannenbaum, *Healers Calling: Women and Medicine in Early New England* (Ithaca: Cornell University Press, 2002), 98; "Complaint against John Pierce, Constable," September 1660, Essex County Court Papers, WPA transcription, vol. 6, 49–1, 2, 50–2/3; Dow, *Quarterly Courts of Essex Co.,* 2:237–38.
67. Norton, *Founding Mothers & Fathers,* 116.
68. Dow, *Quarterly Courts of Essex Co.,* 3:378, 8:411.
69. Dow, *Quarterly Courts of Essex Co.,* 3:224, 225; Essex County Court Papers, WPA transcription, vol. 10, 79, 81–1.

Chapter 2: From "that wicked house"

1. "Case of Elizabeth Emmerson," indictment, September 25, 1691, Massachusetts Archives, Suffolk Files, vol. 31, case 2636; "Examination of Hannah, the wife of Michael Emerson," May 11, 1691, 31:2636; "Examination of Michael Emerson," May 11, 1691, 31:2636; "Examination of Elizabeth Emerson," May 11, 1691, 31:2636; "Examination of Elizabeth Emerson #2," September 25, 1691, 31:2636; "June 8, 1693. Elizabeth Emerson was executed . . . for the murder of [her] children." Massachusetts Archive, Felt Collection, 40:279.
2. "Deposition of Johanah Hasteline, Johanah Corlis, Lidia Lad & Mary Neff," April 19, 1686, Essex County Court Papers, Salem, 46:131; Records of the Court of Common Pleas, Essex County, Massachusetts Archives, microfilm reel 877465, 84; Essex County Quarterly Court File Papers, Massachusetts Judicial Archives, 47:3–4, 104; George Francis Dow, ed., *Records and Files of the Quarterly Courts of Essex Co., Massachusetts,* vols. 1–9 (Salem, 1911–1921), 603.
3. Else Hambleton, *Daughters of Eve: Pregnant Brides and Unwed Mothers in Seventeenth-Century Massachusetts* (New York: Routledge, 2004), xv, xiv, 24, 58, 63, 113; Laura Henigman, *Coming into Communion: Pastoral Dialogues in Colonial New England* (Albany: State University of New York Press, 1999), 57; Nina Dayton, "Taking the Trade: Abortion and Gender Relations in an Eighteenth-Century New England Village," in *Sexual Borderlands: Constructing an American Sexual Past,* ed. Kathleen Kennedy and Sharon Rena Ullman (Columbus: Ohio State University Press, 2003), 52; Hambleton, *Daughters of Eve,* 24.
4. Peter Charles Hoffer and N. E. H. Hull, *Murdering Mothers: Infanticide in England and New England, 1558–1803* (New York: New York University Press, 1981), 13; 21 James I, c. 27 (1624).
5. *The Charter Granted by Their Majesties King William and Queen Mary to the Inhabitants of the Province of Massachusetts-Bay in New-England* (1691; Boston:

Printed by S. Kneeland, 1759), chap. 4, 67; G. S. Rowe and Jack D. Marietta, "Personal Violence in a 'Peaceable Kingdom': Pennsylvania, 1682–1801," in *Over the Threshold: Intimate Violence in Early America*, ed. Christine Daniels and Michael Kennedy (New York: Routledge, 1999), 42; John Acevedo, "Harsh Mercy: Criminal Law in Seventeenth-Century Massachusetts Bay" (PhD diss., University of Chicago, 2013), 17–22; Hoffer and Hull, *Murdering Mothers*, 33, 49; Henigman, *Coming into Communion*, 59; Cotton Mather, *Warnings from the Dead* (Boston, 1693), 69.

6. Laurel Thatcher Ulrich, *Good Wives: Image and Reality in the Lives of Women in Northern New England, 1650–1750* (New York: Vintage Books, 1991), 186, 196. See also G. S. Rowe, "Infanticide, Its Judicial Resolution, and Criminal Code Revision in Early Pennsylvania," *American Philosophical Society* 135, no. 2 (June 1991): 200; Hoffer and Hull, *Murdering Mothers*, 49; Lyle Koehler, *Search for Power: The "Weaker Sex" in Seventeenth-Century New England* (Urbana: University of Illinois Press, 1980), 52–54, 55, 56, 59–60; Sharon M. Harris, *Executing Race: Early American Women's Narratives of Race, Society, and the Law* (Columbus: Ohio State University Press, 2005), 32–36; David B. Baker, *Women and Capital Punishment in the United States: An Analytical History* (Jefferson, NC: McFarland & Co., 2015), 91.
7. Abram Van Engen, *Sympathetic Puritans: Calvinist Fellow Feeling in Early New England* (New York: Oxford University Press, 2015), 20; Martha Saxton, *Being Good: Women's Moral Values in Early America* (New York: Hill and Wang, 2004), 86.
8. John Demos, *A Little Commonwealth: Family Life in Plymouth Colony* (1970; New York: Oxford University Press, 2000), 46–48; Abby Chandler, "At the Magistrate's Discretion: Sexual Crime and New England Law, 1636–1718" (PhD diss., University of Maine, 2008), 17. See also Helena Wall, *Fierce Communion: Family and Community in Early America* (State College: Pennsylvania State University Press, 1990; Dow, *Quarterly Courts of Essex Co.*, vols. 1–9.
9. Chandler, "At the Magistrate's Discretion," 34; Roger Thompson, *Sex in Middlesex: Popular Mores in a Massachusetts County, 1649–1699* (Amherst: University of Massachusetts Press, 1986).
10. Hambleton, *Daughters of Eve*, 91.
11. Dow, *Quarterly Courts of Essex Co.*, vols. 1–9; Records of the Essex County Court, Massachusetts Archives; Records of the General Sessions of the Peace, Massachusetts Archives; Records of the Essex County Court, Massachusetts Archives, file record 22–68–3; "Testimony of Hester Jackson," 1662, Suffolk County Quarterly Court, Supreme Judicial Court, Division of Archives and Records Preservation.
12. Mather, *Warnings*, 42; *The Diary of Samuel Sewall, 1674–1729*, ed. M. Halsey Thomas (New York: Farrar, Straus and Giroux, 1973), 155; Kenneth Silverman, *The Life and Times of Cotton Mather* (New York: Harper & Row, 1985), 308.
13. Thompson, *Sex in Middlesex*,104; Hambleton, *Daughters of Eve*, 70. See Mary Beth Norton, *Founding Mothers & Fathers: Gendered Power and the Forming of American Society* (New York: Alfred A. Knopf, 1996); Henigman, *Coming into*

Communion, 57. See also Daniel S. Scott and Michael S. Hindus, "Premarital Pregnancy in America, 1640–1971: An Overview and Interpretation," *Journal of Interdisciplinary History* 4 (Spring 1975): 554; Edward Elliot, *Power and the Pulpit in Puritan New England* (Princeton: Princeton University Press, 2015), 36; Acevedo, "Harsh Mercy," 199.

14. Chandler, "At the Magistrate's Discretion," 38.
15. Hambleton, *Daughters of Eve,* 163n8; John Noble and John Cronin, *Records of the Court of Assistants of the Colony of the Massachusetts Bay, 1630–1692*, vols. 1–3 (Boston: County of Suffolk, 1901–1928); Dow, *Quarterly Courts of Essex Co.,* vols. 1–9; Chandler, "At the Magistrate's Discretion," 38; Hambleton, *Daughters of Eve*, xiii, xiv, xv; Acevedo, "Harsh Mercy," 24, 33, 49, 197.
16. Dow, *Quarterly Courts of Essex Co.,* 1:337; Hambleton, *Daughters of Eve*, 24, 25, 33.
17. Dow, *Quarterly Courts of Essex Co.,* 2:151.
18. Dow, *Quarterly Courts of Essex Co.,* 2:152, 372–73.
19. Acevedo, "Harsh Mercy," 155, 198, 199.
20. Hoffer and Hull, *Murdering Mothers;* Laurel Thatcher Ulrich, *A Midwife's Tale: The Life of Martha Ballard, Based on Her Diary, 1785–1812* (New York: Vintage Books, 1990), 149; Chandler, "At the Magistrate's Discretion," 58.
21. Dow, *Quarterly Courts of Essex Co.,* 1:71; Noble and Cronin, *Records of Court of Assistants*, 2:137.
22. Paul Donald Marsella, "The Trial and Execution of Elizabeth Atwood in 1720," *Sextant* 7, no. 2 (1997): 9–10.
23. See Jane Kamensky, *Governing the Tongue: The Politics of Speech in Early New England* (New York: Oxford University Press, 1999); Marsella, "Trial and Execution of Elizabeth Atwood," 10.
24. Thompson, *Sex in Middlesex;* Daniel E. Williams, *Pillars of Salt: An Anthology of Early American Criminal Narratives* (Madison, WI: Madison House Publications, 1993), 88; Judith S. Graham, *Puritan Family Life: The Diary of Samuel Sewall* (Boston: Northeastern University Press, 2000), 56.
25. John Rogers, *Death the Certain Wages of Sin* (Boston: G. Green and J. Allen for Samuel Philips, 1701), 122, 124; Allen Hearn, *Legal Executions in New England: A Comprehensive Reference, 1623–1960* (Jefferson, NC: McFarland & Co., 1999), 107.
26. Rogers, *Wages of Sin,* 98, 121, 123; Henigman, *Coming into Communion,* 49.
27. Hoffer and Hull, *Murdering Mothers,* 52; *The General Laws and Liberties of the Massachusetts Bay* (1648), 6.
28. N. E. H. Hull, *Female Felons: Women and Serious Crime in Colonial Massachusetts* (Urbana: University of Illinois Press, 1987), 31; Noble, *Criminal Trials*, 13.
29. David Hackett Fischer, *Albion's Seed: Four British Folkways in America* (New York: Oxford University Press, 1989), 194; Noble, *Criminal Trials,* 11; Noble and Cronin, *Records of Court of Assistants*, 1:70, 114, 115, 234, 240.
30. Noble and Cronin, *Records of Court of Assistants,* 1:71, 252–53.

31. Hambleton, *Daughters of Eve,* 115; Edgar J. McManus, *Law and Liberty in Early New England: Criminal Justice and Due Process, 1620–1692* (Amherst: University of Massachusetts Press, 1993), 142; Dow, *Quarterly Courts of Essex Co.,* 4:269.
32. Dow, *Quarterly Courts of Essex Co.,* 5:143–46.
33. Hearn, *Legal Executions in New England,* 105; Cotton Mather, "Pillars of Salt," in Williams, *Pillars of Salt,* 88.
34. John Williams, *Warnings to the Unclean* (1699), 21; Henigman, *Coming into Communion,* 74; Saxton, *Being Good,* 89.
35. Nan Goodman, *Banished: Common Law and the Rhetoric of Social Exclusion in Early New England* (Philadelphia: University of Pennsylvania Press, 2016); Carolyn B. Ramsey, "Sex and Social Order: The Selective Enforcement of Colonial American Adultery Laws in the English Context," *Yale Journal of Law & the Humanities* 10, no. 1 (January 1998): 208n111, 225.
36. Noble and Cronin, *Records of Court of Assistants,* 2:66, 67, 70, 108; Nathaniel B. Shurtleff, *Records of the Governor and Company of the Massachusetts Bay in New England,* vol. 1 (Boston: William White, 1853), 198.
37. Noble and Cronin, *Records of Court of Assistants,* 1:10.
38. Norton, *Founding Mothers & Fathers,* 27–38; *Ancient Town Records: New Haven Town Records, 1649–1684,* vol. 2, ed. Franklin B. Dexter (1917; New Haven: New Haven Colony Historical Society, 1919), 215; "Examination of Ruth Briggs and other witnesses," February 21–March 4, 1667/8, *Crimes and Misdemeanors,* ser. i, I, doc. 32, Connecticut Archives, Connecticut State Library, Hartford, cited in Norton, *Founding Mothers & Fathers,* 420n16; Hearn, *Legal Execution in New England,* 44; "Bradstreet's Journal, 1664–83," *New England Historical and Genealogical Register* 9 (1855): 44.
39. Hearn, *Legal Execution in New England,* 44; Norton, *Founding Mothers & Fathers,* 37.
40. Chandler, "At the Magistrate's Discretion," 65.
41. Ellen Fitzpatrick, "Childbirth and an Unwed Mother in Seventeenth-Century New England," *Signs* 8, no. 4 (Summer 1983): 747; Graham, *Puritan Family Life,* 56; Hambleton, *Daughters of Eve,* 7.
42. Dow, *Quarterly Courts of Essex Co.,* 4:129.
43. Hambleton, *Daughters of Eve,* xiv, xvii, 19; Elliot, *Power and the Pulpit,* 37.
44. Dow, *Quarterly Courts of Essex Co.,* 2:152, 372, 9:451.
45. Hambleton, *Daughters of Eve,* xi; Suffolk County Quarterly Court, 1662, Supreme Judicial Court, Division of Archives and Records Preservation, 874; Chandler, "At the Magistrate's Discretion," 9.
46. Hambleton, *Daughters of Eve,* 45, 90. See James M. Volo and Dorothy Denneen Volo, *Family Life in 17th- and 18th-Century America* (Santa Barbara, CA: Greenwood Publishing Group 2006), 41–42; Edmund Morgan, *The Puritan Family: Religion and Domestic Relations in Seventeenth-Century New England* (New York: Harper & Row, 1966), 150–60; Philip Greven, *The Protestant Temperament:*

Patterns in Child-Rearing, Religious Experience, and the Self in Early America (Chicago: University of Chicago Press, 1988); Sylvia R. Frey and Marian J. Morton, *New World, New Roles: A Documentary History of Women in Pre-Industrial America* (Santa Barbara, CA: Greenwood Publishing Group, 1986); John F. Woolverton, *Colonial Anglicanism in North America* (Detroit: Wayne State University Press, 1984), 57; Marsha L. Hamilton, *Social and Economic Networks in Early Massachusetts: Atlantic Connections* (University Park: Pennsylvania State University Press, 2009).

47. Noble and Cronin, *Records of Court of Assistants,* 2:137; Hambleton, *Daughters of Eve*, 30.
48. Dow, *Quarterly Courts of Essex Co.*, 1:337; George Chandler, *The Chandler Family, The Descendants of William and Annis Chandler who settled in Roxbury, 1637* (Worcester, MA: Press of Charles Hamilton, 1885); "Statements from John Russ and Abigail Osgood," March 31, 1691, Essex County Quarterly Court; Chandler, "At the Magistrate's Discretion," 34, 49.
49. Sewall, *The Diary of Samuel Sewall,* 151, 399; Mather, *Pillars of Salt*, 89; Hearn, *Legal Executions in New England*, 106.
50. Chandler, "At the Magistrate's Discretion," 53, 54. See also Anne S. Lombard, *Making Manhood: Growing Up Male in Colonial New England* (Cambridge: Harvard University Press, 2003), 68; John Ruston Pagan, *Anne Orthwood's Bastard: Sex and Law in Early Virginia* (New York: Oxford University Press, 2003), 4.
51. Chandler, "At the Magistrate's Discretion," 29, 32, 43–44, 53, 65.
52. "Deposition of William Osgood," May 31, 1687, Essex County Court of General Sessions, File Papers, box 2, Phillips Library, Peabody Essex Museum, Salem; "Deposition of Mary Whittier," May 31, 1687, Essex General Sessions, box 2, Phillips Library; Chandler, "At the Magistrate's Discretion," 61; Clarence Almon Torrey and Elizabeth Petty Bentley, *New England Marriages Prior to 1700* (Baltimore: Genealogical Publishing Company, 1985), 280.
53. "Testimony of Joseph Andrews," 1707, General Sessions of the Peace Papers, box 3, Phillips Library; "Deposition of Jane Andrews," November 25, 1707, box 3, Phillips Library; "Deposition of Joseph Andrews," November 25, 1707, box 3, Phillips Library.
54. E. O. Jameson, *Choats of America* (Boston: Alfred Mudge & Sons Printers, 1896); Chandler, "At the Magistrate's Discretion," 53; *Proctor v. Choat*, Essex General Sessions of the Peace, July 1705, File Papers box 3, Phillips Library.
55. John D'Emilio and Estelle B. Freedman, *Intimate Matters: A History of Sexuality in America*, 3rd ed. (Chicago: University of Chicago Press, 2012), 17; William Burns, *Science and Technology in Colonial America* (Santa Barbara, CA: Greenwood Publishing Group, 2005), 68.
56. Marsella, "Trial and Execution of Elizabeth Atwood," 10; Randolph Roth, "Child Murder in New England," *Social Science History* 25, no. 1 (Spring 2001): 102.

57. "Indictment of Susanna Andrews," Massachusetts Archives, Suffolk Files, 37:3279; "Deposition of John Andrews," 37:3279; "Indictment," 37:3279.
58. "Examination of Michael Emerson," May 11, 1691, Massachusetts Archives, Suffolk Files, 31:2636; "Examination of Hannah, the wife of Michael Emerson," May 11, 1691, 31:2636; "Witness testimony #2—Hanna Swan; Mary Neff," May 11, 1691, 31:2636; "Examination of Elizabeth Emerson," May 11, 1691, 31:2636; "Examination of M. & H. Emerson," 31:2636; "Witness testimony #2—Hanna Swan; Mary Neff," 31:2636.
59. "Deposition by Johanah Hasteltine, Johanah Corlis, Lidia Lad & Mary Neff," April 19, 1686, Essex County Court Papers, 46:131.
60. Hambleton, *Daughters of Eve,* 18; Henigman, *Coming into Communion*, 66.
61. "Testimony of Elizabeth Dressor," Massachusetts Archives, Suffolk Files, 131:14363; "Testimony of Elizabeth Jewitt," 131:14363.
62. "Testimony of Elizabeth Jewitt," Massachusetts Archives, Suffolk Files, 131:14363; "Examination of John West Wife," February 24, 1719, 131:14363; Hearn, *Legal Executions in New England,* 116; Robert Wilhelm, *Murder and Mayhem in Essex County* (Charleston, SC: History Press, 2011), 29; "Testimony of Elizabeth Holden," 131:14363.
63. Chandler, "At the Magistrate's Discretion," 8; Fischer, *Albion's Seed,* 70.
64. *Munn's Case,* May 5–19, 1699, Records of the Court of Assistants and Superior Courts, 1687–1749, vol. 53, Early General Records of Connecticut, Connecticut State Library, 291–93; "Prosecution Summation for Munn Case," *Crimes and Misdemeanors*, 1:223, Connecticut Archives, Connecticut State Library; Edgar J. McManus, *Law and Liberty in Early New England: Criminal Justice and Due Process, 1620–1692* (Amherst: University of Massachusetts Press, 2009), 155; Hoffer and Hull, *Murdering Mothers*, 62.
65. "Deposition of Hannah French," Massachusetts Archives, Suffolk Files, 19:123; "Deposition of Sarah Pratt," no. 1689, 19:123; "Deposition of Hannah Whitmarsh," 19:123–24; Noble and Cronin, *Records of Court of Assistants,* 1:115.
66. *In re Parker,* General Court, Boston, June 12, 1663, Massachusetts Archives, Suffolk Files, 4:532; Melinde Lutz Sanborn, "The Case of the Headless Baby: Did Interracial Sex in the Massachusetts Bay Colony Lead to Infanticide and the Earliest Habeas Corpus Petition in America?" *Hofstra Law Review* 38, no. 1 (2009): 258; Michelle M. Jarrett Morris, *Under Household Government: Sex and Family in Puritan Massachusetts* (Cambridge: Harvard University Press, 2013), 203.
67. "Deposition of Besse Angolas," October 4, 1663, Massachusetts Archives, Suffolk Files, 5:605; "Deposition of Mary Negro, wife of Franck Negro," October 4, 1663, 5:605; "Deposition of Elizabeth Mellows, servant to Parkers," October 4, 1663, 5:605.
68. "Deposition of Zipporah," October 4, 1663, Massachusetts Archives, Suffolk Files, 5:605; "Deposition of Mrs. Sands," October 4, 1663, 5:605; Morris, *Under Household Government,* 197.

69. "Deposition of Mrs. Parker," October 5, 1663, Massachusetts Archives, Suffolk Files, 5:605; "Jury Verdict Regarding the Inquest in the Matter of Zipporah," October 5, 1663, 5:605; Morris, *Under Household Government,* 199, 207; Richard D. Pierce, ed., *The Records of the First Church of Boston, 1630–1868* (Boston: Publication of the Colonial Society of Mass, 1961), 39.
70. Mather, *Pillars of Salt.*
71. Mather, *Warnings,* 56–57, 54; Henigman, *Coming into Communion,* 57; Kathleen Brown, "Murderous Uncleanness: The Body of Female Infanticide in Puritan New England," in *A Centre of Wonders: The Body in Early America,* ed. Janet Moore Lindman and Michele Lise Tartar (Ithaca: Cornell University Press, 2001), 78.

Chapter 3: Almost Inconceivable Foes

1. David Stephen Heidler and Jeanne T. Heidler, *Daily Lives of Civilians in Wartime Early America: From the Colonial Era to the Civil War* (Santa Barbara, CA: Greenwood Publishing Group, 2007), 13; James K. Folsom and Richard Slotkin, *So Dreadfull a Judgment: Puritan Responses to King Philip's War, 1676–1677* (Middletown, Conn.: Wesleyan University Press, 1978), 3; James Axtell, "The Vengeful Women of Marblehead: James Roule's Deposition of 1677," *William and Mary Quarterly,* 3rd ser., 31 (1974): 647–48; Mary Beth Norton, *In the Devil's Snare: The Salem Witchcraft Crisis of 1692* (New York: Alfred A. Knopf, 2002), 92; Christine Heyrman, *Commerce and Culture: The Maritime Communities of Colonial Massachusetts, 1690–1750* (New York: W. W. Norton & Co., 1984), 225; Horace Beck, *The American Indian as a Sea Fighter in Colonial Times* (Mystic, CT: Marine Historical Society, 1959), 31; Increase Mather, letter, May 23, 1677, in Thomas Hutchinson, *The History of the Colony and Province of Massachusetts Bay* (Boston: Thomas and John Fleet at the Heart and Crown in Cornhill, 1764), 307n; "Statement of Robert Roules of Marblehead concerning the capture of fishing vessels at Cape Sable by the Indians," July 17, 1677, Massachusetts Archives, Felt Collection, vol. 69, 158.
2. Increase Mather, "Diary," in *Proceedings of the Massachusetts Historical Society,* ser. 2, 13 (1899–1900), 405; "Roule Deposition," Massachusetts Archives, Felt Collection, 69:158; Yasuhide Kawashima, *Puritan Justice and the Indian* (Middletown, CT: Wesleyan University Press, 1986), 158.
3. Norton, *In the Devil's Snare,* 92, 93, 352n26; Jill Lepore, *The Name of War: King Philip's War and the Origins of American Identity* (New York: Knopf, 1998), 183. Colonial New England society was highly patriarchal and organized around the household. It was through this lens that women defined their roles in society. See John Demos, *A Little Commonwealth: Family Life in Plymouth Colony* (New

York: Oxford University Press, 1970); Laurel Thatcher Ulrich, *Good Wives: Images and Reality in the Lives of Women in Northern New England, 1658–1750* (New York: Vintage Books, 1991).

4. Although many sources mark 1676 as the end of King Philip's War, fighting in the northern theater continued until at least 1678. Ann M. Little, *Abraham in Arms* (Philadelphia: University of Pennsylvania Press, 2007), 1. I am referring to the formal public, composed of adult men, heads of households, and those in charge of official community affairs. Mary Beth Norton, *Founding Mothers & Fathers: Gendered Power and the Forming of American Society* (New York: Alfred A. Knopf, 1996), 20–21; Cotton Mather, *Bethiah: The glory which adorns the daughters of God* (Boston, 1722). In a population of less than fifteen thousand, an increase in attacks by women on colonial officials from a few per decade to at least one per year between 1677 and 1681 is a suggestive trend. Given the small number of cases, however, I cannot claim that this trend is statistically significant. My population estimate of fifteen thousand for late seventeenth-century Essex County is derived from my assumption that the county would not have contained more than one third of the estimated population of the colony of Massachusetts in 1688 (44,000). See Evarts Boutell Green and Virginia Draper Harrington, *American Population before the Federal Census of 1790* (Baltimore: Genealogical Publishing Company, 1993), 14; George Francis Dow, ed., *Records and Files of the Quarterly Courts of Essex Co., Massachusetts,* vols. 1–9 (Salem, 1911–1921); Massachusetts Archive, Court Records, Records of the Essex County Court, Records of the General Sessions of the Peace, Records of the Massachusetts Court of Assistants, Records of the Superior Court of Judicature (after 1686), and Records of the Massachusetts General Court.
5. This misreading stems from misuse of the main source for the event. Historians who discuss the murders reference the antiquarian Samuel G. Drake's nineteenth-century transcription of the Roule deposition rather than the original. Drake rephrased several passages, creating an almost entirely different version of events. Unaware of the discrepancy, historians have used Drake's version to mislabel the event as either a reviled "instance of frontier vigilantism" or an act of female behavior so outrageous that men distanced themselves from its brutality. See S. Drake, "Roule Deposition," MS 252, Edward E. Ayer Collection, the Newberry Library, Chicago; Axtell, "The Vengeful Women of Marblehead," 647–48; Ulrich, *Good Wives,* 194–95; Heyrman, *Commerce and Culture*, 225; Increase Mather, letter, May 23, 1677, in Hutchinson, *The History of Massachusetts Bay*, 307.
6. Lepore calls the incident a "random" and "unprovoked attack" (*The Name of War,* 183); Beck depicts the attack as an expression of women's irrational rage allowed to flourish uncontrolled (*American Indian as a Sea Fighter*); Heyrman argues that the gender of the attackers was relatively unimportant to the incident overall and fails to notice similarities between the attack in Marblehead and

other attacks on officials by colonial women during this period (*Commerce and Culture*, 225).

7. A. Laurence, "Women's Work and the English Civil War," *History Today* 42, no. 6 (1992): 20–25; Charles Carlton, *Going to the Wars: The Experience of the British Civil Wars, 1638–1651* (London: Routledge, 1992); Stevie Davies, *Unbridled Spirits: Women of the English Revolution, 1640–1660* (London: The Women's Press, 1998); Alison Plowden, *Women All on Fire: The Women of the English Civil War* (Stroud: Sutton Publishing, 1998); Roger Hudson, ed., *The Grand Quarrel: Women's Memoirs of the English Civil War* (Stroud: Sutton Publishing, 2000); E. P. Thompson, "The Moral Economy of the English Crowd in the Eighteenth Century," *Past and Present* 50 (February 1971): 116. The Hebrew Bible is also often referred to as the Old Testament in Christian dialogue.
8. Kawashima, *Puritan Justice*, 153–54; Rebecca J. Tannenbaum, *The Healer's Calling: Women and Medicine in Early New England* (Ithaca: Cornell University Press, 2009), 96.
9. An estimated death toll of eight hundred, out of an estimated population for New England of 52,000 English, makes King Philip's War more deadly per capita than the American Revolution, with 180 deaths per 100,000, the Civil War with 857, or World War II with 206. The war was even deadlier for the Native Americans of New England, claiming an estimated 7,900 Indian victims. Kyle F. Zelner, *A Rabble in Arms: Massachusetts Towns and Militiamen during King Philip's War* (New York: New York University Press, 2009), 201; Folsom and Slotkin, *So Dreadfull a Judgment*, 4; Lepore, *The Name of War*, xi. King William's War was almost as deadly. By the end of the war in 1697, at least 650 English colonists were dead, killed in battles, raids, or in captivity. Indian death tolls were even greater, numbering between 600 and 1,300 killed. Richard H. Bayor, ed., *The Columbia Documentary History of Race and Ethnicity in America* (New York: Columbia University Press, 2004), 14; Norton, *Devil's Snare*, 12, 87; David Lovejoy, *The Glorious Revolution in America* (New York: Harper & Row, 1972), 144.
10. Douglass Leach, *Flintlock and Tomahawk: New England in King Philip's War* (New York: Macmillan, 1966), 100; Increase Mather, *An Earnest Exhortation to the Inhabitants of New England* (Boston, 1676), 2.
11. Dow, *Quarterly Courts of Essex Co.*, 6:6, 71, 92–93, 278, 383, 385, 386; Records of the Superior Court of Judicature, Noble transcription, vol. 1, 1692–1695, Massachusetts Archives, Suffolk Files, reel 1, 124, 125, 209–10; Massachusetts Archives, Felt Collection, vols. 68, 69, 70, 71; Vivian Bruce Conger, *The Widows' Might: Widowhood and Gender in Early British America* (New York: New York University Press, 2009), 5; Essex County Court Records, June 1676, Massachusetts Judicial Archives, vol. 5, entry 39,and vol. 6, entry 173; Nathaniel Hubbard, "A Narrative of the Troubles with the Indians," in *History of the Indian Wars in New England*, ed. Samuel Drake, vols. 1 and 2 (repr., Baltimore: Genealogical Publishing Company, 2002), 120n149.

12. Massachusetts Archives, Felt Collection, 61:51, 70:36, 71:130.
13. Steven C. Eames, *Rustic Warriors: Warfare and the Provincial Soldier on the New England Frontier, 1689–1748* (New York: New York University Press, 2011), 10; Heidler and Heidler, *Daily Lives of Civilians*, 13; Alvin Rabushka, *Taxation in Colonial America* (Princeton: Princeton University Press, 2008), 169; Leach, *Flintlock and Tomahawk*, 244; Lyle Koehler, *A Search for Power: The "Weaker Sex" in Seventeenth-Century New England* (Urbana: University of Illinois Press, 1980), 338.
14. George Wingate Chase, *History of Haverhill, From its First Settlement in 1640 to the Year 1860* (Haverhill, 1861), 150; Samuel Ayer to General Court, February 11, 1689, Massachusetts Archives, Felt Collection, 35:232b; Lovejoy, *Glorious Revolution in America*, 196; David Corlett, "Forced to Flee for Our Lives: New England Refugees in King Philip's War," presented at Society for Military History Annual Meeting, February 26, 2005; "Petition for Relief of Service by John Leverrett and Council of Caleb Church of Watertown," June 22, 1676, Massachusetts Archives, Felt Collection, 69:20; "Petition by Hannah Stanley," 1676, Massachusetts Archives, Felt Collection 69:80a.
15. "Petition to the Council from Obedience Curtise of Roxbury," March 1676, Massachusetts Archives, Felt Collection, 69:106a; "Petition for Relief of Payment of Rates by Elizabeth Johnson," March 14, 1682/3, 70:85, "Petition for Relief by Elizabeth Johnson," February 7, 1682, 70:100; "Petition of Sarah Tuckerman," December 14, 1676, 69:86a; "Petition of Elizabeth Bent, widow in Marlborough," May 29, 1679, 69:229; "Petition to of Mary Gardner of Lancaster," June 29, 1705, 71:157–58; "Petition of Hanah Wascarr of Hadley," May 27, 1685, 70:137.
16. Leach, *Flintlock and Tomahawk*, 94, 100–101, 118, 143, 182; Randolph Roth, *American Homicide* (Cambridge: Belknap Press of Harvard University Press, 2009), 51.
17. Dow, *Quarterly Courts of Essex Co.*, 7:41–42; Records of the Essex County Court, Massachusetts Archives, microfilm reel 877464, item 3, entry 35.
18. *Register of the Lynn Historical Society*, vols. 1–9 (Lynn: Lynn Historical Society, 1898), 55, 59; Alonzo Lewis and James Robinson Newhall, *History of Lynn, Essex County, Massachusetts*, vol. 1, 1629–1864 (Lynn: Published at Bookstore of G. C. Herbert, 1890), 230; Levi Daniel Temple, *Some Temple Pedigrees: A Genealogy of the Known Descendants of Abraham Temple* (Boston: D. Clapp & Son, 1900), 9; William Richard Cutter, ed., *Genealogical and Personal Memoirs Relating to the Families of Boston and Eastern Massachusetts*, vol. 2 (Boston: Lewis Historical Publishing Company, 1908), 580; *Obituary Records of Graduates of Yale University* (New Haven, 1911), 14; "Deposition of John Nowall and Thomas Browne," April 1677, Essex County Quarterly Court, File Papers, Massachusetts Judicial Archives, 26:97–2, Dow, *Quarterly Courts of Essex Co.* 6:287, 8:23; "Summons for Clement Coldam," June 19, 1677, Essex County Court, File Papers, 26:97–1.
19. *Publication of the Society of Colonial Wars in the Commonwealth of Massachusetts*, no. 9 (Boston, 1908), 102; Ezra Stearns, William Frederick Whitcher,

and Edward Everett Parker, *Genealogical and Family History of the State of New Hampshire*, vol. 4 (New York: Lewis Publishing Company, 1908), 1632; "Deposition of Thomas Hobbs," July 1680, Essex County Court, File Papers, Massachusetts Judicial Archives, 34 25–2; Dow, *Quarterly Courts of Essex Co.*, 8:21–22; Alice Lapham, *The Old Planters of Beverly in Massachusetts and the Thousand Acre Grant of 1635* (Cambridge: Riverside Press, 1930), 50.

20. George Madison Bodge, *Soldiers in King Philip's War*, 3rd ed. (Boston, 1906), 366; George William Ellis and John Emery Morris, *King Philip's War: Based on Archives and Records of Massachusetts, Plymouth, Rhode Island, and Connecticut* (New York: Grafton Press, 1906), 206, 221; Dow, *Quarterly Courts of Essex Co.*, 7:1.
21. Sidney Perley, ed., *The Essex Antiquarian* 11 (1907): 20; David Webster Hoyt, *Old Families of Salisbury and Amesbury, 1897* (Higginson Book Company, 1990), 527; Bodge, *Soldiers in King Philip's War*, 138; "Testimony of Peater Chiver, constable and Joseph Gatchell," February 3, 1679/1680, Essex County Court Papers, WPA Transcription, vol. 34, 113–1; Dow, *Quarterly Courts of Essex Co.*, 7:329, 332.
22. Tannenbaum, *The Healer's Calling*, 116. Several women like Fox petitioned the General Court for reimbursement after treating wounded men from King Philip's War. See Massachusetts Archives, Felt Collection, 69:86a, 61:333; Stanley M. Aronson and Lucile Newman, "God Have Mercy on This House: Being a Brief Chronicle of Smallpox in Colonial New England," written for *Smallpox in the Americas, 1492 to 1815: Contagion and Controversy*, exhibit at the John Carter Brown Library, Providence (2002); Dow, *Quarterly Courts of Essex Co.*, 6:410, 8:191–92; "Deposition of Thomas Andrews, Deputy Marshal," March 18, 1677, Essex County Court File Papers, Massachusetts Judicial Archives, 36:78–1.
23. Dow, *Quarterly Courts of Essex Co.*, 9:441, 448; Sidney Perley, *The History of Salem, Massachusetts, 1638–1670*, vol. 2 (Salem: S. Perley, 1926), 355; Phyllis Whitman Hunter, *Purchasing Identity in the Atlantic World: Massachusetts Merchants, 1670–1780* (Ithaca: Cornell University Press, 2001), 53; *Diary of William Bentley, 1793–1802*, ed. Joseph Gilbert Waters, Marguerite Dalrymple, and Alice G. Waters (Salem: Essex Institute, 1907), 23; James E. McWilliams, *Building the Bay Colony: Local Economy and Culture in Early Massachusetts* (Charlottesville: University of Virginia Press, 2007), 149.
24. Massachusetts Archives, Felt Collection, vols. 68, 69, 70, 71; Dow, *Quarterly Courts of Essex Co.*, vols. 6–9.
25. See Dow, *Quarterly Courts of Essex Co.*, vols. 1–9; Massachusetts Archive, Court Records, Records of the Essex County Court, Records of the General Sessions of the Peace, Records of the Massachusetts Court of Assistants, Records of the Superior Court of Judicature (after 1686), and Records of the Massachusetts General Court.
26. Rabushka, *Taxation in Colonial America*, 328–29; Lovejoy, *Glorious Revolution in America*, 159, 182–83; Charles Henry James Douglas, *The Financial History of Massachusetts: From the Organization of the Massachusetts Bay Colony to the American Revolution* (New York, 1892), 299; Thomas F. Waters, *Ipswich in the*

Massachusetts Bay Colony (Ipswich: The Ipswich Historical Society, 1905), 239–64; Robert N. Toppan, ed., *Edward Randolph*, vol. 2 (Boston, 1898), 40–49, 307n6.

27. Rabushka, *Taxation in Colonial America,* 330; John Andrew Doyle, *The Puritan Colonies: English Colonies in America,* vol. 3 (New York: Henry Holt and Company, 1889), 239. One example of men's violent resistance to authority figures during this time was a "riot" that occurred during a militia training in Topsfield in 1685. Several men protested when one of their own was taken to the stocks, saying that they would tear the stocks down and destroy the meetinghouse if he was not freed. When the militiamen were reproved for their behavior by the tithingman and threatened with the stocks themselves, one of them replied, "Doe if you dare." Fighting and shooting ensued, and several men were injured. Dow, *Quarterly Courts of Essex Co.,* 9:606.

28. Guy Chet, *Conquering the American Wilderness: The Triumph of European Warfare in the Colonial Northeast* (Boston: University of Massachusetts Press, 2003), 71, 63–64; Alden T. Vaughan, *New England Encounters: Indians and Euroamericans, ca. 1600–1850: Essays Drawn from "New England Quarterly"* (Boston: Northeastern University Press, 1999), 13.

29. "John West to Fitz-John Winthrop," February 23, 1688/9, *Massachusetts Historical Society Collections* 53 (1919–1920): 496–97; William Stoughton et al., "Grievances against Governor Andros," January 27, 1689/90, Massachusetts Archives, Felt Collection, 35:187–92; "List of Evidence against Sir Edmund Andros," 35:255–60; "Evidence that Andros' raid on Pentagoet had Instigated the Conflict," 35:259, entry 107; "Declaration of Silvanus Davis," n.d. [after October 15, 1690], in *Documentary History of the State of Maine,* vol. 5 (Portland: Lefavor-Tower Company, 1907), 144; "Brief Relation" (1689), in "Hutchinson Papers," *Massachusetts Historical Society [MHS] Collections* 21 (1825): 100; Stoughton, "Grievances against Andros," 35:191; and "Testimonies of Joseph Graves, Mary Graves and John Rutter," Sudbury, January 3, 1689, 4:446–47; "Statement of Thomas Browne, John Gooenow, Jonathan Stanhope, John Paramenter," 4:447; "Testimony of Stephen Greenleaf Junr." April 9, 1689, 6:472–73; "Testimony of George Little," 6:473, all in *Documentary History of the State of Maine.*

30. Chet, *Conquering the American Wilderness,* 74–75; Norton, *Devil's Snare*, 96; Cotton Mather et al., "Declaration of the Gentlemen, Merchants, and Inhabitants of Boston," in *The Andros Tracts: Being a Collection of Pamphlets and Official Papers*, ed. William Henry Whitmore, vol. 2 (Boston: Prince Society, 1874), 17–18; "Joint Depositions of Joseph Emerson & Jacob Whitaker of Haverhill relative to the treatment, accorded to the soldiers at Pemaquid under Andros Goverment," December 17, 1689, Massachusetts Archives, Felt Collection, 35:128.

31. Lovejoy, *Glorious Revolution in America,* 240–41; Cotton Mather et al., "Boston Declaration of Grievances" (1689), in *The Glorious Revolution in America: Documents on the Colonial Crisis of 1689,* ed. Michael G. Hall, Lawrence H. Leder, and Michael Kammen (Chapel Hill: University of North Carolina Press, 2012), 42–46; "Letter from Samuel Prince to Thomas Hinckley," Boston, April 22, 1689,

Hinckley Papers, *MHS Collections,* ser. 4, vol. 5 (Boston, 1861),192–96; "A Letter from a Gentlemen of the City of New York" (1698). in *Narratives of the Insurrections, 1675–1690,* ed. Charles McLean Andrews (New York: Charles Scribner's Sons, 1915), 362n1; John Riggs, "A Narrative of the Proceedings at Boston in New England upon the Ihabts seizing the Governmt there," *Colonial Board of Trade Reports, 1679–88,* vol. 5 (1679–1688): 904–5; John Fiske, *The Beginnings of New England, or the Puritan Theocracy* (Cambridge: Riverside Press, 1889), 272; Nathaniel Byfield, "An Account of the Late Revolution in New-England," in Andrews, *Narratives,* 170–75; Whitmore, *The Andros Tracts,* 2:8.

32. Chet, *Conquering the American Wilderness,* 63–64; "Testimony of Ester Waldron Elkins Lee," *Documentary History of the State of Maine,* 9:60.
33. Chet, *Conquering the American Wilderness,* 63–64, 74–75; "Letter from Saltonstall and others Regarding Haverhill," 1677, Massachusetts Archives, Felt Collection, 69:152; Chase, *History of Haverhill,* 158–59, 199.
34. Chet, *Conquering the American Wilderness,* 62, 74–75; Eames, *Rustic Warriors,* 9–10, 13; Mary Pray to James Oliver, October 20, 1675, *MHS Collections,* ser. 5, vol. 1 (1871): 105–10.
35. Chet, *Conquering the American Wilderness,* 80, 83–84, 86; Norton, *Devil's Snare,* 98, 103–5; Jenny Hale Pulsipher, *Subjects unto the Same King: Indians, English and the Contest for Authority in Colonial New Englan*d (Philadelphia: University of Pennsylvania Press, 2005), 255–58; Hutchinson, *The History of Massachusetts Bay,* 2:61–62; Samuel Adams Drake, *The Border Wars of New England* (New York: Charles Scribner's Sons, 1910), 96–101, 102nI.
36. Heidler, *Daily Lives of Civilians in Wartime Early America,* 13; "Act to Prevent the deserting of the Frontier of this Province," 1699, Massachusetts Archives, Felt Collection, 70:457.
37. Benjamin L. Mirick and John Greenleaf Whittier, *The History of Haverhill, Massachusetts* (Haverhill: A. W. Thayer, 1832), 223; Emma Lewis Coleman, *New England Captives Carried to Canada: Between 1677 and 1760 during the French and Indian Wars,* vol. 1 (Portland, ME: Southworth Press, 1925), 345.
38. "Letter by Lieutenant George Ingersol," in John James Babson, *Notes and Additions to the History of Gloucester: Part First, Early Settlers* (Gloucester: M. V. B. Perley, 1876), 39.
39. Little, *Abraham in Arms,* 98; Cotton Mather, *Decennium Luctuosum* (1699), in *Narratives of the Indian Wars, 1675–1699,* ed. Charles H. Lincoln (New York: Charles Scriber's Sons, 1913), 94.
40. Marie L. Ahearn, *The Rhetoric of War: Training Day, the Militia, and the Military Sermon* (New York: Greenwood Press, 1989), 58; Chet, *Conquering the American Wilderness,* 13, 21; Alden T. Vaughan, *The Puritan Tradition in America, 1620–1730* (New York: Harper & Row, 1972), 90–91; Nathaniel B. Shurtleff, *Records of the Governor and Company of the Massachusetts Bay in New England,* vol. 1 (Boston: William White, 1853), 25–26; Louis Effingham DeForest and Anne Lawrence DeForest, *Captain John Underhill: Gentleman, Soldier of Fortune* (New York:

Underhill Society of America Education and Publishing Fund, 1985), 9; Chase, *History of Haverhill*, 66.

41. Chet, *Conquering the American Wilderness*, 58. Preferably, garrisons were designed with a second floor that projected out over the first, forming an overhanging gallery that enabled defenders to fire on attackers storming the doors and windows below. Edward M. Cook Jr. in discussion with the author, February 2014.
42. Mather, *Decennium Luctuosum*, 237; Jeremy Belknap, *The History of New Hampshire*, vol. 1 (Philadelphia, 1784), 338–39.
43. Ulrich, *Good Wives*, 179; Chet, *Conquering the American Wilderness*, 58. See Patrick Malone, *Skulking Way of War: Technology and Tactics among the New England Indians* (Lanham, MD: Madison Books, 1991); Chase, *History of Haverhill*, 66, 152; Samuel Penhallow, *The History of the Wars of New England with the Eastern Indians* (Boston, 1726), 28; Cotton Mather, *Good Fetch'd Out of Evil* (Boston, 1706), 38.
44. "Deposition of Mary Logia," June 1677, Essex County Court Papers, WPA transcription, vol. 26, 107–3; "Deposition of John King against Joseph Indian," June 1677, 26:107–5.
45. Essex County Court Records, July 1677, entry 43, Massachusetts Archives, microfilm reel 877462; Dow, *Quarterly Courts of Essex Co.*, 6:295; Kawashima, *Puritan Justice*, 152, 154, 162–63, 237; Alden T. Vaughan, *New England Frontier: Puritans and Indians, 1620–1675*, rev. ed. (New York: Norton, 1979), 320.
46. Increase Mather, *A Brief History of the Warr with the Indians in New England* (1676); Daniel R. Mandell, *King Philip's War: Colonial Expansion, Native Resistance, and the End of Indian Sovereignty* (Baltimore: Johns Hopkins University Press, 2010), 11; Mary Rowlandson, *The Sovereignty and Goodness of God: Being a Narrative of the Captivity and Restoration of Mrs. Mary Rowlandson* (1682), in Lincoln, *Narratives*, 107–66; Little, *Abraham in Arms*, 53.
47. Vaughan, *New England Frontier*, 316; *Diary of Samuel Sewall*, vol. 1 (Boston: Massachusetts Historical Society, 1878–1882), 23; Roth, *American Homicide*, 46n41; Edmund B. O'Callaghan, ed., *Documents Relative to the Colonial History of the State of New York* (Albany, 1853–1887), 412–14.
48. John Underhill, *Nevves from America; or, A New and Experimentall Discoverie of New England: Containing, a True Relation of their War-like Proceedings these two yeares last past, with a figure of the Indian fort, or Palizado . . .* (London, 1638), 2–8.
49. Underhill, *Nevves from America*, 22, 23, 26, 29–34, 36–40.
50. Cotton Mather, *Magnalia Christi Americana or The Ecclesiastical History of New England* (Hartford: Silas Andrus & Son, 1853), 648; Judges 5:24–31; "Hannah Dustin's Letter to Elders of The Second Church of Haverhill" (1724), Haverhill Historical Society Collection, Haverhill, MA.
51. Eames, *Rustic Warriors*, 3; Chase, *History of Haverhill*, Charles Henry Pope, *The Haverhill Emersons* (Boston: Murray and Emery Company, 1913); "Joint Depositions of Joseph Emerson & Jacob Whitaker of Haverhill relative to the

treatment, accorded to the soldiers at Pemaquid under Andros Goverment," December 17, 1689, Massachusetts Archives, Felt Collection, 35:128

52. Everett Schermerhorn Stackpole, Lucien Thompson, and Winthrop Smith Meserve, *The History of the Town of Durham, New Hampshire (Oyster River Plantation)*, vol. 2 (Durham: Vote of the Town, 1913), 89; Pope, *Haverhill Emersons*, 28; Coleman, *New England Captives Carried to Canada*, chap. 10; *Collections of Maine Historical Society* ser. 2, vol. 5 (Portland: Maine Historical Society, 1894), 516. Judith is listed among the "Captiues yet in the Indians hands" as of January 24, 1689/9 as "Judah Emmerson of oyester River." *Collections of Maine Historical Society*, ser. 2, 5:317.
53. Cotton Mather, *Humiliations Follow'd with Deliverances* (Boston: B. Green & J. Allen for Samuel Phillips, 1697), 43.
54. Francis W. Cronan, *Red Sunday: The Saltonstalls, the Dustons, and the Fighting Ayers* (Haverhill: Anundsen, 1965), 75; Chase, *History of Haverhill*, 200; "A List of the Frontier Garisons Reviewed by Order of His Excellency the Governour," November 1711, Massachusetts Archives, Felt Collection, 71:871; Chet, *Conquering the American Wilderness*, 71; Chase, *History of Haverhill*, 52.
55. Cronan, *Red Sunday*, 73; *Vital Records of Haverhill, Massachusetts, to the End of the Year 1849*, vol. 2 (Topsfield, MA: Topsfield Historical Society, 1911), 450; "William Neff, Estate Inventory," May 14, 1689, Essex County Probate Records, Massachusetts Archives, 304:208; "Men killed & wounded in the Sako Expedition," August 7, 1691, Massachusetts Archives, Felt Collection, 37:105; James Otis Lyford, *History of the Town of Canterbury, New Hampshire, 1727–1912*, vol. 2 (Concord, NH: Rumford Press, 1912),93; Chase, *History of Haverhill*, 128, 145, 160, 199, 201; "Letter from Nathaniel Saltonstall, re: Attack and Capture of John Roby of Haverhill," 1691–92, Felt Collection, 37:41a; "Letter Regarding Roby, Injuries & Death," 1691–92, 37:43
56. Stackpole, Thompson, and Meserve, *History of Durham*, 89, 99–100; Pope, *Haverhill Emersons*, 28; Mather, *Magnalia Christi Americana*, 636.
57. "An Inventory of the Estate of Mrs Hannah Dusten, late of Haverhill," March 10, 1737/8, Essex Probate, Massachusetts Archives, 325:145–46; "The Will of Thomas Dustin," 1724, Essex Probate, 319:348–50; "An Inventory of the Estate of Mr. Thomas Dustin late of Haverhill," Essex Probate, Vol. 319:341; Vaughan, *New England Frontier*, 316.
58. "William Neff, Estate Inventory," May 14, 1689, Essex Probate, Massachusetts Archives, 304:208; Mather, *Magnalia Christi Americana*, 635; John Grenier, *The First Way of War: American War Making on the Frontier, 1607–1814* (Cambridge: Cambridge University Press, 2008), 42, 41; Michael A. Bellesiles, ed., *Lethal Imagination: Violence and Brutality in American History* (New York: New York University Press, 1999), 20; Ward Churchill, *A Little Matter of Genocide: Holocaust and Denial in the Americas, 1492 to the Present* (San Francisco: City Lights, 1997), 180; "An Act for the encouragement of the prosecution of the Indian Enemy and Rebels," October 19, 1697, Massachusetts Archives, Felt Collection,

30:435, 435a; Thomas Duston, "Petition for Scalp Bounty," June 8, 1697, Felt Collection, 70:350; "Petition by Joseph Neff (son) to General Court," May 1739, Felt Collection, 31:261.

59. Samuel Adams Drake, *The Border Wars of New England* (New York: Charles Scribner's Sons, 1897), 9–10, 136–37; Rabushka, *Taxation in Colonial America,* 365.
60. Penhallow, *The History of the Wars of New-England,* 28; Mather, *Good Fetch'd Out of Evil*, 38; Chase, *History of Haverhill*, 216; Cronan, *Red Sunday,* 72; Coleman, *Captives Carried to Canada*, 348–49.
61. Chase, *History of Haverhill;* Records of the General Sessions of the Peace for Essex County, Massachusetts Archives, microfilm reel 0877466, 169; Heyrman, *Commerce and Culture,* 250; "Petition of the Inhabitants of Marblehead," 1668/9, Massachusetts Archives, Felt Collection, 60:39; Perley, *Essex Antiquarian,* 3:175; General Sessions of the Peace, Massachusetts Archives, microfilm reel 0877466, 169.
62. General Sessions of the Peace, Massachusetts Archives, microfilm reel 0877466, 212. There are no attacks by women against colonial officials in the court records for Essex County for at least seven years after 1709. General Sessions of the Peace, microfilm reel 0877466; Massachusetts Archives, Felt Collection, 68:97; Charles Henry Pope, *The Pioneers of Massachusetts* (1900; repr., Westminster, MD: Heritage Books, 2010), 156; Coleman, *Captives Carried to Canada,* 352.

Chapter 4: "The Devil will Bless himself, to find such a convenient Lodging"

1. George Francis Dow, ed., *Records and Files of the Quarterly Courts of Essex Co., Massachusetts,* vols. 1–9 (Salem, 1911–1921), 7:43, 44, 47–48, 51, 54–55.
2. Marilynne K. Roach, *The Salem Witch Trials: A Day-by-Day Chronicle of a Community under Siege* (New York: Taylor Trade Publications, 2004), 273; Dow, *Quarterly Courts of Essex Co.* 7:46.
3. Carol Karlsen, *The Devil in the Shape of a Woman: Witchcraft in Colonial New England* (New York: Norton, 1987); *Sarah Bibber v. Dorcas Hoar,* July 2, 1692, Essex County Court Archives, Salem, Witchcraft, vol. 1, no. 209; "Examination of Dorcas Hoar," May 2, 1692, Essex County Archives, Witchcraft, 1:77.
4. *Historical Collections of the Essex Institute,* vol. 2 (Salem: Published for the Essex Institute by Henry Whipple and Son, 1860), 32, 79, 246, 247.
5. Dow, *Quarterly Courts of Essex Co.,* vols. 1–9; Cotton Mather, "A Brand Pluck'd Out of Burning" (1693), in *Narratives of the Witchcraft Cases, 1648–1706,* ed. George Lincoln Burr (New York: Scribner's Sons, 1914), 253–85; Cotton Mather, "Another Brand Pluck'd Out of the Burning, or More Wonders of the Invisible World" (1693), in Burr, *Narratives,* 308–25; C. Mather, *The Wonders of the Invisible World* (London: John Russell Smith, 1862), 89.

6. Mary Beth Norton, *In the Devil's Snare: The Salem Witchcraft Crisis of 1692* (New York: Alfred A. Knopf, 2002), 8.
7. Norton, *Devil's Snare;* Paul Boyer and Stephen Nissenbaum, *Salem Possessed: The Social Origins of Witchcraft* (Cambridge: Harvard University Press, 1974).
8. Case of Goodwife Seager (Elizabeth Seager), Connecticut State Library, State Archives, Samuel Wyllys Papers; Samuel Adams Drake, *A Book of New England Legends and Folk Lore* (Boston: Little, Brown and Company, 1901), 315–18; John Demos, *Entertaining Satan: Witchcraft and the Culture of Early New England* (New York: Oxford University Press, 1982), 92, 186.
9. Mather, "A Brand Pluck'd Out of Burning," 262.
10. Norton, *Devil's Snare,* 28, 42; Richard Bernard, *A Guide to Jury Men* (London, 1627), 228, 239; Deodat Lawson, "A Brief and True Narrative of Witchcraft at Salem Village," in Burr, *Narratives,* 155, 156; Olma Alyagon Darr, "Experiments in the Courtroom: Social Dynamics and Spectacles of Proof in Early Modern English Witch Trials," *Law & Social Inquiry* 39, no. 1 (Winter 2014): 152–75.
11. Mather, "A Brand Pluck'd Out of Burning," 264–65; "Examination of Dorcas Hoar"; Darr, "Experiments in the Courtroom."
12. Jane Kamensky, *Governing the Tongue: The Politics of Speech in Early New England* (New York: Oxford University Press, 1999), 10; Lyle Koehler, *A Search for Power: The "Weaker Sex" in Seventeenth-Century New England* (Urbana: University of Illinois Press, 1980), 171, 399; "Examination of Rebecca Nurse," March 24, 1692, Essex County Archives, Witchcraft, 1:72.
13. Elizabeth Pleck, *Domestic Tyranny: The Making of American Social Policy against Family Violence from Colonial Times to the Present* (New York: Oxford University Press, 1987), 19; Koehler, *A Search for Power,* 139; Edward Bever, "Witchcraft, Female Aggression, and Power in the Early Modern Community," *Journal of Social History* 35, no. 4 (2002): 955–88; Karlsen, *Devil in the Shape of a Woman,* 129–30, 150; Demos, *Entertaining Satan*, 93–121; Laurel Thatcher Ulrich, *Good Wives: Image and Reality in the Lives of Women in Northern New England, 1650–1750* (New York: Vintage Books, 1991), 29; Garthine Walker, *Crime, Gender and Social Order in Early Modern England* (Cambridge: Cambridge University Press, 2003), 85.
14. David D. Hall, *Witch-Hunting in Seventeenth-Century New England: A Documentary History, 1638–1693* (Boston: Northeastern University Press, 2005), 19–20,
15. John Murrin, "Coming to Terms with the Salem Witch Trials," *Proceedings of the American Antiquarian Society* 110, no. 2 (2003): 309–47; Boyer and Nissenbaum, *Salem Possessed;* Margo Burns and Bernard Rosenthal, "Examination of the Records of the Salem Witch Trials," *William and Mary Quarterly* 65, no. 3 (2008): 401–22; Demos, *Entertaining Satan*; Richard Godbeer, *The Devil's Dominion: Magic and Religion in Early New England* (New York: Cambridge University Press, 1992); Peter Charles Hoffer, *The Salem Witchcraft Trials: A Legal History* (Lawrence: University Press of Kansas, 1997); Karlsen, *Devil in the Shape of a Woman*; Norton, *Devil's Snare*; Bernard Rosenthal et al., eds., *Records of the Salem Witch-Hunt* (New York: Cambridge University Press, 2009).

16. Murrin, "Coming to Terms," 319.
17. Murrin, "Coming to Terms," 317; Hall, *Witch-Hunting,* 21–25, 270–71.
18. Helena Wall, *Fierce Communion: Family and Community in Early America* (State College: Pennsylvania State University Press, 1990); E. F. Crane, *Witches, Wife Beaters, and Whores: Common Law and Common Folk in Early America* (Ithaca: Cornell University Press, 2011), 83; Karlsen, *Devil in the Shape of a Woman*, 128, 217.
19. Clive Holmes, "Women: Witnesses and Witches," *Past & Present,* no. 140 (1993): 46; Murrin, "Coming to Terms."
20. Dow, *Quarterly Courts of Essex Co.*, 1:11, 108, 199, 2:163, 305, 313, 3:414; Karlsen, *Devil in the Shape of a Woman*, 8.
21. John Hale, *A Modest Enquiry into the Nature of Witchcraft* (Boston, 1702), 17; *The Journal of John Winthrop*, vol. 2, ed. Richard S. Dunn, James Savage, and Laetitia Yeandle (Cambridge: Belknap Press, 1996), 344–45; Demos, *Entertaining Satan*, 92; Keith Thomas, *Religion and the Decline of Magic: Studies in Popular Beliefs in Sixteenth and Seventeenth Century England* (Oxford: Oxford University Press, 1971); John Noble and John Cronin, *Records of the Court of Assistants of the Colony of the Massachusetts Bay, 1630–1692*, 2 vols. (Boston: County of Suffolk, 1901–1928), 2:242.
22. Dow, *Quarterly Courts of Essex Co.*, 3:352–53, 413, 421; Crane, *Witches, Wife Beaters, and Whores,* 83.
23. Dow, *Quarterly Courts of Essex Co.*, 2:65, 66, 143, 157–58, 159, 160, 3:10, 27, 39, 120, 121–22; Noble and Cronin, *Records of Court of Assistants*, 3:151–52, 158–61; John Demos, "John Godfrey and His Neighbors: Witchcraft and the Social Web in Colonial Massachusetts," *William & Mary Quarterly* 33, no. 2 (1976): 245, 246, 250, 252, 253.
24. Essex County Quarterly Court File Papers, Massachusetts Judicial Archives, 15:63–1, 63–2; Dow, *Quarterly Courts of Essex Co.*, 4:207–9; Hall, *Witch-Hunting*, 185; Rebecca Tannenbaum, *Healers Calling: Women and Medicine in Early New England* (Ithaca: Cornell University Press, 2002), 130; Demos, *Entertaining Satan*, 84.
25. "Testimony of William Hannum continued, and Testimony of Sarah Bridgeman," August 11, 1656, East Cambridge Archives, courtesy of the University of Massachusetts, Amherst; "Testimony on behalf of Sarah Bridgeman by William Hannum's wife," September 30, 1656, East Cambridge Archives; "John Mathews testifies before John Pynchon," East Cambridge Archives; Demos, *Entertaining Satan,* 250–61.
26. "Testimony of Samuell Bartlett against Mary Parsons," September 29, 1674, Hampshire County Court, courtesy of Hampshire County Court Registry of Probate, Northampton, MA; "Appearance of Mary Parsons," January 5, 1675, Hampshire County Court; Noble and Cronin, *Records of Court of Assistants,* 1:31, 33; Goody Parson's witchcraft case exhibit, University of Massachusetts, Amherst.
27. Robert E. Cray Jr. "'Weltering in their Own Blood': Puritan Causalities in King Philip's War," *Historical Journal of Massachusetts* 37, no. 2 (Fall 2009): 107–23; Norton, *Devil's Snare;* Godbeer, *The Devil's Dominion,* 186–97.

28. Norton, *Devil's Snare,* 12; Koehler, *A Search for Power,* 343; Karlsen, *Devil in the Shape of a Woman*; Emerson W. Baker and James Kences, "Maine, Indian Land Speculation, and the Essex County Witchcraft Outbreak of 1692," *Maine History* 40, no. 3 (Fall 2001): 159–189; James Kences, "Some Unexplored Relationships of Essex County Witchcraft to the Indian Wars of 1675 and 1689," *Essex Institute Historical Collections* 120, no. 3 (July 1984): 179–212.
29. Godbeer, *The Devil's Dominion,* 204.
30. Karlsen, *Devil in the Shape of a Woman,* 118; Martin Ingram, "'Scolding women cucked or washed': A Crisis in Gender Relations in Early Modern England?," in *Women, Crime and the Courts in Early Modern England,* ed. Jennifer Kermode and Garthine Walker (London: Routledge, 1994), 66; Christina Larner, *Witchcraft and Religion: The Politics of Popular Belief,* ed. Alan MacFarlane (Oxford: Basil Blackwell, 1985), 86; Ann Kibbey, "Mutations of the Supernatural: Witchcraft, Remarkable Providences, and the Power of Puritan Men," *American Quarterly* 34, no. 2 (1982): 147.
31. Elizabeth Reis, *Damned Women: Sinners and Witches in Puritan New England* (Ithaca: Cornell University Press, 1997), 2.
32. Boyer and Nissenbaum, *Salem Possessed,* 51, 156, 163; Norton, *Devil's Snare,* 17.
33. Norton, *Devil's Snare,* 18, 332n9; Larry D. Gragg, *The Quest for Security: The Life of Samuel Parris, 1653–1720* (Westport, CT: Greenwood Press, 1990), 42–43, 60–68; James F. Cooper and Kenneth P. Minkema, eds., *The Sermon Notebook of Samuel Parr*is (Charlottesville: University of Virginia Press, 1993), 2–3, 18–19; church records from 1689 to 1691, in *Salem-Village Witchcraft: A Documentary Record of Local Conflict in Colonial New England,* ed. Paul Boyer and Stephen Nissenbaum (Boston: Northeastern University Press, 2016), 268–77. Late in 1691, the church had sixty-two members and the village approximately 215 adult residents. Boyer and Nissenbaum, *Salem Possessed,* 164; Benjamin C. Ray, *Satan and Salem: The Witch-Hunt Crisis of 1692* (Charlottesville: University of Virginia Press, 2015), 189.
34. Boyer and Nissenbaum, *Salem Possessed,* 168, 177, 185; Ray, *Satan and Salem,* 189.
35. Norton, *Devil's Snare,* 18; "Sermon from January 3, 1691," in *Sermon Notebook of Samuel Parris,* ed. Benjamin Ray (Charlottesville: University of Virginia Library, 2016), 133–39.
36. John Hale, "A Modest Enquiry into the Nature of Witchcraft," in Burr, *Narratives,* 413.
37. Boyer and Nissenbaum, *Salem Possessed,* 114, 139.
38. Ray, *Satan and Salem;* Norton, *Devil's Snare,* 30, Rosenthal, *Records of Salem,* 31; Boyer and Nissenbaum, *Salem Possessed,* 115, 126, 128.
39. Norton, *Devil's Snare,* 22; Elizabeth Reis, *Spellbound: Woman and Witchcraft in America* (Lanham, MD: Rowman and Littlefield, 1998), 86.
40. "Examination of Sarah Good, Sarah Osborn, & Tituba, as Recorded by Ezekiel Cheever," March 1, 1692, in Rosenthal, *Records of Salem,* 127–28; Norton, *Devil's Snare,* 59; Cotton Mather, *The Wonders of the Invisible World* (1693).

41. "Examination of Sarah Good, Sarah Osburn, & Tituba," 126–29; Norton, *Devil's Snare*, 27.
42. Boyer and Nissenbaum, *Salem Possessed,* 149, Norton, *Devil's Snare,* 44, 48–51.
43. Boyer and Nissenbaum, *Salem Possessed,* 147; Dow, *Quarterly Courts of Essex Co.,* 7:10–21, 8:116–21, 319–23; Norton, *Devil's Snare,* 47; Boyer and Nissenbaum, *Salem Possessed*, 182.
44. David Thomas Konig, *Law and Society in Puritan Massachusetts: Essex County, 1629–1692* (Chapel Hill: University of North Carolina Press, 1979), 180.
45. "Deposition of Ann Putnam Sr. v. Martha Corey and Rebecca Nurse and Testimony of Ann Putnam Jr. v. Rebecca Nurse and Martha Corey," March 24, 1692, Essex Institute Collection, Salem, Massachusetts; Boyer and Nissenbaum, *Salem Possessed,* 147–48; Deodat Lawson, "A Brief and True Narrative of Witchcraft at Salem Village," (1692), in Burr, *Narratives*, 157; Testimony of Abigail Williams v. Rebecca Nurse and Sister Cloyse, Essex County Archives, Witchcraft, 1:73.
46. "Samuel Perley, et ux v. Elizabeth Howe," June 1, 1692, Essex County Archives, Witchcraft, 1:146; Dow, *Quarterly Courts of Essex Co.,* 3:403.
47. "Samuel Perley, et ux v Elizabeth Howe," June 30, 1692, Essex County Archives, Witchcraft, 1:146; "Joseph Safford v Elizabeth Howe and Bridget Bishop," June 30, 1692, 1:152.
48. "Nehemiah Abbott v Elizabeth How, Testimony," June 30, 1692, Essex Institute Collection; "Samuel Perley, et ux v Elizabeth Howe," June 30, 1692, Essex County Archives, Witchcraft, 1:146.
49. "Deposition of Isaac Cummings, Sr. v. Elizabeth Howe," Essex County Archives, Witchcraft, 1:330; "Testimony of John How v. Elizabeth Howe," 1:335.
50. Emerson W. Baker, *A Storm of Witchcraft: The Salem Trials and the American Experience* (Oxford: Oxford University Press, 2015), 83; Boyer and Nissenbaum, *Salem Possessed*, 148; Dow, *Quarterly Courts of Essex Co.,* 7:10–21, 8:116–21, 319–23; "Examination of Elizabeth Howe," May 31, 1692, Essex County Archives, Witchcraft, 1:144.
51. Dow, *Quarterly Courts of Essex Co.,* 1:179, 3:66, 118; "Deposition of John Gould and Zacheus Perkins v. Mary Wilds," Essex Institute Collection; "John Wilds for Sarah Wilds," Essex County Archives, Witchcraft, 1:55; "Thomas Dorman v Sarah Wilds Deposition," Essex Institute Collection; "Testimony of Ann Putnam Jr. v. Sarah Wilds," June 30, 1692, Essex Institute Collection; "Deposition of John Gould and Zacheus Perkins v. Mary Wilds," Essex Institute Collection.
52. "Humphrey Clark v Sarah Wilds Deposition," Essex Institute Collection, "Elizabeth Symonds v Sarah Wilds," Essex Institute Collection; Alice Peterson Towne and Marietta Clark, "Topsfield in the Witchcraft Delusion," *Historical Collections of the Topsfield Historical Society* 13 (1908): 31.
53. "Deposition of Edward Putnam v. Martha Corey," March 21, 1692, in Rosenthal, *Records of Salem,* 152–53; Cotton Mather, *Memorable Provinces*, in Burr, *Narratives*, 108; "Ann Putnam Jr v. George Burroughs," August 2, 1692, Essex County

Archives, Witchcraft, 2:24; Norton, *Devil's Snare,* 135; Boyer and Nissenbaum, *Salem Possessed*, 174.

54. "Examination of Abigail Hobbs," May 12, 1692, Essex County Archives, Witchcraft, 1:50; Baker, *Storm of Witchcraft,* 23; Norton, *Devil's Snare,* 80, 119, 128.
55. Norton, *Devil's Snare,* 130; "Ann Putnam Jr v. George Burroughs," August 2, 1692, Essex County Archives, Witchcraft, 2:24; Peter Charles Hoffer, *The Devil's Disciples: Makers of the Salem Witchcraft Trials* (Baltimore: Johns Hopkins University Press, 1996), 48; Frances Hill, *A Delusion of Satan: The Full Story of the Salem Witch Trials* (New York: Da Capo Press, 1995), 59.
56. Norton deduces that Lewis and Hubbard were the afflicted girls from Salem sent to Andover; Norton, *Devil's Snare,* 233. Rosenthal speculates they were Elizabeth Hubbard and Mary Warren; Rosenthal, *Records of Salem*, 468.
57. Baker, *Storm of Witchcraft*, 33, 158; Ray, *Satan and Salem*, 105, 107; "Examination of Ann Foster, Mary Lacy Sr., & Mary Lacy Jr.," July 21, 1692, in "The Witchcraft Delusion of 1692. By Gov. Thomas Hutchinson," ed. William Frederick Poole, *New England Historical and Genealogical Register* 24, no. 4 (October 1870): 399–401; "Examinations of Mary Lacy Jr., Mary Lacy Sr., & Ann Foster," Andover Examinations Copy, July 21, 1692, Essex Institute Collection, 24, 1r–3r.
58. "Examination of Ann Foster," Friday, July 15, 1692, in Rosenthal, *Records of Salem,* 467–68; "Examination of Deliverance Hobbs in Prison," April 23, 1692, Essex County Archives, Witchcraft, 2:102; "Examination of Sarah Cloyse and Elizabeth Proctor," April 11, 1692, in Thomas Hutchinson, *The History of the Province of Massachusetts Bay,* vol. 2, ed. Lawrence Shaw Mayo (Cambridge: Harvard University Press, 1936), 21–23; Mary Beth Norton, "The Refugee's Revenge," *The Common Place* 2, no. 3 (April 2002), https://www.common-place-archives.org/vol-02/no-03/norton/.
59. Cotton Mather, "The Trial of Martha Carrier at the Court of Oyer and Terminer," August 2, 1692, in *Wonders of the Invisible World* (Boston, 1693), 138; Karlsen, *Devil in the Shape of a Woman*, 99–100; Ray, *Satan and Salem*, 105–6.
60. "Testimony of Benjamin Abbot and Deposition of Sarah Abbot v Martha Carrier," August 3, 1692, in Rosenthal, *Records of Salem,* 509–10.
61. "Statement of Samuel Preston v Martha Carrier," August 3, 1692, in Rosenthal, *Records of Salem,* 512; "Deposition of Phoebe Chandler and Testimony of Bridget Chandler v Martha Carrier," August 3, 1692, in Rosenthal, *Records of Salem*, 510–11.
62. Ray, *Satan and Salem,* 106; Baker, *Storm of Witchcraft,* 24, 33; "Examination of Martha Carrier," May 31, 1692, Essex County Archives, Witchcraft, 1:311; Rosenthal, *Records of Salem*, editor's note, 482.
63. "Declaration of Mary Osgood, Mary Tyler, Deliverance Dane, Abigail Barker, Sarah Wilson Sr. & Hannah Tyler," January 3, 1693, in Rosenthal, *Records of Salem,* 737–38; Hutchinson, *History of Massachusetts Bay,* 2:31–32.
64. Enders A. Robinson, *Salem Witchcraft and Hawthorne's House of Seven Gables* (Bowie, MD: Heritage Books, 1992), 154.

65. Ray, *Satan and Salem*, 110–12; Robinson, *Salem Witchcraft*; Baker, *Storm of Witchcraft*, 153; "Petition for Mary Osgood, Eunice Frye, Deliverance Dane, Sarah Wilson, Sr., & Abigail Barker," January 3, 1693, in Rosenthal, *Records of Salem*, 38–39; and Hutchinson, *History of Massachusetts Bay*, 2:32–33.
66. The Massachusetts governor sent none other than the deputy governor, Thomas Danforth, and four other assistants to Salem—where they were joined by assistants John Hathorne and Jonathan Corwin. That such high-ranking men were involved in the trials indicates the level of seriousness with which they were regarded by Massachusetts leadership. Baker, *Storm of Witchcraft*, 22, 170, 185.
67. Rosenthal, *Records of Salem*, 17, 23; Norton, *Devil's Snare*, 24, 25.

Chapter 5: Female Violence

1. Teresa A. Toulouse, *The Captive's Position: Female Narrative, Male Identity, and Royal Authority in Colonial New England* (Philadelphia: University of Pennsylvania Press, 2007), 2–3; David D. Hall, *Worlds of Wonder, Days of Judgement: Popular Religious Belief in Early New England* (New York: Alfred A. Knopf, 1989), 32; Peter Charles Hoffer and N. E. H. Hull, *Murdering Mothers: Infanticide in England and New England, 1558–1803* (New York: New York University Press, 1981), 56; Toulouse, *The Captive's Position*, 108.
2. Perry Miller, *The New England Mind: The Seventeenth Century* (1939; Boston: Beacon Press, 1961), vii, 472; Michael Wigglesworth, *God's Controversy with New-England* (1662), in *The Puritans in America: A Narrative Anthology*, ed. Alan Heimert and Andrew Delbanco (Cambridge: Harvard University Press, 2009), 229–36; Joshua Moody, *Souldiery Spiritualized, Or the Christian Souldier Orderly, and Strenuously Engaged in the Spiritual Warre* (Cambridge, 1674); Increase Mather, *The Day of Trouble is Near* (Cambridge, 1673); Eleazer Mather, *A Serious Exhortation to the Present and Succeeding Generation in New-England* (Cambridge, 1678).
3. Richard P. Gildie, *The Profane, the Civil, and the Godly: The Reformation of Manners in Orthodox New England* (University Park: Pennsylvania State University Press, 2010), 13, 19–22; William T. Youngs, *The Congregationalists* (Westport, CT: Greenwood Press, 1990), 64, 66; Miller, *The New England Mind*, 168–69, 472–73.
4. Hall, *Worlds of Wonder*, 7, 46, 57, 80, 81.
5. See John Demos, *Entertaining Satan: Witchcraft and the Culture of Early New England* (New York: Oxford University Press, 1982); Mary Beth Norton, *In the Devil's Snare: The Salem Witchcraft Crisis of 1692* (New York: Alfred A. Knopf, 2002); Richard Godbeer, *The Devil's Dominion: Magic and Religion in Early New England* (New York: Cambridge University Press, 1992); Erika Gasser, *Vexed with Devils: Manhood and Witchcraft in Old and New England* (New York: New York University Press, 2017), 137.

6. Richard Slotkin, *Regeneration through Violence: The Mythology of the American Frontier, 1600–1860* (Middletown: Wesleyan University Press, 1973), 114, 139; Janice Knight, "Telling It Slant: The Testimony of Mercy Short," *Early American Literature* 37, no. 1, "Interiority in Early American Literature" (2002): 63n6.
7. Cotton Mather, *Magnalia Christi Americana* (Hartford, 1820), bk. 6, 390–91. An account of the possession also appeared in Increase Mather's *Essay for the Recording of Illustrious Providences* (1684), and Willard's recollections were later published as "A Brief account of a strange and unusual providence of God befallen to Elizabeth Knapp of Groton by me, Samuel Willard," in Samuel A. Green, *Groton in the Witchcraft Times* (Groton, MA, 1883), 7–21.
8. Carol Karlsen, *The Devil in the Shape of a Woman: Witchcraft in Colonial New England* (New York: Norton, 1987), 236; Demos, *Entertaining Satan*, 126.
9. "A Brief account of a strange and unusual providence of God befallen to Elizabeth Knapp of Groton by me, Samuel Willard," in *Witch-Hunting in Seventeenth-Century New England: A Documentary History,* ed. David D. Hall (Boston: Northeastern University Press, 1999), 200, 207; Mather, *Magnalia Christi Americana,* bk. 6, 390.
10. Karlsen, *Devil in the Shape of a Woman,* 240.
11. Willard, "A Brief account" (Hall ed.), 199, 200, 207; Mather, *Magnalia Christi Americana,* bk. 6, 390–91.
12. Willard, "A Brief account" (Hall ed.), 212, 212n7; Mather, *Magnalia Christi Americana,* bk. 6, 391; Karlsen, *Devil in the Shape of a Woman*, 241.
13. Knight, "Telling It Slant," 42; Cotton Mather, "A Brand Pluck'd Out of Burning" (1693), in *Narratives of the Witchcraft Cases, 1648–1706,* ed. George Lincoln Burr (New York: Scribner's Sons, 1914), 259; Karlsen, *Devil in the Shape of a Woman*, 227.
14. Mather, "A Brand Pluck'd Out of Burning," 259–60.
15. Mather, "A Brand Pluck'd Out of Burning," 260, 261, 264–65, 271, 278.
16. Cotton Mather, "Another Brand Pluck'd Out of the Burning, or More Wonders of the Invisible World" (1693), in Burr, *Narratives of the Witchcraft Cases,* 310–12, 318.
17. Mather, "A Brand Pluck'd Out of Burning," 260n4, 261, 268–69; Mather, "Another Brand Pluck'd Out of the Burning," 312; Knight, "Telling It Slant," 50, 55.
18. Mather, "A Brand Pluck'd Out of Burning," 261, 282–83.
19. Mather, "A Brand Pluck'd Out of Burning," 257, 259–60, 267–68, 281–82; Mather, "Another Brand Pluck'd Out of the Burning," 312, 316–17; Gasser, *Vexed with Devils,* 144.
20. Mather, "A Brand Pluck'd Out of Burning," 287; *The Diary of Cotton Mather,* ed. Worthington Chauncey Ford, 2 vols. (Boston: Massachusetts Historical Society, 1911–12), 1:160.
21. Mather, "A Brand Pluck'd Out of Burning," 285, 260; Mather, "Another Brand Pluck'd Out of the Burning," 318.

22. Mather, "Another Brand Pluck'd Out of the Burning," 310, 311, 312, 313, 315, 316, 318.
23. Knight, "Telling It Slant," 41; Diane E. Foulds, *Death in Salem: The Private Lives behind the 1692 Witch Hunt* (Guilford, CT: Globe Pequot Press, 2010), 152, 154–55; Mather, "Another Brand Pluck'd Out of the Burning," 312–15, 318, 319–20.
24. Kathleen Brown, "Murderous Uncleanness: The Body of Female Infanticide in Puritan New England," in *A Centre of Wonders: The Body in Early America,* ed. Janet Moore Lindman and Michele Lise Tartar (Ithaca: Cornell University Press, 2001), 82; Daniel A. Cohen, "In Defense of the Gallows: Justifications of Capital Punishment in New England Execution Sermons, 1674–1825," *American Quarterly* 40, no. 2 (1988): 147; Daniel E. Williams, *Pillars of Salt: An Anthology of Early America Criminal Narratives* (Madison, WI: Madison House Publishers, 1993), 19–20; Stuart Banner, *The Death Penalty: An American History* (Cambridge: Harvard University Press, 2002), 32–34; Mark Winston Brewin, "The New England Execution Sermon: Texts, Rituals, and Power," *Observatorio Journal* 5, no. 2 (2011): 135–36.
25. Brown, "Murderous Uncleanness," 78.
26. Mather, *Diary,* 1:165.
27. Mather, *Diary,* 1:164–65.
28. *The Diary of Samuel Sewall, 1674–1729,* vol. 1 (Boston: Massachusetts Historical Society, 1878), 400, 486; N. E. H. Hull, *Female Felons: Women and Serious Crime in Colonial Massachusetts* (Urbana: University of Illinois Press, 1987), 122; Mather, *Diary* 1:139; Samuel Williard, *Impenitent Sinners Warned of their Misery* (Boston, 1698, repr., 2010); Increase Mather, *The Folly of Sinning, Opened & Applied* (Boston, 1699).
29. Hull, *Female Felons,* 123–24; Williams, *Pillars of Salt,* 3.
30. Cotton Mather, *Warnings from the Dead* (Boston, 1693), 35–36.
31. Mather, *Warnings,* 1–2, 35–36, 75; Williams, *Pillars of Salt,* x, 2; Daniel A. Cohen, *Pillars of Salt, Monuments of Grace: New England Crime Literature and the Origins of American Popular Culture, 1674–1800* (New York: Oxford University Press, 1993), 7; Toulouse, *The Captive's Position,* 108; Hull, *Female Felons,* 56, 123, 124–25; Jodi Schorb, "Hard-Hearted Women: Sentiment and Scaffold," *Legacy* 28, no. 2 (2011): 290–311.
32. Cotton Mather, "Pillars of Salt," in Williams, *Pillars of Salt,* 2, 3, 5, 69.
33. Brown, "Murderous Uncleanness," 82; Mather, *Warnings,* 71.
34. Mather, "Pillars of Salt," 88–89. When fleeing from the destruction of Sodom and Gomorrah, Lot's wife disobeyed the angel's command not to look back on the cities as God rained fire and brimstone upon them. She looked back and was turned into a pillar of salt. Genesis 19:26.
35. John Williams, *Warning to the Unclean* (Boston, 1699), 4, 6, 12, 15, 17, 22, 24, 30, 32, 42; Mather, "Pillars of Salt," 88.
36. Mather, *Diary,* 1:164–65; Mather, *Warnings,* 71, 73; Massachusetts Archives, Records of the Court of Common Pleas, Essex County, microfilm reel 877465, 84.

37. Mather, "Pillars of Salt," 88.
38. *The Diary of Samuel Sewall,* 1:486; Mather, preface to *Pillars of Salt;* Cohen, *Pillars of Salt,* 55; Samuel Willard, *Impenitent Sinners Warned of their Misery and Summoned to Judgment* (Boston, 1698), unpaginated.
39. Mather, *Warnings,* 36, 56–57, 84–85; Brown, "Murderous Uncleanness," 84.
40. See Phillips D. Carleton, "The Indian Captivity," *American Literature* 15, no. 2 (May 1943): 169–80; Roy Harvey Pearce, "The Significances of the Captivity Narrative," *American Literature* 19 (1947): 1–20; June Namias, *White Captives: Gender and Ethnicity on the American Frontier* (Chapel Hill: University of North Carolina Press, 1993); Tara Fitzpatrick, "The Figure of Captivity: The Cultural Work of the Puritan Captivity Narrative," *American Literary History* 3 (1991): 1–26; Kathryn Z. Derounian-Stodola and James A. Levenier, *The Indian Captivity Narrative, 1550–1900* (New York: Twayne, 1993); Kathryn Z. Derounian-Stodola, ed., *Women's Indian Captivity Narratives* (New York: Penguin Books, 1998); Gary L. Ebersole, *Captured by Texts: Puritan to Postmodern Images of Indian Captivity* (Charlottesville: University of Virginia Press, 1995); Williams, *Pillars of Salt,* 12.
41. "Thomas Dustin Petition for Bounty," Massachusetts Archives, Felt Collection, vol. 70, 350; Annette Kolodny, *The Land before Her: Fantasy and Experience of the American Frontiers, 1630–1860* (Chapel Hill: University of North Carolina Press, 1984), 24.
42. Cotton Mather, *Humiliations Follow'd with Deliverances* (Boston: B. Green & J. Allen for Samuel Phillips, 1697), 43, 46; Mather, *Wonders of the Invisible World,* 80.
43. Cotton Mather, *Humiliations,* 44–47. Jael is a heroine from the book of Judges who killed a powerful general, Siseria, an enemy of the Israelites, by driving a tent stake through his skull as he slept. Judges 5:23–27.
44. Mather, *Humiliations,* 37, 40, 43–46.
45. Mather, *Humiliations,* 46, 49.
46. Mather, *Humiliations,* 4–5, 6, 9, 10, 47, 49.
47. Mather, *Humiliations,* 5–6, 14–15, 16–17, 18–19.
48. Hannah Dustin's letter petitioning church elders to join the Second Church of Haverhill is dated 1724, almost thirty years after her escape from the Indians in 1697. "Hannah Dustin's Letter to Elders of the Second Church of Haverhill," 1724, Haverhill Historical Society Collection, Haverhill, MA; George Francis Dow, ed., *Records and Files of the Quarterly Courts of Essex Co., Massachusetts,* vols. 1–9 (Salem, 1911–21), 6:141, 9:603; Dustin Family Letters, HB2.D97.15, Records of the Dustin Family, Haverhill Public Library Special Collections, Haverhill, MA; Massachusetts Archives, Common Pleas, no. 877465, 84; Massachusetts Archives, Suffolk County Court Records, Early Files, vol. 31, case 2636.
49. Mather, *Humiliations,* 21; Williams, *Pillars of Salt,* 13.
50. Mather, *Humiliations,* 33, 42–43; Randolph A. Roth, *American Homicide* (Cambridge: Harvard University Press, 2009), 79.

51. Mather, *Humiliations,* 34, 44; Roth, *American Homicide,* 79.
52. Cotton Mather, *Decennium Luctuosum. An History of Remarkable Occurrences* (Boston: Green & Allen, 1699), 160–61.
53. Kenneth Silverman, *The Life and Times of Cotton Mather* (New York: Harper & Row, 1984), 75, 80–81.
54. Mather, *Decennium Luctuosum,* 93, 94, 96; Teresa A. Toulouse, "Bodies in Discourse," in Lindman and Tartar, *A Centre of Wonders,* 206. The details of Cotton Mather's account of the incident should be taken with a grain of salt, argues Ann Little. "Mather never went anywhere near the frontier during the war," she notes, "instead preferring to write his hawkish screeds in favor of invading the St. Lawrence River valley from the comfort and safety of Boston." Ann M. Little, *Abraham in Arms: War and Gender in Colonial New England* (Philadelphia: University of Pennsylvania Press, 2007), 41. I argue that Mather's distance from the actual event would have given him even greater freedom to craft the narrative to suit his political goals.
55. Mather, *Decennium Luctuosum,* 98, 161.
56. Howard Peckman, *The Colonial Wars, 1689–1762* (Chicago: University of Chicago Press, 1964), 84; Samuel Penhallow, *History of the Wars of New-England with the Eastern Indians, or a Narrative of their Continued Perfidy and Cruelty* (1726), 49.
57. Penhallow, *History of the Wars of New-England,* 107; Patrick Malone, *The Skulking Way of War: Technology and Tactics in New England Indian Warfare* (Lanham, MD: Madison Books, 1993); Little, *Abraham in Arms,* 27; Joyce Chaplin, *Subject Matter: Technology, the Body, and Science on the Anglo-American Frontier, 1500–1676* (Cambridge: Harvard University Press, 2001), 252. This woman from Oxford was not alone in stepping outside the boundaries of her sex and using guns for protection in the seventeenth and eighteenth centuries. New Hampshire Historical Society records indicate that Philip Moodey purchased a half pound of gunpowder for his mother in Nicholas Perryman's store in Exeter in 1722. Nicholas Perryman Ledger, Exeter, NH, 1723–1754, MS, New Hampshire Historical Society Records, 7.
58. A. Laurence, "Women's Work and the English Civil War," *History Today* 42, no. 6 (1992): 20–25; Charles Carlton, *Going to the Wars: The Experience of the British Civil Wars, 1638–1651* (London: Routledge, 1992); Stevie Davies, *Unbridled Spirits: Women of the English Revolution, 1640–1660* (London: Women's Press, 1998); Alison Plowden, *Women All on Fire: The Women of the English Civil War* (Stroud: Sutton Publishing, 1998); Roger Hudson, ed., *The Grand Quarrel: Women's Memoirs of the English Civil War* (Stroud: Sutton Publishing, 2000); Little, *Abraham in Arms,* 88–89.
59. Jack Green, "Recent Developments in the Historiography of Colonial New England," *Acadiensis* 17, no. 2 (1988): 71; Philip J. Greven, *Four Generations: Population, Land, and Family in Colonial Andover, Massachusetts* (Ithaca: Cornell University Press, 1970), 41–71; Kenneth A. Lockridge, *A New England Town,*

The First Hundred Years: Dedham, Massachusetts, 1636–1736 (New York: Norton, 1985), 79–118, and Lockridge, "Land, Population and Evolution of New England Society, 1630–1790," *Past & Present* 39 (1968): 62–80.

60. Jabez Fitch, *Brief Narrative of Several Things Respecting the Province of New Hampshire in New-England* (Boston: Massachusetts Historical Society, 1728–29), 4; Jabez Fitch, letter, September 22, 1724, Belknap Papers, *Collections of the Massachusetts Historical Society* (1891): 3–4; Jeremy Belknap, *The History of New Hampshire,* vol. 1 (Philadelphia, 1784), 338–39.
61. "Journal of the Rev. John Pike," in *Collections of the New Hampshire Historical Society,* vol. 3 (Concord: Printed by Jacob B. Moore, 1832), 40, 55; Vern L. Bullough and Bonnie Bullough, *Cross-Dressing, Sex, and Gender* (Philadelphia: University of Pennsylvania Press, 1993), chap. 4; see also Little, *Abraham in Arms,* 59.
62. Jill Lepore, *The Name of War: King Philip's War and the Origins of American Identity* (New York: Alfred A. Knopf, 1998), chap. 3; Penhallow, *History of the Wars of New-England,* 104; Little, *Abraham in Arms,* 108.
63. Penhallow, *History of the Wars of New-England,* 11. Bradley was lucky compared to other pregnant women who fell into Indian hands, as Penhallow described in his history. "Teeming Women, in cold Blood have been ript open; others fastned to Stakes and burnt alive," he wrote. Penhallow, *History of the Wars of New-England,* 37.
64. Penhallow, *History of the Wars of New-England,* 10–11; Robert Wilhelm, *Murder and Mayhem in Essex County* (Charleston, SC: History Press, 2011), 46.
65. Penhallow, *History of the Wars of New-England,* 11; Benjamin Mirick, *The History of Haverhill, Massachusetts* (Haverhill, 1832), 109–10; Abiel Abbot and Ephraim Abbot, *A Genealogical Register of the Descendants of George Abbot, of Andover, etc.* (Boston, 1847).
66. Fitch, *Brief Narrative,* chap. 4.

INDEX